The Visual Investor

How to Spot Market Trends

John J. Murphy

JOHN WILEY & SONS, INC.

New York • Chichester • Brisbane • Toronto • Singapore • Weinheim

To Patty, who has now survived the writing of three books.

To Clare and Brian, who asked: "Dad, if your first two books were so good, why do you need to write a third one?"

And to Kae and Jim, who always compliment me on my ties.

This text is printed on acid-free paper.

Copyright © 1996 by John J. Murphy
Published by John Wiley & Sons, Inc.

ISBN 0-471-14447-9 (Cloth)

Printed in the United States of America

10 9 8 7 6 5 4

Contents

Preface

I've been pretty lucky as a writer. Ten years ago, I completed my first book, *Technical Analysis of the Futures Markets* (New York Institute of Finance/Prentice-Hall, 1986), which has been described by many as the Bible of technical analysis. That 600-page volume has since been translated into six foreign languages, including Chinese, German, Italian, Japanese, Polish, and Spanish. That book introduced many readers to the world of market analysis and also introduced to the investing community many of the computerized indicators that have since become so popular.

Five years ago, I completed *Intermarket Technical Analysis* (John Wiley & Sons, 1991). That second book has been described as a landmark publication because of its emphasis on linkages between financial markets and asset classes. I'm happy to say that the Market Technicians Association now considers *intermarket* analysis an official branch of market analysis. Both books have been labeled bestsellers, which always provides a certain degree of satisfaction as well as financial rewards.

This latest book, *The Visual Investor,* has been the most enjoyable one to write and, at the same time, the most challenging. It has been enjoyable because I've been able to focus on only those techniques I've come to favor over the years. It's been the most challenging because I'm writing for people who have no idea what I'm talking about. Well, that's probably an exaggeration. Let's just say that this book has been written for the average person who invests in the stock market (or is thinking about it), who likes mutual funds (but is overwhelmed by so many), who owns a computer (or is thinking of owning one), and has bought a charting software package (or is thinking of buying one), but isn't sure how to use it.

This book is written primarily for the thousands (hopefully millions) of viewers of CNBC, where I've served as technical analyst for the past five years. My television work on CNBC has been both rewarding and frustrating. Rewarding because I've been given a platform to explain how markets work, utilizing many of the visual tools that professionals have been using for decades. Judging from the large numbers of cards and letters I have received over the years from CNBC viewers, my efforts in that direction have helped many viewers gain a better understanding of how the financial markets work and have improved their investing results.

Television work has been frustrating because of time constraints and the constant struggle to explain market movements in a space of five minutes to an audience that may not even understand the visual tools shown on the screen. If I explain the visual tools, there isn't time to get to the main conclusion or the reason for the story. If I jump to the main conclusion, I lose those viewers who are still trying to figure out what those "squiggly lines" mean in the first place. Then there are the "this just in" stories that seem to appear just as I'm getting to my punchline.

Thanks to a lot of coaxing by Myles Thompson at John Wiley & Sons, and a lot of consultation with my editor, Pamela van Giessen, we decided that it was time someone wrote a book explaining what all those squiggly lines really mean. And who better to do it than the guy who has been showing those squiggly lines for the past few years on television and leaving more than a few viewers wondering "What the heck is that guy talking about and does he really expect us to believe that those lines mean anything?" Then after a while thinking to themselves: "Then again, he does seem to be right *most* of the time. Maybe there's something to it. I just wish he'd slow down and explain where he gets those lines from and where I can get them and learn how to read them myself."

The term *squiggly lines* comes from Ted David, my colleague and anchor at CNBC. Ted, along with Sue Herera and other anchors I've had the pleasure of working with at CNBC, has taught me the need to avoid jargon and get to the point as quickly as possible (and to make sure that I have a point). Sue has taught me never to underestimate the value of a woman's intuition. Sue has a way of asking a question about a market in such a way that I know what she already thinks is the right answer. I've learned never to disagree with her, because she's usually right. Of course, there are years of market experience behind that female intuition.

My years of working with Ted David have taught me two other valuable lessons. One is that it is possible to have a little fun with market analysis without taking away from its serious side. The second is that a little knowledge can be a dangerous thing. If you've ever been exposed to Ted's occasional attempts at chart reading, you'll know what I mean. The fact of the matter is that Ted went to the trouble to attend a 15-week course on chart analysis and knows more about the subject than some of the people he interviews.

We decided to call this book *The Visual Investor.* We didn't do that just for cosmetic reasons. What I do on CNBC is look at pictures of markets in much the same way that meteorologists look at pictures of weather maps. It's all visual. There's no point calling it anything else. I started calling what I do *visual analysis* to lessen the fear factor of producers at CNBC, who seem terrified by the subject. It's a funny thing. Every commentator at CNBC uses a chart to explain a market story. I know, because I provide them with most of the charts. When I use the *same* chart during my segment, however, it is often described as "too technical."

So here it is: My attempt to slow down and explain what all those squiggly lines mean. It's not that difficult. I've gone to great lengths to keep it simple. I've deliberately chosen those indicators that I believe to be most useful. I also tell you where to get the same charts that I use. If you can read a *line* on a chart and learn to tell *up* from *down,* you won't have any trouble grasping what *visual analysis* is all about. You'll also learn why markets usually *lead* the news, why they react to fundamental news the way they do, and why much of what happens actually makes sense if you know what to look for.

As you begin to understand what visual analysis is all about, you may notice an increase in your own self-reliance. You may find that you don't really need to listen to all those analysts and economists who like to explain why the markets did what they did yesterday (which they didn't know or didn't bother telling you about the day *before* yesterday). You may even get to the point where you won't need to watch CNBC anymore. (Oops, shouldn't have said that. Sorry, CNBC.)

I would like to express my deep gratitude to Greg Morris for his invaluble assistance in the production of this book. Greg has been developing trading systems and indicators for 20 years and has an extensive knowledge of what software products are available to the average investor today (because he developed some of them himself). Greg's insights add immeasurably to the value of this book. Greg is also largely responsible for the production of the charts in this book. He wrote the Appendixes on *Market Breadth* and *Japanese Candlesticks*. He has authored two books of his own and made my work on this one a good deal easier.

We started out to make this a *visual* book. We wanted to show a lot of pictures of markets that could tell a story on their own. As a result, you're going to see a lot of charts. The charts we chose were taken from the most recent market data available to us. They weren't chosen to depict perfect textbook examples, but to show *real life* examples of visual principles at work in the current market environment. I hope we've chosen wisely.

Even after you've become a pretty fair visual analyst yourself, there's no reason why you can't still tune in to keep an eye on my squiggly lines. After reading this book, you'll even know what they mean.

Acknowledgments

In order to perform visual analysis in the simplest and most efficient way possible, the investor needs charting software and access to an online data service. With that in mind, the charts used throughout this book were developed with only those software and data services readily available (and reasonably priced) to the investing public. Most of the charts were developed with the two heavyweights of charting software, *MetaStock* from Equis International and *SuperCharts* from Omega Research. Our primary data sources are two popular online services, *Dial Data* and *Telescan*. In the section on mutual funds, we also make reference to two services that specialize in that area, *FastTrack* and *TeleChart 2000*. Both of those firms provide data and charting capability for mutual funds, which is an important part of this book. A special word of thanks goes to Knight-Ridder for the use of their *Tradecenter* terminal, which proved most helpful in the research for this book. More information can be found on each of these fine products in the Resources section of this book.

SECTION 1

Introduction

Traders and investors have been using a visual approach to investing for over a century. Up until the past decade, the use of visual analysis as a serious method of trading and investing was pretty much limited to professionals and full-time traders. Most successful traders would never think of making a trade without first consulting the pictures on their charts. Even the Federal Reserve Board now uses price charts to aid in deciding when to intervene in the foreign exchange markets.

WHAT HAS CHANGED?

For the average investor, however, the world of visual trading had been largely closed. The intimidating jargon and complicated formulas were beyond the reach and, indeed, the interest of the nonprofessional investor. A couple of important factors have changed that in the past decade. The most important is the availability of inexpensive *computers* and corresponding *software* packages. The investing public now has an impressive array of technological and visual tools that weren't even available to the professional community 20 years ago.

The second development has been the dramatic expansion of the *mutual fund* industry to the point where more mutual funds exist than stocks

1

now traded on the New York Stock Exchange. This phenomenal growth has produced both benefits and challenges for the average investor. The challenge lies in the fact that the job of choosing among mutual funds has been greatly complicated. In a very real sense, the mutual fund growth has made the task of the individual investor more difficult. The original purpose of mutual funds was to *simplify* investing. If someone didn't have the time or expertise to pick stocks, that task could be turned over to a mutual fund manager. Besides professional management, instant diversification was provided. An investor could buy one fund and be in the market. Now, however, mutual funds are so segmented that the investor has a bewildering set of choices to make.

MUTUAL FUND CATEGORIES

Domestic stock funds are categorized by goal and style—*aggressive growth, growth, growth and income,* and *equity income.* Mutual funds are also divided by the size or capitalization of the stocks included in their portfolios. *Large-cap stock funds* limit their portfolios to those stocks included in the Standard & Poor's 500 stock index. *Midsize funds* focus on stocks included in the S&P 400 Mid-Cap Index or the Wilshire Mid-Cap 750. *Small-cap funds* choose their portfolios from the Russell 2000 or the S&P 600 Small-Cap Index. Mutual funds can be further identified by their specialization in various stock market sectors, such as *technology, basic industry, health care, financial services, energy, precious metals,* and *utilities.* Stock *sectors* can be further subdivided into *industries* with even more specified mutual funds. The technology sector, for example, would include funds that emphasize *computers, defense and aerospace, communications, electronics, software, semiconductors,* and *telecommunications.* Fidelity Investments offers as many as 35 sector funds for the individual to choose from.

GLOBAL FUNDS

Another dimension has been the growing popularity of global investing. Investors can now trade in individual foreign countries or geographic regions by selecting the appropriate mutual fund. As a result, investors are forced to keep abreast of market developments not just in the United States, but all over the world. While overseas investing carries more risk than domestic funds, the rewards are well worth it. During 1995, international funds rose a modest 5 percent, while U.S. funds soared 30 percent.

During 1993, however, American investors who invested overseas were rewarded with gains of 38 percent, while the American market rose a relatively modest 5 percent. *Emerging market funds* are the riskiest of all. Since 1989, however, emerging market funds have gained 18 percent annually versus average gains of 15 percent for the U.S. market. Overseas investing provides diversification from the U.S. market, which is why financial advisors recommend leaving as much as a third of one's portfolio abroad to improve returns and lessen risk.

INVESTORS NEED TO BE BETTER INFORMED

For many investors, *mutual fund* investing has replaced *individual stock* selection. However, with the degree of segmentation that has taken place in the mutual fund industry, investors have little choice but to become better informed and more actively involved in the mutual fund selection process. Investors must be aware of what different sectors of the American market are doing as well as how global markets are faring. The number of choices available to the investor is a mixed blessing.

So, too, are the technological advances of the past decade. The investor can run software on his or her PC, paying as little as $29.95 for a charting program. The problem is knowing how to select and use the resources that are available. The technology has outpaced the public's ability to use the new data in the most efficient way. Which brings us to the purpose of this book—to help the average investor get acclimated to visual trading in the quickest and simplest way possible. And, second, to show how these relatively simple principles can be applied to the problem of sector investing primarily through mutual funds.

BENEFITS OF VISUAL INVESTING

The bright side of the increased specialization among mutual funds is that the investor has never before been provided with so many vehicles to choose from. Individuals who favor a certain market sector or industry, but don't want to choose which stocks to buy, can now buy the whole group. Sector funds also provide additional ways to diversify one's core stock holdings and to pursue more aggressive growth opportunities with a portion of one's assets. That's where visual analysis comes in.

The tools explained in this text can be applied to any market or fund anywhere in the world. With the aid of a computer and easy access to price data, the task of monitoring and analyzing mutual funds has been made immeasurably easier. The power of the PC can also be harnessed for such things as *monitoring* portfolios, *back-testing* rules for buying and selling decisions, *scanning* charts for attractive opportunities, and *ranking* mutual funds by relative performance. While the challenges of learning how to apply new technology to mutual fund and sector investing are there, so are the rewards. If you're in the market, you've already accepted the challenge. This book will show you how to reap the rewards.

STRUCTURE OF THE BOOK

The book is divided into four sections. Section 1 explains what visual analysis is and how it can be blended with more traditional forms of investment analysis. The critically important subject of *market trend* is explained, along with some visual tools to help identify the trend. You may be surprised to discover how much value lies in some of the simplest tools that are covered in the first section.

Section 2 covers some of the more popular market indicators in use today. We stress the *concepts* behind the various indicators and how they are *interpreted*. We limit our coverage to only the most useful tools. For those wishing to explore the world of indicators more fully, reference sources are given in the Resources section at the end of the book.

Section 3 introduces the idea of *market linkages*. This is especially important in order to appreciate why stock market investors should also monitor movements in commodity prices, bond prices, and the dollar. *Intermarket analysis* is also helpful in understanding asset allocation and the process of sector rotation within the stock market. Along the way, you'll gain some insight into policy-making decisions of the Federal Reserve. You'll be able to watch many of the same things the Fed watches.

Section 4 focuses on sector analysis and mutual funds. *Relative strength* analysis is shown to play an important role in the selection process. We also show you how to analyze the global markets.

The Resources section is devoted to helping you get started on your own visual analysis. It names some important publishing and educational resources that will help you get going, as well as listing some of the more highly regarded software products and data vendors that you will need in your quest to become a truly visual investor.

1

What Is Visual Investing?

They say a picture is worth a thousand words. Maybe they should have said a thousand dollars. After all, we're talking here about using pictures to make money. And that's really what this book is all about. It's that simple. A stock either goes up or down. If it goes up, and you own it, that's good. If it goes down, and you own it, that's bad. You can talk all you want about what a stock *should* be doing or *why* it isn't doing what it *should* be doing. You can talk about inflation, interest rates, earnings, and investor expectations. Ultimately, however, it comes down to the picture. Is the stock going up or down? Knowing the reasons behind a stock's movement is interesting, but not critical. If your stock goes up on a given day, they won't take the money away from you if you don't know why it went up. And if you can explain why it went down, they won't give you back your lost money. All that really matters is a picture, a simple line on a chart. The trick to visual investing is learning to tell the difference between what is going up and what is going down. The goal of this book is to help you tell that difference.

WHY MARKET ANALYSIS?

As the various chapters unfold, you will be provided with some relatively simple visual tools to aid you in market analysis and timing. Notice our use of the term *market analysis.* Whatever you choose to call it, the bulk of this book deals with visual analysis of the financial markets by utilizing price and volume charts. Analysis of fundamental data, such as earnings expectations and the state of the economy, helps determine what a stock *should* be doing. Market analysis tells us what the stock actually *is* doing. The two approaches are very different. The use of earnings estimates comes under the general heading of *fundamental* analysis. The use of market analysis comes under the heading of *chart,* or *visual,* analysis. Most investors are more familiar with the fundamental approach, because that is what they are taught in school and what they read about in the media. There's no question that the fundamentals are what ultimately move a stock or group of stocks. It's just a question of how one goes about studying those fundamentals and their effect on the stock.

THE TREND IS TO BLEND

The fact of the matter is that most successful traders and money managers use some blend of the visual and the financial. The more recent trend is toward a blending of the chart and fundamental disciplines. The use of *intermarket analysis,* the study of *market linkages* (discussed in Section 3), blurs the line between those two disciplines even further. The intention here is simply to explain how the two approaches differ, and to increase the reader's understanding of why the charting (or visual) approach should be a part of any investment or trading decision.

WHAT'S IN A NAME?

Visual analysis (also called *chart* or *technical analysis*) refers to the study of the market itself. Price charts can show individual stocks, industry groups, major stock averages, international markets, bond prices, commodity prices, and currencies. Visual analysis of open- and closed-end mutual funds can also be accomplished. Many people are intimidated by the term *technical analysis.* As a result, they deprive themselves of the benefits of a very useful form of analysis. If that is the case with you, simply call it *visual analysis* because that's what it is. The dictionary defines *visual* as "capable of being seen by the eye; visible." *Technical* is defined as "abstract or theoretical." Believe me, there's nothing abstract or theoretical about this form of analysis. I'm often amazed at the number of people who are terrified by technical analysis but look at price charts all the time. They're scared more by the name than the analysis. To relieve that anxiety, we'll use the terms *visual analysis, market analysis,* and *chart analysis* throughout this book.

WHY STUDY THE MARKET?

Let's suppose an investor has some money to invest in the stock market. The first decision is whether or not this is a good time to put new funds into the market. If it is, which sector of the market would be most suitable? An investor has to study the market in order to make an informed decision. The question is how to accomplish that task.

An investor can read the newspapers, plow through a lot of earnings reports, call up his or her broker on the phone, or subscribe to some financial publication or newsletters. All of those things should probably be done as part of the process anyway. But there's a quicker and easier way: Instead of wondering what the market should be doing, why not look at what it is doing? Begin by studying the price trend of major stock averages. Then, look at the charts of the various stock sectors to see which way they're trending. Both steps can be accomplished in a matter of minutes by looking at the appropriate chart pictures.

CHARTISTS ARE CHEATERS

In a way, using chart analysis is a form of cheating. After all, why does a stock go up or down? It goes up because its fundamentals are bullish. It goes down because its fundamentals are bearish. Or, at least, that is how the market perceives a stock's fundamentals. How many times have you seen a stock fall in price in the face of a bullish piece of news? One striking recent example was the decline in the price of Microsoft and most technology stocks immediately after the widely heralded August 1995 release of Windows 95 software. What matters isn't always the actual news, but what the market was expecting and what it thinks of that news.

Why, then, is chart analysis cheating? Because it is a shortcut form of fundamental analysis. It enables a chartist to analyze a stock or industry group without doing all of the work of the fundamental analyst. And how does it do that? Simply by telling the chartist whether the fundamentals of a stock are bullish or bearish by the direction its price is moving. If the market perceives the fundamentals as bullish, the stock will be rewarded with a higher price. A negative market evaluation of a stock's inherent fundamental value will punish the stock by pushing its price lower. All the chartist has to do is study the direction of the stock to see if it is going up or down. It almost seems like cheating, but it really isn't. It's just smart.

IT'S ALWAYS JUST SUPPLY AND DEMAND

The simplest way to understand the difference between the two approaches is to consider *supply and demand.* Simple economics tells us that when demand increases relative to supply, prices rise. When supply exceeds demand, prices fall. The same principle applies to stocks, bonds, currencies, and commodities. However, how does one tell what those supply and demand figures are? The ability to tell which is greater is obviously the key to price forecasting. The hard way is to actually study all of the supply and demand factors, individually and collectively, to determine which is greater. The easier way is to let the price itself tell us. If the price is rising, demand is greater. If the price is falling, supply is probably greater.

CHARTS ARE JUST FASTER

An excellent example of the difference between the two approaches was provided to me early in my career as a market analyst. Our portfolio manager called me and a fundamental analyst into his office one day and gave us both the same assignment: to analyze the historic value levels for a list of stocks that he was considering purchasing for the company's investment portfolio. He wanted to know at what level each stock was overvalued and which were at more reasonable historic levels and more suitable for purchase.

I went back to my office and got out a long-term chart book showing price histories, going back several decades, for each stock. I simply noted the price levels where the stocks had peaked and troughed in the past, and which stocks were closest to those peaks and troughs. The entire project was completed the same afternoon.

However, my report wasn't submitted for another two weeks, which was how long it took my fundamental counterpart to complete his report. When both lists were submitted, the funny thing was that we both came up with essentially the same results. He had taken all of the fundamental factors, including historic price/earnings ratios and the like, into consideration to determine his numbers for historic valuations. I simply looked at the price histories of the stocks. We came up with the same numbers, but my task took two hours while his took two weeks. I learned two things from that. First, both approaches often give us the same results, demonstrating the enormous overlap between the two. Second, the chart approach is much quicker and doesn't require much knowledge of the stocks in question.

CHARTS DO LOOK AHEAD

The market is always looking ahead. It is a *discounting mechanism.* We don't always know why a market is rising or falling. When we do find out, the market often goes in the opposite direction. During September 1995, semiconductor stocks suddenly started to drop sharply. Up until that point, they had been among the stock market's best performers. Security analysts interviewed on CNBC seemed uniformly bullish. One analyst was asked why the charts looked so bad if the fundamentals were so bullish. He replied that the charts tell us where a market has been, not where it is going. In other words, they weren't very helpful. Within four months, however, semiconductor stocks had lost 45 percent of their value. During January 1996, many security analysts downgraded the chip stocks as a result of negative earnings "surprises." By then, Micron Technology had lost two thirds of its value (see Figure 1.1). Obviously, the market (and those who studied it) knew something well before the analysts did.

PICTURES DON'T LIE

Since fundamentals are discounted in the market, market analysis is just another form of fundamental analysis—a more visual approach, if you will. Often when I'm asked why a market is rising, I will respond by saying that the fundamentals are bullish. I may have no idea what those fundamentals are. But I can feel confident that a rising price signals that the market is taking a bullish view of its fundamentals. It is this very point that makes the case for market analysis so compelling.

It also demonstrates why studying the market visually is such a vital part of the investing process. It suggests why fundamental analysis shouldn't be used in a vacuum. Market analysis can alert an investor to changes in a market's supply/demand equation, which would then prompt a reevaluation of that market's fundamentals. Or, market analysis can be used as a check or filter on fundamental assessments. Either way, there is plenty of room for both disciplines to complement each other's strengths.

Figure 1.1   This chart shows both an uptrend and a downtrend in the same stock. The price increased 500 percent during the first three quarters of 1995. Try telling those investors who bought at 90 that the subsequent downtrend was not real. *(MetaStock, Equis International, Inc.)*

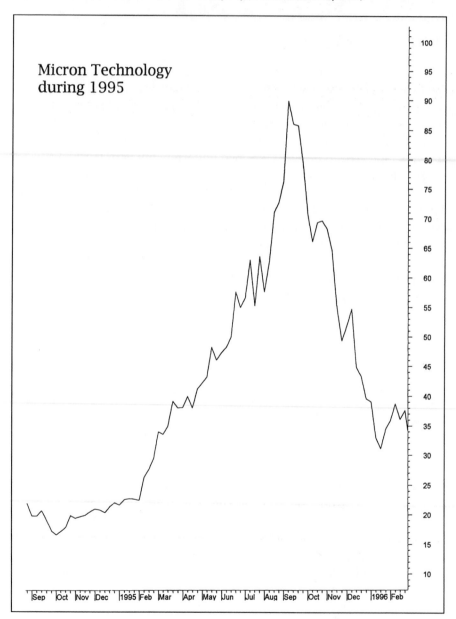

Micron Technology
during 1995

PICTURE ANYTHING YOU WANT

One of the greatest strengths of the visual approach to market analysis is its ability to monitor a large number of markets at the same time and to cross over into other investment mediums. It is possible for an investor with a chartbook or some simple software and a data base to track markets all over the world. Global stock and bond markets, foreign currencies, stock sectors, individual stocks, bonds, and commodities can easily be monitored. In addition, the principles of chart analysis can be applied to any and all of those markets with little knowledge of the respective fundamentals of the markets themselves. Given the trend toward global investing, and the myriad investment choices now available to the individual investor, this is no small achievement. And the beauty of it is that one can do a creditable job of analyzing those markets by mastering a relative handful of visual tools.

THE MARKET'S ALWAYS RIGHT

Charts work for two reasons. First, they reflect the market's assessment of the value of a given stock. How many times have you heard the expression "You can't fight the tape"? If you're bullish on a stock, and it is falling, you're wrong in your opinion of that stock (or, as forecasters sometimes like to say, "early"). If you are short on the stock and it is rising, you're wrong again. The market gives us a daily report card. Analysts sometimes say that a market is rising or falling for the wrong reasons (usually when the analyst has been wrong on the stock's direction). There's no such thing as a market moving for the wrong reasons. The market is always right. It's up to us to get in sync with it. I've been told a few times in my career that I was right, but for the wrong reasons—usually by someone who was wrong for the right reasons. I'd rather be right for the wrong reasons than wrong for the right reasons any day. How about you?

IT'S ALL ABOUT TREND

The second reason that charts work is that markets trend. If you don't believe it, look at the chart of the Dow Jones Industrial Average in Figure 1.2. If you're still not convinced, all you have to do to prove it to yourself is buy a stock that is falling. The existence of a downward trend will be painfully apparent. Figure 1.1 shows Micron Technology rising from 15 to 90—an uptrend—during the first nine months of 1995, only to drop all the way back to 30 over the ensuing four months—a downtrend. The study of trend is what visual chart analysis is all about. From this point on, the tools and indicators that we employ will have one purpose in mind—to identify the trend of a stock or market, either up or down.

ISN'T THE PAST ALWAYS PROLOGUE?

Critics of charting claim that past price data can't be used to predict the future, or that charts work because of a "self-fulfilling prophecy." Consider whether the first claim makes any sense: What form of forecasting doesn't use past data? Doesn't all economic and financial forecasting involve the study of the past? Think about it. There is no such thing as future data. All anybody has is past data.

   If you are concerned about the self-fulfilling prophecy, turn on CNBC and listen to the conflicting opinions of market analysts. As with any method of forecasting, market analysts often differ as to how they interpret the same data. I'm often asked why charts work. Does it really matter? Isn't it enough that they do work? Keep in mind that charts are nothing more than a visual history of a stock's performance. It's virtually impossible for a stock to trend in any direction without that trend being revealed on the price chart. It naturally follows that if trends can be seen, they can also be acted upon.

TIMING IS EVERYTHING

Our intention in this first chapter is not only to explain how the visual approach differs from traditional forms of financial analysis, but also to show how they can be blended together. Consider the problem of timing: Suppose your fundamental analysis identifies a stock that appears attractive for purchase. Do you just go in and purchase it? Maybe the analysis is right, but the timing is wrong. In such cases, the application of some basic charting can help determine if now is the best time to begin buying, or if purchases should be deferred until a more opportune time. In this way, the two disciplines can be combined quite nicely.

SUMMARY

The point of this chapter is to present some of the philosophical ground on which visual chart analysis is based and to demonstrate how and why it should be incorporated into one's analysis. The logic and simplicity

Figure 1.2   Anyone who doesn't believe that markets trend might want to study this chart. A lot of money was made in the past decade by those investors who believe in trends. *(MetaStock, Equis International, Inc.)*

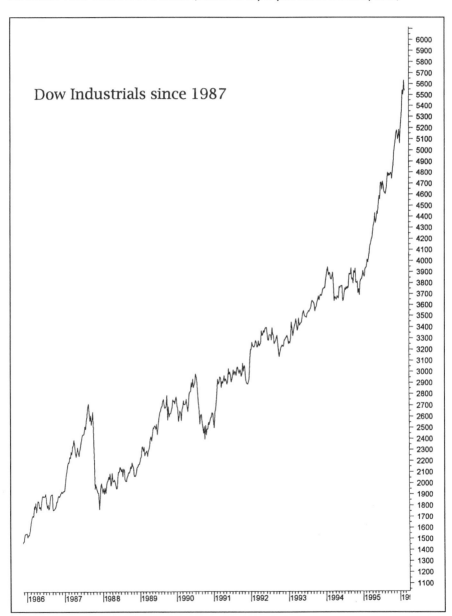

behind the visual approach is both appealing and compelling. At the same time, it seems worthwhile for anyone just beginning a study of this approach to understand and appreciate its true value.

Consider the plight of someone who doesn't use any form of visual analysis: Picture a bus driver operating the vehicle without looking out the windows and at the rear view mirror. Imagine a surgeon operating on a patient blindfolded or without first looking at an X ray. Have you ever seen a meteorologist do a weather forecast without maps? All these people are using visual tools and skills. Would you undertake any serious venture with your eyes closed? Would you go on a trip without a map? Why, then, would you consider investing your money in any stock or mutual fund without first looking at a picture of how it is doing?

In the next chapter, we begin showing you what you can see in that picture.

2
The Trend Is Your Friend

As we stated at the outset, markets trend. They usually move in a specific direction, either up or down. There are periods when a market will move sideways for a while in an apparently trendless fashion. Such cases represent interim periods of indecision, but are still important. Sideways movements are often nothing more than a pause in the existing trend, after which the prior trend resumes. At other times, a sideways movement can signal an important reversal of the trend in progress. It's important to be able to tell the difference between the two. But first, let's define just what a trend is and provide some guidelines for determining when a trend is in motion, when it is likely to continue, and when it is likely to reverse.

WHAT IS A TREND?

Since our primary task in visual analysis is the study of trend, we need to explain just what a trend is. Simply put, *trend* represents the direction a market is moving. It's important to recognize that no market moves in a straight line. If we observe the strong bull market in stocks that began in 1982, it is easy to spot several periods of downward correction (as in 1987 or 1990) or a sideways consolidation in the bull trend (as in 1994 [Figure 2.1]). An uptrend is most often represented by a series of rising peaks (highs) and troughs (lows). As long as each succeeding peak is higher than the prior peak, and as long as each successive trough is higher than the preceding trough, the uptrend remains intact (see Figure 2.2). Any failure to exceed a previous high is an early warning of a possible trend reversal. Any downside violation of a prior low is usually a confirmation that a trend reversal has in fact taken place (see Figure 2.3). A downtrend is just a mirror image of an uptrend and is characterized by a series of declining peaks and troughs (see Figure 2.4). The ability of a price to hold above a previous low point followed by an upside penetration of a prior high point is necessary to signal a reversal of the preceding downtrend.

SUPPORT AND RESISTANCE LEVELS

Fortunately, these peaks and troughs have names which are self-explanatory (see Figure 2.5). *Support* refers to a reaction low, or trough, that was formed sometime in the past. Analysts often speak of prices bouncing off a support level. They're usually referring to nothing more than a prior low formed sometime in the last week, month, or year. Remember that support is always *below* the market. What the market does at that support is very important. If the market closes below the support level (referred to as *breaking support*), the downtrend is resumed. The ability of prices to bounce off that support level (referred to as a successful *test of support*) is usually the first sign that the downtrend is ending and that prices are beginning to bottom.

Resistance is the name assigned to any previous peak. You may hear analysts speak of prices approaching an overhead resistance level. They are simply referring to some price level at which a prior peak was formed. The ability of prices to exceed that prior peak is critical. If prices close above the peak, the uptrend is maintained. If prices back off again from the prior peak, a warning signal is given of a possible trend failure (see Figure 2.6). Resistance is a barrier above the market.

ROLE REVERSAL

This is a market phenomenon that you should be aware of. After support and resistance levels are penetrated by a reasonable amount, they often reverse roles. In other words, a broken support level (prior bottom) becomes a resistance barrier above the market. During an uptrend, a broken resistance level (prior peak) usually becomes a new support level on subsequent market corrections. Figures 2.7 and 2.8 show examples of how this happens. Figure 2.7 shows Federal Express bouncing off new support

Figure 2.1   Markets don't trend in a straight line. The major uptrend in the Dow Industrials was interrupted by a sideways consolidation during 1994, after which the major bull market resumed. *(MetaStock, Equis International, Inc.)*

Figure 2.2   The uptrend in semiconductor stocks during most of 1995 was identified by a series of rising peaks and troughs. *(SuperCharts, Omega Research)*

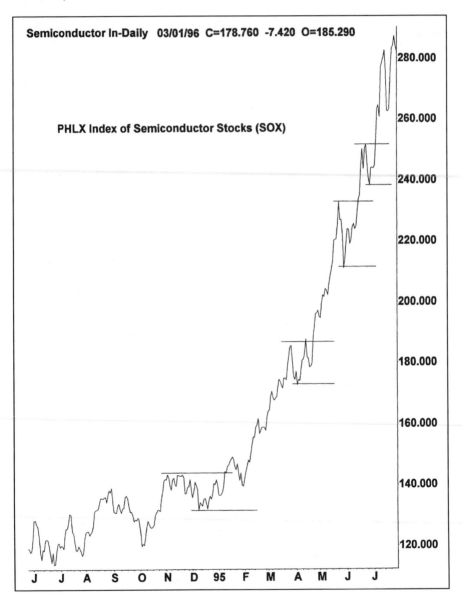

Figure 2.3   Example of trend reversal in semiconductor stocks. A second peak (C) failed to rise above the first peak (A). Prices then fell below the prior trough (B). The pattern of rising peaks and troughs has been reversed. (MetaStock, Equis International, Inc.)

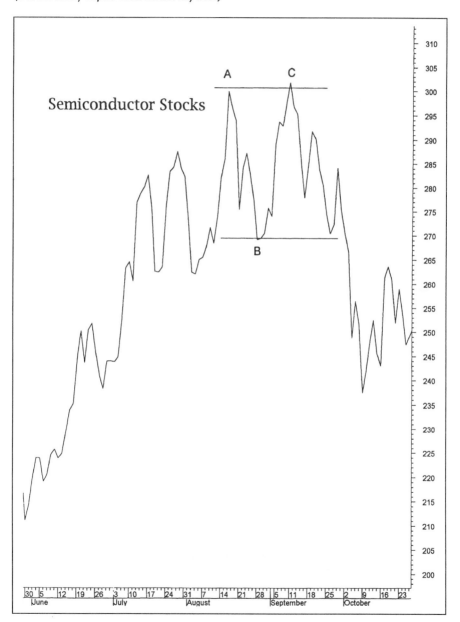

Figure 2.4 An uptrend turning into a downtrend. The pattern of rising peaks and troughs (points 1 to 2) has turned into a pattern of falling peaks and troughs (points 2 to 3). *(SuperCharts, Omega Research)*

Figure 2.5   Example of a downtrend turning into an uptrend. *(MetaStock, Equis International, Inc.)*

Figure 2.6   Resistance is seen at peaks (A and C). Support is seen at trough (B). This is an example of an uptrend turning into a downtrend. *(SuperCharts, Omega Research)*

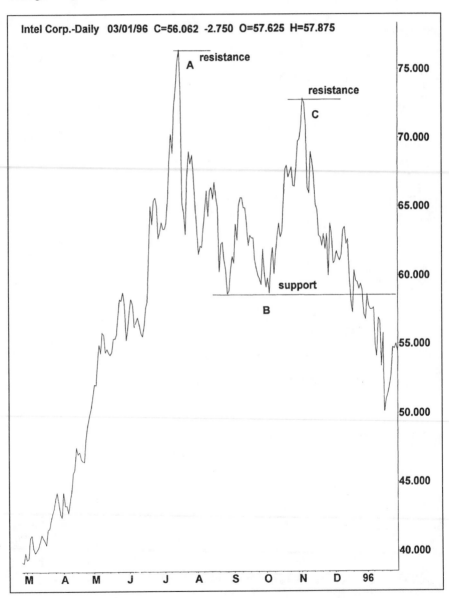

at its mid-1995 peak near 70. Market analysts look for support to function near a prior market peak. Figure 2.8 shows what usually happens in a downtrend. During October 1995, Motorola broke a prior low around 68. Once that prior support level was broken, it became a resistance barrier above the market.

The rationale behind this tendency to reverse roles stems from investor psychology. If support exists at a prior low, that means investors have bought at that level. Once that level is decisively broken and investors realize they've made a mistake, they're usually anxious to break even. In other words, they will sell where they previously bought. Prior support becomes resistance. During an uptrend, investors who sold near a prior peak only to watch the stock trend higher are now anxious to take advantage of a second chance to buy where they once sold. Prior resistance becomes new support on market dips.

SHORT VERSUS LONG TERM

Many investors are confused by the terms *short term* and *long term,* which are so casually tossed around by market professionals. The distinction is actually fairly simple, but requires an understanding of the fact that there are many different degrees of trend interacting with each other. A *major trend,* as the name implies, refers to an important trend that lasts anywhere from six months to several years. When analysts speak of the major trend of the stock market, they are referring to the *longer-term trend* of the market, which is the most important to stock investors. The major trend is also called the *primary trend.*

The second most important trend is the *secondary,* or *intermediate, trend.* This refers to a correction in the major trend that can last from one to six months. In other words, it is not long enough to qualify as a major trend, but too long to be considered a short-term trend. The third degree of trend is the *short-term,* or *minor, trend.* This usually refers to a correction or consolidation phase that lasts less than a month and is measured in days or weeks. It usually represents nothing more than a pause in the intermediate or major trend. The short-term trend is generally of most importance to market traders as opposed to investors (see Figures 2.9 and 2.10).

Breaking down market trends into three categories is really an oversimplification. There are an infinite number of trends to measure at any one time, from an intraday chart showing hourly changes, to a 50-year trend measured on annual charts. However, for purposes of convenience and simplification, most analysts use some version of the three just men-

Figure 2.7   A prior resistance peak (A) usually provides support on subsequent declines (B). *(MetaStock, Equis International, Inc.)*

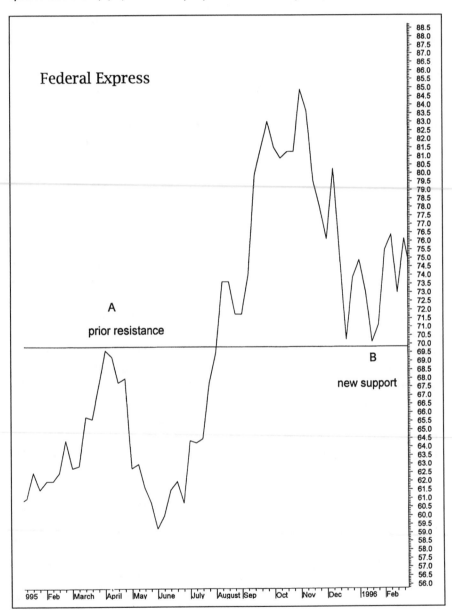

Figure 2.8   Once a support level is broken (A), it often provides resistance on subsequent bounces (B). *(SuperCharts, Omega Research)*

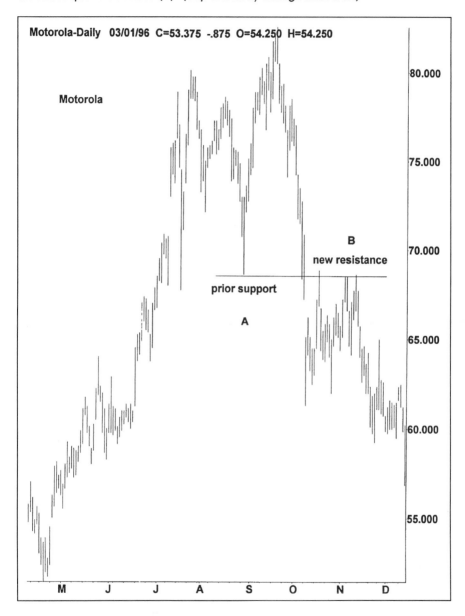

Figure 2.9   The decline from point A to point B lasted five months and was an intermediate (secondary) correction within a major uptrend. *(MetaStock, Equis International, Inc.)*

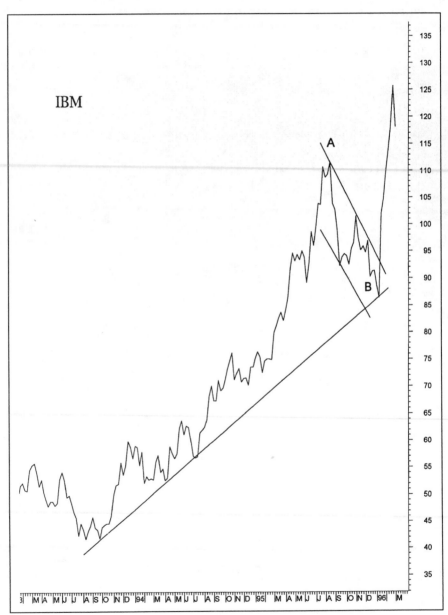

Figure 2.10   The decline from point A to point B (five months) qualifies as a secondary correction in a longer-term uptrend (see Figure 2.9). The bounce from points 1 to 2 (four weeks) was a short-term bounce in a secondary decline. *(MetaStock, Equis International, Inc.)*

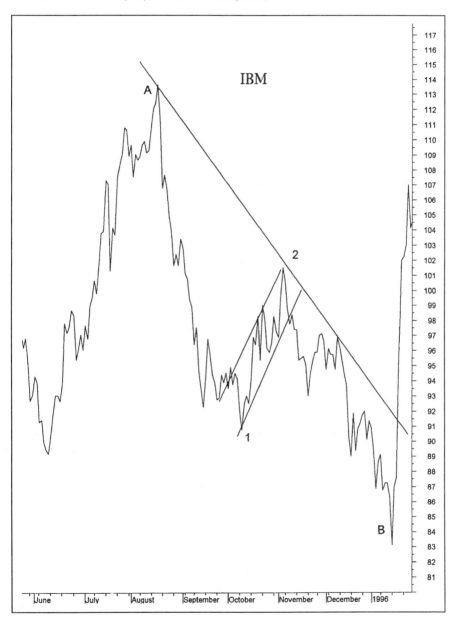

tioned. Bear in mind that different analysts may use different time parameters to determine trend significance. Some measure short-term trends in days, intermediate trends in months, and major trends in years. The precise definition isn't that important. What *is* important is that you understand the basic difference between the three degrees of trend.

For example, an analyst may be bullish on a stock, but bearish short term. That simply means that although the most important trend (the major trend) is still up, the stock will probably experience some short-term downward pressure (often called *volatility*). This may mean different things to different people. A short-term trader might sell a stock that is entering a downside correction. A longer-term investor would probably use a short-term correction in a major uptrend as a buying opportunity.

DAILY, WEEKLY, AND MONTHLY CHARTS

An appreciation of what each trend is doing is important. For this reason, it's necessary to use price charts that monitor the different trends. In order to gain a long-term perspective, *monthly charts* showing 20 years of price history are a good place to start. *Weekly charts* that cover at least five years are recommended to get a closer picture of the major trend. *Daily charts* going back a year are necessary to study the shorter-term trends. While monthly and weekly charts are most helpful in determining a generally bullish or bearish attitude on a market, daily charts are most helpful in the timing of various trading strategies. You'll see why it's important to use all three (see Figures 2.11 and 2.12).

RECENT VERSUS DISTANT PAST

Time is important in market analysis. Generally speaking, the longer a trend has been in motion, the more important it is. A five-day trend is clearly not as significant as a five-month or a five-year trend. The same is true of support and resistance levels, since they measure those different degrees of trend. A support or resistance level that was formed a couple of weeks ago is not nearly as important as one formed two years ago. As a general rule, the further back in time that a support or resistance level was formed, the more significant it becomes. As a second rule, the more times a support or resistance level has been "tested," the more important it becomes. Sometimes a market will back off from a resistance level three or four times. Clearly, any subsequent penetration of that barrier carries much more significance. The number of times a price tests support or

Figure 2.11   A 10-year perspective shows IBM breaking a major down trendline. *(MetaStock, Equis International, Inc.)*

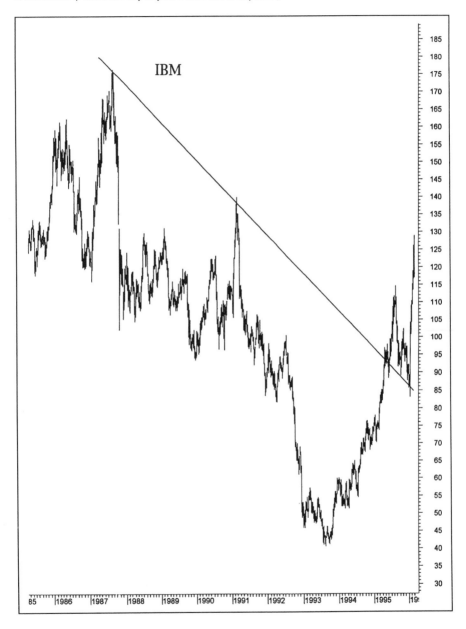

Figure 2.12   A 20-year perspective shows that major support existed in IBM near 40, a good thing to know in 1993. *(MetaStock, Equis International, Inc.)*

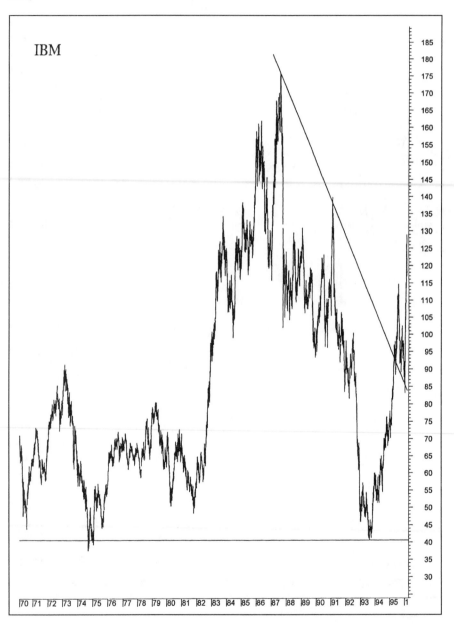

resistance is also important in the identification of *price patterns,* which will be covered in the next chapter.

TRENDLINES

The simple *trendline* is possibly the most useful tool in the study of market trends. And you'll be happy to know that they're extremely easy to draw. Chart analysts use trendlines to determine the slope of a market trend and to help determine when that trend is changing. Although horizontal trendlines can be drawn on a chart, the most common usage refers to up trendlines and down trendlines. An *up trendline* is simply drawn under the rising reaction lows. A *down trendline* is drawn above the declining market peaks. Markets often rise or fall at a given slope. The trendline helps us to determine what that slope is.

Once a valid trendline is drawn, markets will often bounce off it several times. For example, in an uptrend, markets will often pull back to the up trendline and bounce off it. Retests of up trendlines often present excellent buying opportunities (see Figure 2.13). Prices in a downtrend will often bounce back to the falling trendline, presenting a selling opportunity. Analysts often refer to *trendline support and resistance.*

How to Draw a Trendline

The most common way to draw a trendline is to make sure that it includes all of the price action. On a bar chart (where the price range is marked by a vertical bar), the up trendline is drawn in such a way that the trendline rests on the bottom of the bars (see Figure 2.14). A down trendline touches the top of the price bars. Some analysts prefer to connect only the closing prices instead of the individual price bars. For longer-range trend analysis, it doesn't make too much difference. For shorter-term analysis, I prefer connecting the tops and bottoms of the individual price bars.

It takes two points to draw a line. An up trendline can't be drawn until two troughs are visible. Even then, the trendline is not necessarily a *valid* trendline. Prices should test the trendline, and bounce off it, to confirm that the trendline is valid. Preferably, prices should touch a trendline three times. (Sometimes, however, the market isn't as accommodating as we would like and a trendline is touched only twice.) The more times a trendline is tested, the more significant it becomes. Once the analyst feels confident about a trendline, then any decisive violation of that line is an early warning of a possible change in trend.

Figure 2.13   An up trendline is drawn under reaction lows. After three tests, the line is considered valid. Notice IBM stock bouncing off up trendline in early 1996. *(SuperCharts, Omega Research)*

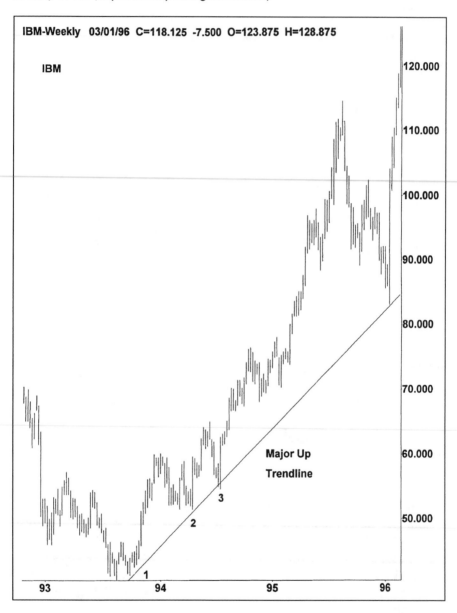

Figure 2.14   Examples of shorter-term trendlines at work. Violation of up trendline at (A) signaled start of correction. Break of down trendline at (B) signaled end of correction. *(MetaStock, Equis International, Inc.)*

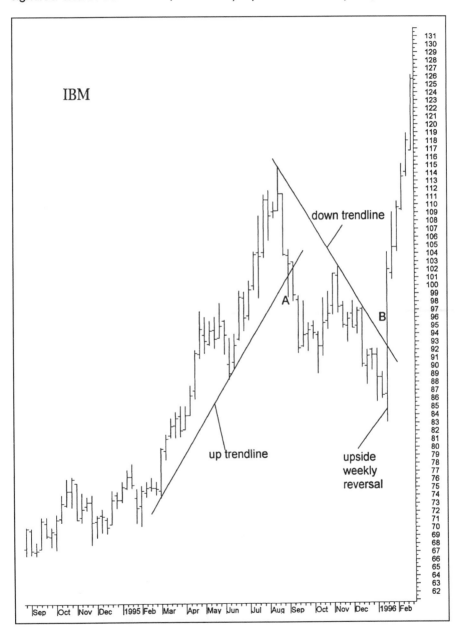

Most analysts draw several lines on their charts. Sometimes the original trendline proves to be incorrect, in which case a new trendline must be drawn. Another reason for having several trendlines is that they measure different trends. Some measure the short-term trend, some the longer trend. As with trends themselves, longer-term trendlines carry more significance than shorter-term trendlines (see Figures 2.13 and 2.14).

CHANNEL LINES

Channel lines are easily drawn on price charts and often help identify support and resistance levels. Markets will often trend between two parallel trendlines, one above and one below the price action. During a downtrend, you must first draw a conventional down trendline along two market peaks. Then move your cursor to the bottom of the intervening trough and instruct the computer to draw a line parallel to the declining trendline. You'll wind up with two declining trendlines, one above the price action and one (the channel line) below (see Figure 2.15). A stock will often find support when it touches the lower channel line.

To draw a rising trendline (during an uptrend), you must first draw a conventional up trendline along two market lows. By moving your computer cursor to the peak between the two troughs, you can draw another rising trendline exactly parallel to the lower trendline—except that the channel line is rising above the price trend, while the conventional up trendline is below. It's usually a good idea to know where rising channel lines are located, since markets will often stall at that level.

While the channel technique doesn't always work, it's usually a good idea to know where the channel lines are located. A move above a rising channel line is a sign of market strength, while a decline below a falling channel line is a sign of market weakness. Most software packages refer to channel lines as *parallel lines.*

RETRACING OUR STEPS BY ONE-THIRD, ONE-HALF, AND TWO-THIRDS

One of the simplest and most useful market tendencies to be aware of is the *percentage retracement.* We've already stated that markets generally don't trend in a straight line. Trends are characterized by zig-zags, which are identified by successive peaks and troughs. Intermediate trends represent corrections to major trends, while short-term trends represent corrections to intermediate trends. Those corrections, or interruptions,

Figure 2.15   Prices will often find support at a channel line drawn parallel to the down trendline. *(MetaStock, Equis International, Inc.)*

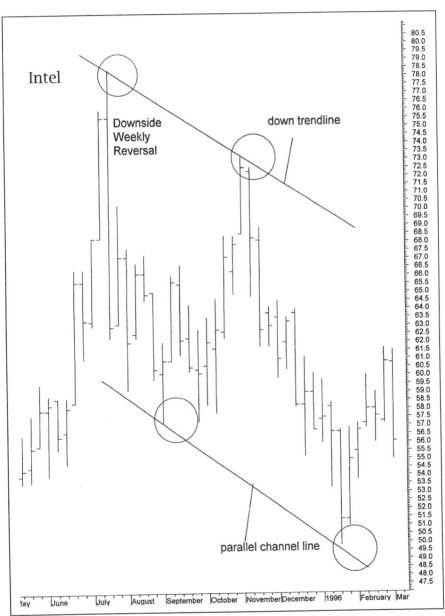

usually retrace the prior trend by predictable percentage amounts. The best known is the *50-percent retracement*. A stock that's traveled from 20 to 40 will often retrace about 10 points (50 percent) before resuming its advance. Knowing this, an investor might consider purchasing a stock that has lost about half the amount of its prior advance. In a downtrend, stocks will often regain half of the prior losses before resuming their decline. This tendency for prices to retrace the prior trend by certain percentages is true in all degrees of trend.

One-Third to Two-Thirds Retracements

Usually a market will retrace a *minimum one-third* of its prior move. A rally from 30 to 60 will often be followed by a 10-point correction (one-third of the 30-point gain). This minimum retracement tendency is particularly helpful in the timing of purchases or sales. In an uptrend, an investor can determine in advance where a one-third retracement lies, and use that level as a potential buy point. In a downtrend, a one-third bounce could represent a selling area. Sometimes a severe correction will retrace as much as *two-thirds* of the prior move. That level becomes very significant. If the correction is just that, prices rarely retrace more than two-thirds. That area represents another useful support area on the charts. If a market moves beyond the two-thirds point, then a total trend reversal is most likely taking place.

Most charting software packages allow the user to identify retracement levels on a chart. This is done in two ways. After the user has identified the beginning and end of a move with a cursor, a table appears which tells the user at what price levels the various percentage retracements will occur. A second option draws horizontal lines that highlight the levels on the price chart at which the various percentage retracements will occur. These retracement lines help function as support levels in an uptrend and resistance levels in a downtrend. The user can preset the percentage retracements to any levels desired. The levels most commonly used are 33 percent, 38 percent, 50 percent, 62 percent, and 66 percent.

Why 38 Percent and 62 Percent?

These two retracement levels are derived from a number series known as the *Fibonacci numbers*. This series begins with the number 1 and adds each two succeeding numbers together (e.g., $1 + 1 = 2$, $1 + 2 = 3$, and so on). The most commonly used Fibonacci numbers are 1, 2, 3, 5, 8, 13, 21, 34, 55, and

89. *Fibonacci ratios* are very important. The two most important are 38 percent and 62 percent. Each Fibonacci number is approximately 62 percent of the next higher number (e.g., ⅝ = .625); hence, the 62 percent retracement level. 38 is the inverse of 62 (100 − 62 = 38); hence, the 38 percent retracement number. This is probably all you need to know at this point about these numbers. They are very popular among professional traders and are widely used to determine how far corrections will retrace. Figure 2.16 shows the 38 percent, 50 percent, and 62 percent retracement lines applied to a chart of IBM. (For a more in-depth explanation, see *Elliott wave analysis* in the Glossary.)

Doubling and Halving

This simple technique can prove useful in determining when to sell a rising stock and when to buy a falling stock. Consider selling at least a portion of a stock that has doubled in price. The flip side of that is to consider buying a portion of a stock that has lost half of its value. This is sometimes called the *cut in half rule*, which differs from the 50-percent retracement rule. The 50-percent retracement refers to a stock that loses half of its prior advance. A 50-percent retracement of a stock that has risen from 50 to 100 would be a decline to 75. The cut in half rule refers to a stock that loses half of its total value, which would mean a fall all the way to 50 in this example.

WEEKLY REVERSALS

The *weekly reversal* is another simple market formation that's worth looking out for. Two prominent weekly reversals can be seen in Figures 2.14 and 2.15. An *upside weekly reversal* occurs during a market decline and can be seen only on a weekly bar chart (Figure 2.14). A stock starts the week with a lot of selling and usually breaks under some type of support level. By week's end, however, prices have turned dramatically upward and close above the previous week's price range. The wider the weekly price bar, and the heavier the trading volume, the greater the significance of the turnaround. The fact that IBM achieved a massive upside weekly reversal during January 1996 (Figure 2.14) signaled the probable end of its downward correction. Lending even more importance to the upward turnaround was its location. IBM was bouncing off a major up trendline (Figure 2.13) and was at a 38 percent retracement level (Figure 2.16).

A *downside weekly reversal* is just the opposite. Prices open the week sharply higher and then collapse at week's end. A huge downside weekly

Figure 2.16   The computer calculates the various percentage retracement
lines which can then be viewed as support levels. *(SuperCharts, Omega
Research)*

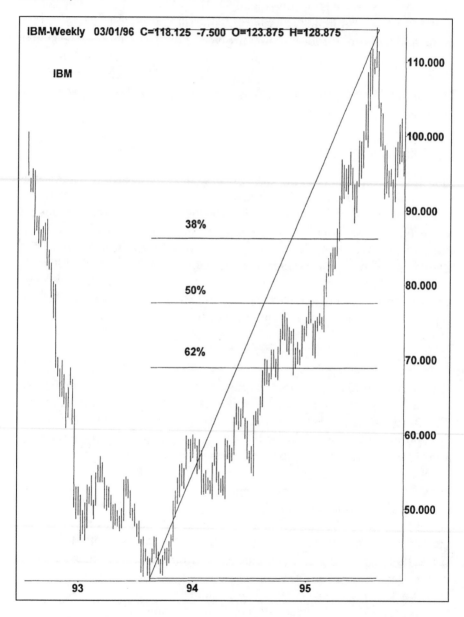

reversal was formed by Intel at its 1995 summer peak (Figure 2.15). While that pattern alone isn't usually enough to turn the chart bearish, it is enough to warrant closer study of the situation and to consider taking some type of defensive action. Weekly reversals take on more significance if they occur in the vicinity of historic support or resistance levels. The daily version of the weekly reversal is referred to as a *key reversal day* (see Glossary). While daily reversals can be important, weekly reversals carry much more significance.

SUMMARY

The most important goal of the visual trader is to be able to identify the *trend* of a market and spot when that trend is changing. The entire point of visual analysis is to participate in significant uptrends and to avoid significant downtrends. There are different categories of trend, however. The *major trend* (usually more than six months) measures the most important trend of a market. The *intermediate trend* (lasting from one to six months) tracks less important trends that represent corrections within the major trend. The *minor trend* (usually lasting less than a month) is the least important of the three and measures shorter-term swings in a market. This shorter trend is extremely important for timing purposes. It's important to watch all three trends for a proper perspective. For this reason, it's necessary to utilize daily, weekly, and monthly charts.

An *uptrend* represents a series of rising peaks (resistance) and troughs (support). A *downtrend* represents a series of declining peaks (resistance) and troughs (support). *Resistance levels* are always above the market. *Support levels* are always below the market. *Trendlines* drawn along those peaks and troughs are one of the simplest ways to measure market trends. Another useful technique is *50-percent retracement.* Other important percentage retracements are 33 percent, 38 percent, 62 percent, and 66 percent. A *doubling in price* usually marks an *overbought* market. A *halving in price* usually signals that a market is *oversold.* The next chapter shows how simple trendlines, along with support and resistance levels, are combined to form predictive *price patterns.*

3
Pictures That Tell a Story

Having learned how to identify a trend, to spot support and resistance levels, and to draw a trendline, the visual investor is ready to look for price patterns. Prices have a tendency to form patterns or pictures that often indicate which way a stock is going to trend. It should be obvious that the ability to distinguish between patterns that represent nothing more than an *interruption* in the primary trend and those that signal an impending trend *reversal* is a valuable skill to acquire. In order to accomplish a complete analysis of any chart, it is important to take both price and volume (trading activity) into consideration. We'll show you how to incorporate volume into your chart analysis. But first, a quick word on the types of charts available for visual analysis.

CHART TYPES

The Bar Chart

We're going to confine our discussion to the most popular chart types, beginning with the bar chart. A daily *bar chart* represents each day's price action with a vertical bar and horizontal price ticks, one to the left and one to the right of the vertical bar (see Figure 3.1). The vertical bar connects the high price of the day to the low price. The vertical bar measures the stock's daily *price range*. A small horizontal tick is placed to the left of the bar, which represents the *opening price*. The small horizontal tick to the right of the vertical bar represents the *closing price*. The price bar tells us where the stock opened (left tick), where it closed (right tick), and the highest and lowest prices reached during the day (top and bottom of the vertical price bar). On a weekly bar chart, the bar measures the price range for the entire week, with the left tick showing Monday's open and the right tick Friday's close.

The Line Chart

The most important price of the day is the closing price, because that is the market's final judgment for that day as to what a stock is worth. When you turn on your nightly news report to see what's happened to your stock portfolio, you will learn where a stock closed and its change from the previous day. They'll tell you that IBM, for example, closed at 110, down 2 points from the previous day; or that the Dow Jones Industrials rose 10 points to close at 5,450. To many analysts, the final price is all that really matters. Those analysts usually employ a simpler type of chart that uses just the closing prices. They simply draw a line that connects the successive closing prices for each day. They wind up with a single line, which is referred to as a *line chart*. While the line chart shows only closing prices, the bar chart includes each day's high, low, and opening prices in addition to the closing price (see Figure 3.1).

Both types of chart can be used to perform virtually any type of visual analysis. As mentioned in the previous chapter, it makes very little difference where longer-range price trends are being studied. However, for shorter time periods most analysts prefer the bar chart, which provides a more complete summary of the price action. The same holds true for trendline analysis. For shorter-term study, we'll employ bar charts most of the time. For longer-range trends, we'll use both types.

The Candlestick Chart

This is a Japanese version of the bar chart that has become extremely popular with market analysts in recent years. The candlestick chart uses the same price data as the bar chart—open, high, low, and close—but the candlestick presents the data in a more useful visual format (see Figures 3.2 and 3.3). In the candlestick chart, a thin bar represents the daily price range

Figure 3.1   Merck: (*a*) Each bar represents the daily price range. The tick to the left of each bar is the open and the tick to the right is the close price. (*b*) A line chart covering the same data as chart (*a*). A line chart simply connects the closing prices for each day. *(MetaStock, Equis International, Inc.)*

Figure 3.2 Merck: (a) Daily bar chart showing price range (bar), open price (left tick), and close price (right tick). (b) Candlestick chart of the same data as shown in (a). The thin lines (shadows) show the price range. The fat portion (body) marks the area between open and close. Clear or empty bodies represent close price higher than open price. (MetaStock, Equis International, Inc.)

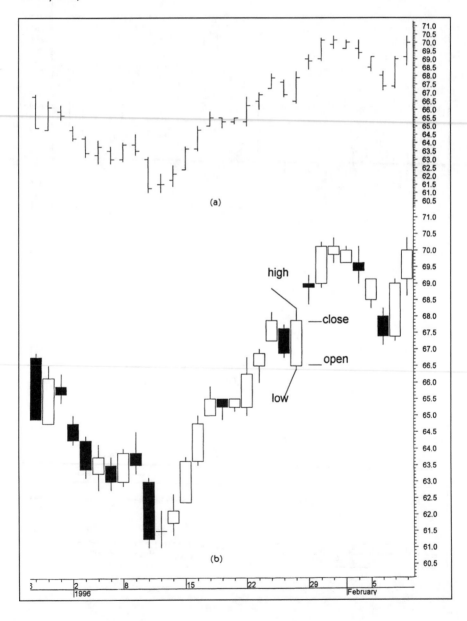

Figure 3.3   Daily candlestick chart of Merck. The color of the rectangle (body) is determined by the relationship between the open and the close price. A white body (bullish) occurs when the close is higher than the open. A dark body (bearish) means the close is under the open. Notice the frequency of black bodies during downtrends and the frequency of white bodies during uptrends. *(MetaStock, Equis International, Inc.)*

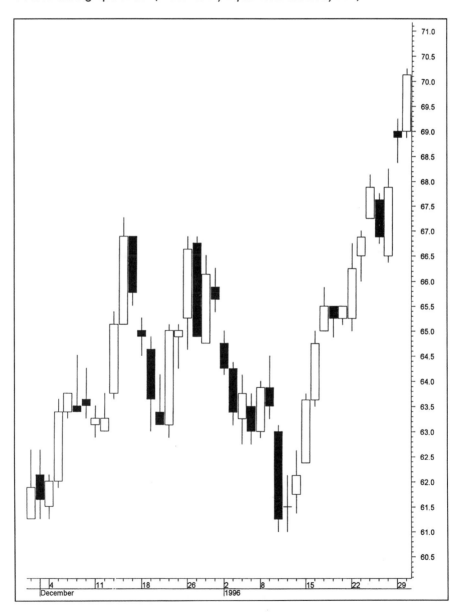

(called the *shadow*). The fatter portion of the bar (called the *real body*) includes the distance between the opening and closing prices. If the closing price is higher than the opening price, the fat portion of the candlestick is white. A white candlestick is bullish. If the closing price is lower than the opening, the fat portion is black. A black candlestick is considered bearish.

The Japanese place considerable importance on the relationship between the opening and closing prices. The attraction of the candlestick chart is that it provides the same information as the Western bar chart, but with an added dimension. Not only does the color of the bars reveal a bullish or bearish bias in a given market, but the shape of the candles reveals bullish or bullish patterns that aren't visible on the bar chart. In addition, all of the techniques that can be applied to the bar chart can also be applied to the candlestick. (Appendix B provides a more extensive explanation of candlesticks for those wishing to study them further.)

TIME CHOICES

In the previous chapter, we pointed out that monthly and weekly charts can be constructed for longer-range trend analysis. Daily charts can be used for shorter-term study. Intraday charts, measuring hourly price changes, can even be employed for short-term trading purposes. We were primarily referring there to the line and bar charts. Candlestick charts can be time adjusted with each candlestick representing one hour, one day, one week, or one month in the same way as one would adjust a bar chart. Daily line charts connect daily closes, weekly line charts connect weekly closes, and so on. All of the chart types described can be adjusted for both short-term and long-term analysis simply by adjusting the time sensitivity (see Figures 3.4 and 3.5).

In addition, the basic charting principles are applied the same way in each time dimension. In other words, one would analyze a weekly chart in the same way as a daily chart. One of the real advantages of employing charting software is the ability to shift between daily and weekly charts with a keystroke to gain a different time perspective, and to move back and forth between bar, line, or candlestick charts with another keystroke. The choices then are which type of chart to employ and over what time period. But there are other choices to consider.

SCALING

The most commonly used price charts present two types of information—*price* and *time*. Time is shown horizontally, with dates along the bottom of

Figure 3.4   (a) Daily bar chart of Merck showing short-term break of support. (b) Weekly bar chart of Merck showing that short-term decline was just a dip in the uptrend. *(SuperCharts, Omega Research)*

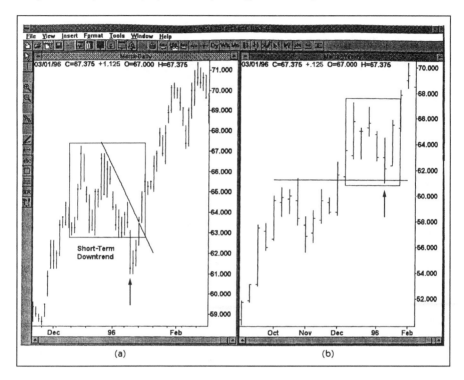

the chart moving from left to right. The price scale is shown vertically, moving from the lower prices upward to higher prices. There are two ways to show the vertical price data. The most common is by using a linear, or arithmetic, scale. On a linear stock chart, for example, each price increment is measured equally. Each one-point advance looks the same as any other one-point advance. An advance from 10 to 20 looks the same as an advance from 50 to 60. Each represents a 10-point advance and takes up the same distance on the vertical scale. This is the chart scale most of us are familiar with. The other type is the log scale (see Figure 3.6).

Logarithmic or *semilog charts* measure price changes by percentages instead of by units. In other words, a move from 10 to 20 looks much larger than a move from 50 to 60. The reason is that, in percent terms, a rally from 50 to 60 is not nearly as significant as a move from 10 to 20. An investor who buys a stock at 10 and watches it rise to 20 has doubled his or her money—a 100 percent gain. An investor purchasing a stock at 50 and

Figure 3.5   (*a*) Monthly bar chart of Merck. The decline in the weekly bars to the right didn't even register on the monthly chart. (*b*) Weekly bar chart of Merck showing short-term dip at beginning of 1996. *(SuperCharts, Omega Research)*

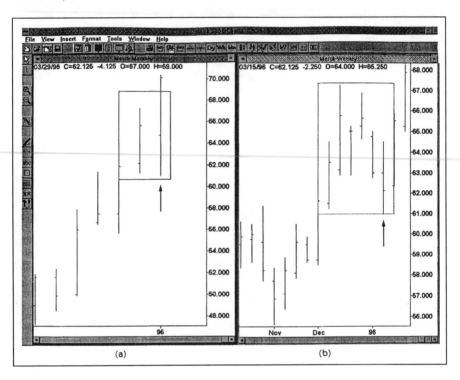

(a)   (b)

watching it rise to 60 has only gained 20 percent, despite the fact that both stocks rallied 10 points. In order to match the same 100 percent gain from 10 to 20, the other stock would also have to also double in price, rising from 50 to 100 (for a 100 percent gain). Log charts, therefore, are constructed in such a way that the gain from 10 to 20 (100 percent) measures the same distance as the move from 50 to 100 (100 percent).

Generally speaking, the difference between the two types of charts isn't that significant for shorter time periods. Most traders still employ the more familiar arithmetic scale for that purpose, and there's no reason why you shouldn't do the same. The differences on longer range charts can, however, be significant. On a semilog chart, successive price increases look smaller in comparison to earlier moves. As a result, trendlines drawn on log charts will be broken much quicker. There's no absolute answer as

Figure 3.6   (*a*) Monthly chart of Merck with linear (arithmetic) scale. With a linear scale, all moves are equal; the space from 60 to 65 is the same as the space from 30 to 35. (*b*) Monthly chart of Merck with semilog (logarithmic) scale. Logarithmic scaling compares percentage increases; the space from 60 to 65 is much smaller than the space from 30 to 35. *(SuperCharts, Omega Research)*

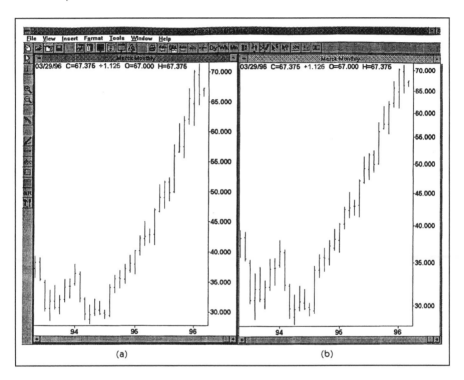

to which technique is better. For most of our work in this text, we employ the simpler arithmetic scaling. However, it's usually a good idea to look at the chart both ways when doing longer-range work. The computer lets you switch back and forth quite easily.

VOLUME ANALYSIS

Most price charts also show *volume bars* along the bottom of the chart. On a bar chart, for example, the vertical volume bars along the bottom horizontal part of the chart correspond to each price bar in the upper end of the chart (see Figure 3.7). Heavier volume is shown by larger volume bars

Figure 3.7   Barrick Gold (weekly): Notice the tendency for volume bars (bottom of chart) to get bigger during market upmoves (points A, B, and C). This is considered bullish if prices rise on rising volume. *(SuperCharts, Omega Research)*

and, of course, lighter volume can be identified by smaller volume bars. By scanning the chart, the analyst can see which days (or weeks) had the heaviest volume. This is important because volume tells us a lot about the strength or weakness of the price trend. Generally speaking, when a stock price is in an uptrend, buying pressure should be greater than selling pressure. In a healthy uptrend, volume bars are generally larger when prices are rising and smaller when prices are falling. In other words, volume is confirming the price trend. When the analyst notices that price pullbacks are accompanied by heavier volume than is evident on rallies, that is an early warning that the uptrend is losing momentum. As a general rule of thumb, *heavier volume should be evident in the direction of the existing trend.*

Granville's On-Balance Volume

This useful indicator was first described by Joseph Granville in his 1963 book, *Granville's New Key to Stock Market Profits.* What makes *on-balance volume (OBV)* so useful is that it presents a more visually helpful way to view the volume flow and to compare it with the price action (see Figure 3.8). Volume should increase in the direction of the price trend. Granville's indicator makes it easier to make sure that is happening. The construction of on-balance volume is extremely simple. Every day that a stock trades, it closes up or down on a certain amount of trading activity. If the stock closes higher, that day's volume is given a positive value and is added to the previous day's volume. If the stock drops, its volume is considered to be negative and is subtracted from the previous day's volume. On days when the stock is unchanged, the volume line also remains unchanged. In other words, *on-balance volume is a running cumulative total of positive and negative volume numbers.*

Eventually, the on-balance volume line will take a direction. If the direction is up, the line is bullish, meaning that there is more volume on up days than on down days. A falling OBV line signals that volume is heavier on down days, and is considered to be bearish. By including the OBV line along the bottom of the chart (or overlayed right on top of the price action), the analyst can easily see if the price and volume lines are moving in the same direction. If both are moving up together, the uptrend is still healthy. In that case, volume is *confirming* the price trend. However, if prices are moving higher while the volume line is dropping, a negative *divergence* exists, warning that the price uptrend may be in trouble. It is when the price and volume lines begin to diverge from each other and travel in opposite directions that the most important warning signals are given.

Figure 3.8   The on-balance volume (thin) line led prices higher and antici-
pated the bullish breakout in Barrick Gold (heavy line). *(MetaStock, Equis International, Inc.)*

It is the direction of the OBV line that matters, not the numerical value of the line. The OBV values will change depending on when the line was begun (how far back you are looking). Concentrate on the trend, not the numbers. Software packages will compute and draw the OBV line for you.

CHART PATTERNS

Reversal or Continuation

A number of chart patterns that carry some predictive value have been identified by chart analysts over the years. We're going to confine our comments here to a handful of the more easily recognizable and more reliable ones. Under the category of *reversal patterns*, the three most important are the *double top and bottom,* the *triple top and bottom,* and the *head and shoulders top and bottom.* These patterns can be spotted quite easily on most charts and, when properly identified, can warn that a trend reversal is taking place. Under the category of *continuation patterns,* we're going to study the *triangle.* When this pattern is clearly evident on the chart, it usually implies that a market is just consolidating within its prior trend and will most likely resume that trend. This is why it is called a *continuation* pattern. All you really need to spot these patterns is an ability to see peaks (resistance levels) and troughs (support levels) and the ability to draw some trendlines.

Volume

Volume is important in the interpretation of chart patterns. During a topping pattern, for example, volume will display a tendency to lighten during rallies and increase during pullbacks. During the latter stages of a downtrend, prices will display heavier volume bars during rallies and lighter volume during price dips. At important breakouts, particularly bullish breakouts, heavy volume is an essential ingredient. An upside breakout in any market that is not accompanied by a noticeable increase in trading activity is immediately suspect. During continuation patterns, such as the *triangle,* volume generally becomes much lighter, reflecting a period of indecision. Volume should pick up noticeably once the pattern has been resolved and prices break free of the prior trading range.

On-Balance Volume

On-balance volume can be very helpful in the study of price patterns. Since these sideways price patterns usually represent a period of indecision in the market, the analyst is never sure whether the stock in question is truly reversing or just resting. The volume line can often help answer that question by showing which way the heavier volume is flowing. That can help the analyst determine earlier on whether the stock is undergoing accumulation (buying) or distribution (selling). Many times, the on-balance line will break out before prices do (as happens in Figure 3.8). That's usually an early signal that prices will follow in the same direction. It's a good idea to keep an eye on the OBV line, especially in the study of price patterns, to confirm that the price chart is telling the true story and warn when it is not.

Double Tops and Bottoms

These patterns are self-explanatory. Picture an uptrend which is a series of rising peaks and troughs. Each time a stock rallies back to its old high at a previous peak, one of two things will happen: Either the price will go through that peak, or it won't. If price closes through the prior peak, the uptrend is resumed and everything is fine. If, however, the stock fails to exceed its prior peak and starts to weaken, caution flags are being waved. What the analyst then has is a possible *double top* in its earliest stages. A double top is nothing more than a price chart with two prominent peaks at about the same price level (see Figure 3.9).

Trading Ranges

The chart in Figure 3.10 shows why we never know for sure if that pullback is the beginning of a double top or just a natural hesitation at a prior resistance level. Prices will often do nothing more than trade sideways for a while between the prior peak and the prior trough before finally resuming the uptrend. We normally refer to that sideways pattern as a *consolidation* or a *trading range*. In order for an actual double top to be present, something else has to happen. Not only does the stock have to stall at a previous peak—the price also has to fall enough to close below its previous trough. Once that happens, the pattern of higher peaks and troughs has been reversed and the analyst is left with a double top reversal pattern. The double top is also referred to as an *M pattern* because of its shape (take another look at Figure 3.9).

Although we've described a topping pattern, the bottoming pattern is just a mirror image. A *double bottom* is present when a market forms two prominent lows around the same price level, followed by an upside close through the prior peak. A new uptrend has been started, especially if the

Figure 3.9   Double top in paper and forest product stocks in 1995. Double tops are marked by two prominent peaks around the same level (points 1 and 2), which is followed by a breaking of support (point 3). *(MetaStock, Equis International, Inc.)*

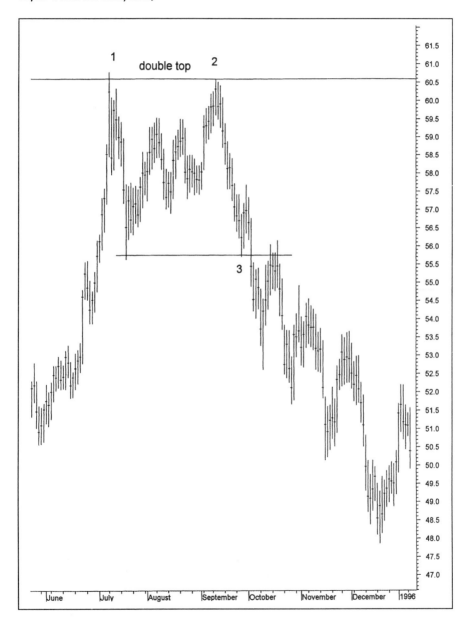

Figure 3.10   NASDAQ Composite Index: example of sideways consolidation pattern. This chart shows why it's important to wait for prices to fall below the low at point A to label a chart as a double top. If the decline at point B bounces off the support line, the pattern usually represents nothing more than a pause in the uptrend. *(SuperCharts, Omega Research)*

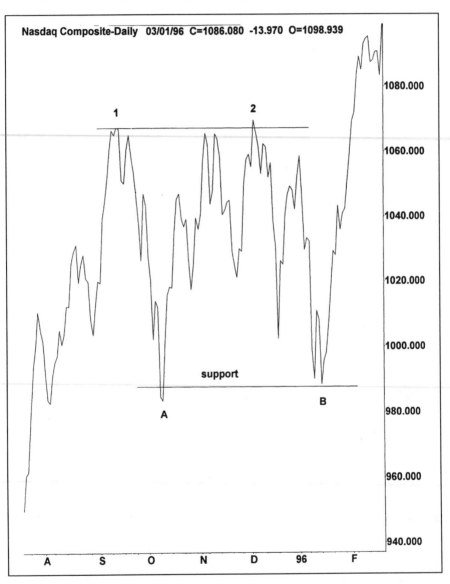

upside breakout takes place on heavy volume. Here again, chartists like to see the on-balance volume line confirm whatever prices are doing. The double bottom is also called a *W pattern* (see Figures 3.11 and 3.12).

Triple Tops and Bottoms

As you might expect, *triple tops* show three prominent tops instead of two. This simply means that the sideways period of price movement is carried on much longer. However, the interpretation is the same. If prices that had been in an uptrend eventually close at a new high, the uptrend is resumed. If, however, three prominent peaks are visible around the same price level and prices break below the previous reaction low, then a triple top reversal pattern has probably occurred. A *triple bottom* would naturally show three prominent troughs at about the same price level, followed by an upward penetration of the previous peak (see Figure 3.13). As you can see, these patterns are pretty self-explanatory and are easily spotted. If you look at any library of market charts, you will spot countless examples of these patterns. Generally speaking, double tops and bottoms are much more frequent. Triple tops and bottoms are less frequent, but they can be found. Another popular variation of the triple top and bottom is the *head and shoulders* reversal pattern.

Head and Shoulders Pattern

You've probably gotten the idea by now that there isn't anything terribly complicated about these price patterns and the names assigned to them. The same is true of the *head and shoulders* pattern. This bottoming pattern is basically the same as the triple bottom in the sense that there are three prominent lows. Where they differ is in how the three lows are formed. The triple bottom shows three lows at about the same price level (see Figure 3.13). The head and shoulders pattern gets its name from the fact that it shows one prominent low in the middle (the head) surrounded on each side by two slightly higher lows (the shoulders [see Figures 3.14 and 3.15]). It resembles a person standing on his or her head.

In a bottoming pattern, a trendline (neckline) is drawn above the two intervening peaks. Once that line is broken on the upside, the pattern has been completed and a new uptrend has been signaled. The bottom version is called an *inverse* head and shoulders.

The top is just a mirror image of the bottom (see Figure 3.16). While a top is being formed, the middle peak (head) is slightly higher than the sur-

Figure 3.11 This chart shows how a double bottom looks. Notice that the second trough (point 2) is itself, a small double bottom. *(MetaStock, Equis International, Inc.)*

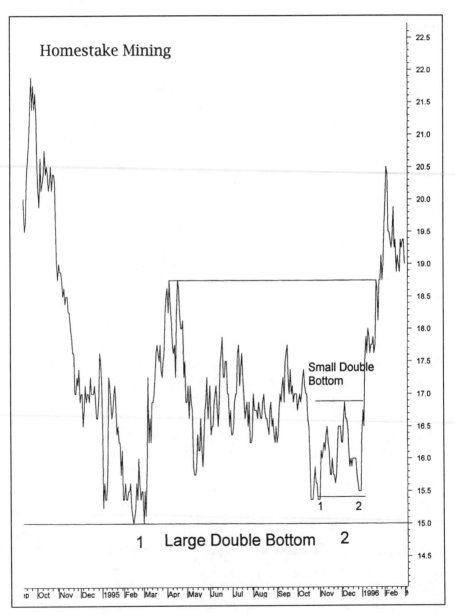

Figure 3.12   A longer-range view of Homestake Mining shows that the completion of the double bottom coincided with the breaking of an important down trendline. *(MetaStock, Equis International, Inc.)*

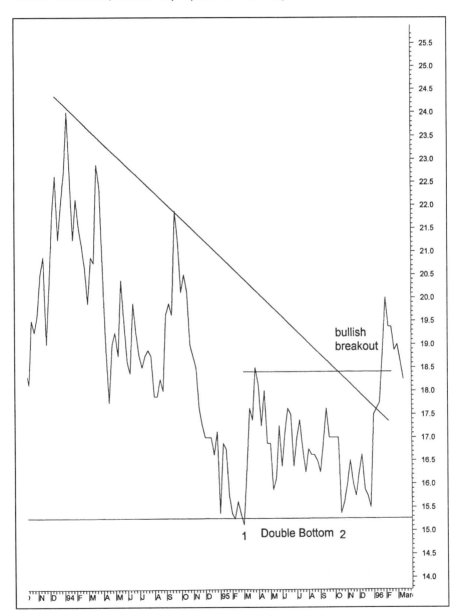

Figure 3.13   Example of triple bottom formed over a period of three years. (MetaStock, Equis International, Inc.)

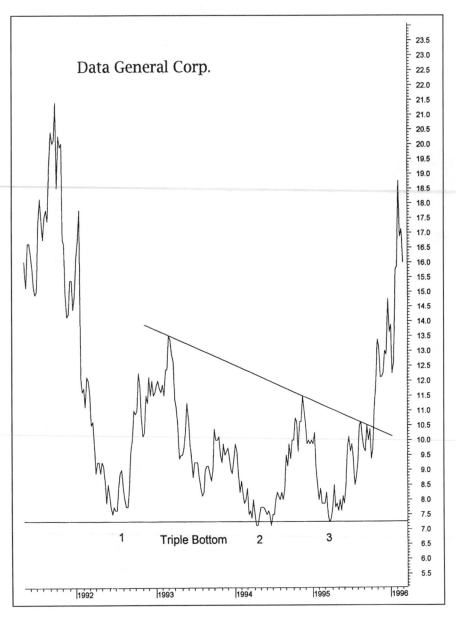

Figure 3.14   This bullish breakout in late 1995 completed a three-year inverse head and shoulders bottom. *(MetaStock, Equis International, Inc.)*

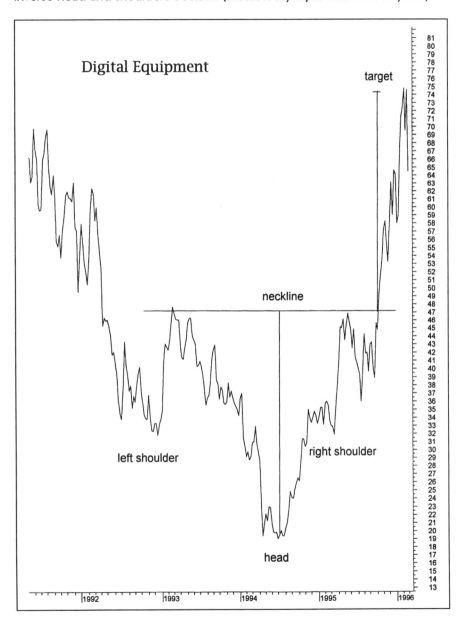

Figure 3.15   Gold stocks (XAU) with inverse head and shoulders bottom.
(SuperCharts, Omega Research)

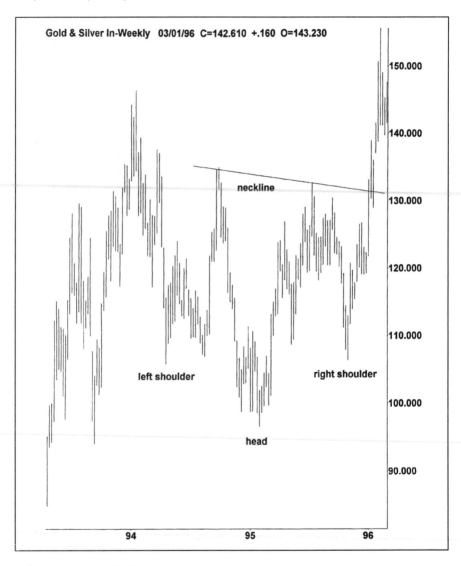

rounding peaks (shoulders). A trendline (neckline) is drawn below the two intervening troughs. Once prices fall below that trendline, a new downtrend has been signaled.

In all of these reversal patterns, it's important to study the volume pattern to confirm what prices are doing. An on-balance volume line is espe-

Figure 3.16   Example of head and shoulders top. *(MetaStock, Equis International, Inc.)*

cially helpful while these patterns are forming and at their completion, to make sure that the volume flow is confirming the price action. Keep in mind that heavier volume is more critical on the upside than on the downside.

MEASURING TECHNIQUES

Price patterns often tell us how far a market will run. These measurements are simply meant to give an approximation of the minimum distance a market can be expected to travel after a pattern has been completed. The general rule of thumb for the three patterns covered here is that *the height of the pattern determines the market's potential.* In other words, simply measure the height of the sideways trading range and project that distance from the breakout point. If the height of a double or triple top is 20 points, that would imply that prices will probably drop at least 20 points from the point where the previous reaction low was violated. For example, if the trading range measured from 50 to 70, a break to the downside would imply a target to 30.

The measurement for the head and shoulders is a bit more precise. At a top, the vertical distance from the top of the head to the neckline is subtracted from the level where the neckline is broken on the downside (see Figure 3.16). At a head and shoulders bottom, the vertical distance from the bottom of the head to the neckline is added to the point where prices exceed the neckline (see Figure 3.14). Bear in mind, however, that these are not precise measurements and only help to approximate the minimum potential for a market move.

EVEN THE FED IS CHARTING

During the summer of 1995, the central banks launched a successful intervention in support of the U.S. dollar. The financial press attributed part of that success to the fact that the central bankers had actually employed some technical trading methods on the markets. That the Federal Reserve Board was taking the chart approach more seriously was confirmed by the release of an August 1995 Staff Report, "Head and Shoulders: Not Just a Flaky Pattern." I was also pleasantly surprised to see my first book, *Technical Analysis of the Futures Markets* (Prentice-Hall, 1986), quoted frequently throughout the report as a primary source of information. The final conclusion of the report was that the head and shoulders pattern produces statistically and economically significant profits when applied to currency trading. The report's introduction states:

Technical Analysis . . . has been shown to generate statistically significant profits despite its incompatibility with most economists' notions of "efficient markets."
(Federal Reserve Bank of New York, C. L. Osler and P. H. Kevin Chang, Staff Report, No. 4, August 1995.)

Who are we to argue with the Fed?

THE TRIANGLE

This pattern differs from the previous ones in that the *triangle* is usually a continuation pattern. Its formation signals that a trend has gotten ahead of itself and needs to consolidate for a while. Once that consolidation has been completed, the prior trend usually resumes in the same direction. In an uptrend, therefore, a triangle is usually a bullish pattern. In a downtrend, a triangle is usually bearish. The shape of the triangle can take various forms. The most common is the *symmetrical triangle* (see Figure 3.17). This pattern is characterized by sideways movement on the chart where the price action gradually narrows. Trendlines drawn along its peaks and troughs appear to *converge* on each other. Each trendline is usually touched at least twice and often three times. Usually, about two-thirds to three-quarters of the way into the pattern, prices will break out in the direction of the prior trend. If the prior trend was up, prices will probably break out on the upside.

Ascending and Descending Triangles

These two variations of the triangle generally have a more decisive predictive quality. In an *ascending triangle,* the line drawn along the upper end of the price range is flat, while the line along the bottom of the range is rising (see Figure 3.18). This is considered to be a bullish pattern. A *descending triangle* has a flat lower line and a falling upper line, and is considered to be bearish (see Figure 3.19). The resolution of all three types of triangle takes place when one of the two trendlines (either above or below the pattern) is broken decisively. Here again, a pickup of volume is important, especially if the breakout is to the upside.

There are ways to determine how far prices will probably go after completion of the triangle. The simplest way is to measure the vertical height at the triangle's widest part (on the left) and project that distance from the point where the breakout actually occurs on the right (see Figure 3.19). As in

Figure 3.17   Example of bullish symmetrical triangle with converging trend-lines. *(SuperCharts, Omega Research)*

Figure 3.18   Two triangles on the same stock. *(MetaStock, Equis International, Inc.)*

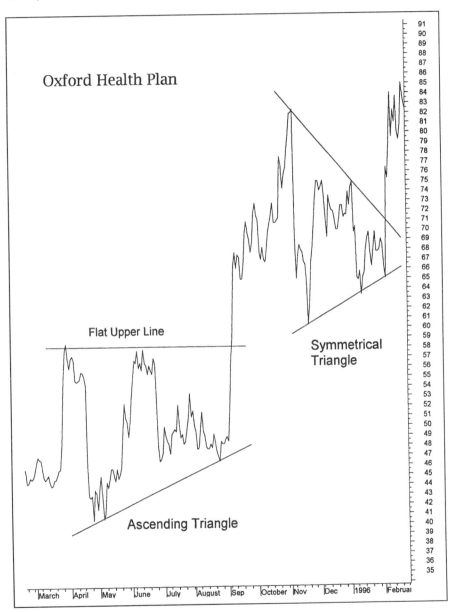

Oxford Health Plan

Flat Upper Line

Symmetrical
Triangle

Ascending Triangle

Figure 3.19   An example of bearish descending triangle with a flat lower line and falling upper line. (*MetaStock, Equis International, Inc.*)

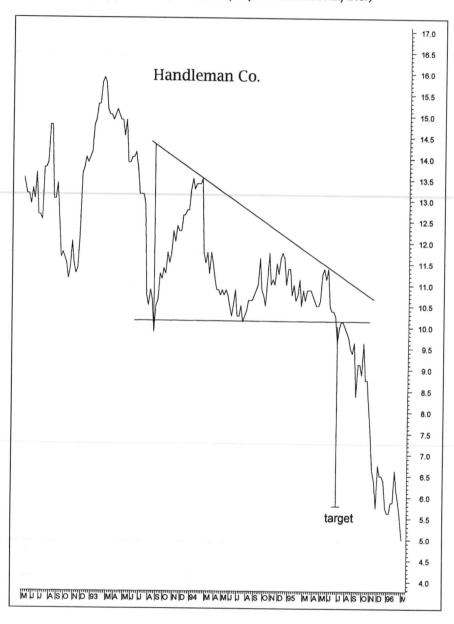

Figure 3.20   When prices gap higher (usually a sign of strength), that gap area will usually provide support on price dips. *(MetaStock, Equis International Inc.)*

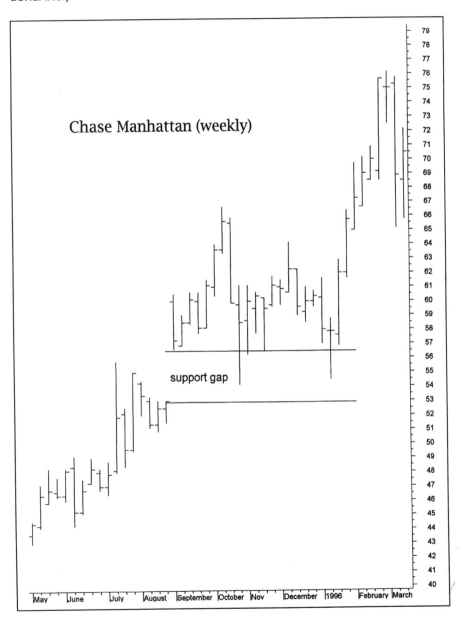

Chase Manhattan (weekly)

support gap

the case of the reversal patterns mentioned previously, the larger the vertical height (volatility) of the pattern, the greater the price potential.

One other measuring rule has to do with the horizontal size of all these patterns. A pattern that has been forming for two weeks isn't as significant (and doesn't carry the same potential) as a pattern that has been forming for two months or two years. Generally speaking, *the longer any price pattern has been forming, the more important it is.*

PRICE GAPS

Price gaps are simply open spaces that appear on bar charts. When a market is unusually strong (or after a piece of bullish news), prices will sometimes open sharply higher the next morning, usually well above the previous day's highest price. As a result, a space or *gap* appears. Generally speaking, *up gaps* are considered positive and *downside gaps* are considered negative. Prices sometimes retrace a sufficient amount to fill all or part of a price gap on a chart after it has formed.

Generally speaking, *a price gap below the market should provide support on any price dip* (see Figure 3.20) and usually provides a good buying opportunity. Price gaps above a falling market usually produce selling or resistance on any subsequent price rebounds.

Other types of gaps that appear at different stages of the trend are beyond our needs here. Refer to the Glossary for an explanation of *breakaway, measuring,* and *exhaustion gaps,* as well as *island reversals.*

SUMMARY

The visual analyst has several chart formats to choose from, with the most popular being the *bar* and *line charts. Candlesticks* are also gaining in popularity. The chart reader can employ *arithmetic* or *logarithmic* scaling, with the latter most helpful for longer-range analysis. Price patterns are formed by the interaction of successive peaks and troughs. The two major categories are *reversal* and *continuation* patterns. The two most common reversal patterns are *double tops and bottoms* and the *head and shoulders* pattern. Among the continuation patterns, *triangles* are very common. (Some shorter term continuation patterns, such as *flags* and *pennants,* are explained in the Glossary.) Volume plays an important role in confirming price patterns. Granville's *on-balance volume* is one of the simplest and most effective tools for that purpose.

SECTION 2

Indicators

4

Your Best Friend in a Trend

The first three chapters cover a fair amount of ground. You could stop reading here and still do a fair job of visual market analysis simply by studying the trend of the markets, knowing where the support and resistance levels are located, drawing some trendlines, and being able to spot important chart patterns. There are additional indicators, however, that help the analyst track existing trends and that signal when those trends are reversing or losing momentum. This brings us to the moving average, which works especially well in a trending market.

TWO CLASSES OF INDICATORS

Moving averages, like trendlines, help measure the direction of existing trends and can help determine when a trend change has taken place. Moving averages also act as support and resistance levels. Moving averages, as helpful as they are, are *lagging indicators.* They confirm that a trend change has occurred, but only after the fact. Another class of indicator—*oscillators*—helps determine when a market has reached an important extreme on either the upside or the downside. The oscillator tells us when a market is *overbought* or *oversold.* The major value of oscillators is that they are anticipatory in nature. They warn us in advance that a market has rallied too far, and are often able to anticipate a market turn before it actually happens.

In this chapter, we explain the various ways moving averages can be used as a trend-following indicator. You'll also learn how moving averages can be used to arrive at price objectives and to measure market extremes. The next two chapters in this section show how to use some of the more popular oscillators. That discussion is supplemented with coverage of another indicator that uses moving averages, while also functioning as an oscillator, to give you the best of both worlds.

THE MOVING AVERAGE

There's good news and bad news related to the moving average. The bad news is that it won't tell you in advance that a trend change is imminent. The good news is that it will help you determine if an existing trend is still in motion and help to confirm when a trend change has taken place. It may be helpful to think of a moving average as a *curving trendline*. A moving average can serve the same purpose as a trendline in the sense that it provides support during selloffs in an uptrend and resistance to bounces in a downtrend. The breaking of the moving average line usually carries the same meaning as the breaking of a trendline in the sense that it implies a trend change. The main advantage of the moving average over the trendline is the former's ability to combine more than one moving average line to generate additional trading signals.

THE SIMPLE AVERAGE

Chart packages offer a wide variety of ways to plot moving averages. For example, the user can plot one moving average line by itself, or combine two lines to generate *crossover* signals. The *length* of the lines can also be varied, depending on whether the analyst is plotting shorter- or longer-term trends. The first choice to be made, however, is which *type* of moving average to employ. Let's explain why.

A moving average is simply an average of a market's closing prices over a selected time span. The best known example is the *200-day moving average,* which is applied to stock charts to monitor the *major trend.*

To construct the 200-day average, the computer adds the last 200 closing prices for a stock and divides that sum by 200. Each day, a new number is added to the total (the latest price) and an old number is dropped off (the price 201 days back). Since the average moves with each passing day, it is called a *moving* average. A 50-day average would use the last fifty days while a 10-day average would use the last 10 days. This is called a *simple average* because each day's price is given equal weight.

WEIGHTING THE AVERAGE OR SMOOTHING IT?

While the simple average is most commonly used, some analysts prefer giving extra weight to the more recent price action. This is the idea behind a *weighted* moving average. The weighted average assigns more weight to recent price data and lesser weight to prices further back in time. For that reason, the weighted average is more sensitive than the simple average and tends to hug the price trend more closely. The *exponentially smoothed average* is the most popular of the weighted averages. This average assigns a percentage value to the last day's price, which is then added to a percentage of the previous day's value. For example, the last day's close could be assigned a value of .10. This means that the last day's closing price would be given a value of 10 percent, which is then added to 90 percent of the previous day's value. A value of .05 would give the last day's price a smaller 5 percent weighting and the previous day's a larger 95 percent. The higher the percentage assigned to the last price, the more sensitive the line becomes to more recent price action.

Computers allow the user to convert these percentage weightings into time periods for easier comparison. For example, the 5-percent exponential weighting is equivalent to a 40-day moving average. A 10-percent weighting would be the equivalent of a more sensitive 20-day moving average. The person who wants to use a 40-day moving average, for example, can choose between a simple average, a weighted average, or an exponentially smoothed average by making a keystroke. If you do choose to experiment with weighted averages, this explanation should help you understand the differences. Another reason for explaining the exponentially smoothed average here is to prepare you for our discussion in Chapter 6 of a popular indicator, the MACD, that utilizes the exponential smoothing technique.

MOVING AVERAGE LENGTHS

What length moving average should one employ? That depends on what trend the analyst is tracking. For long-term trends, the 200-day average is most popular. The 50-day average is most commonly used on stock charts to track the intermediate trend. Traders who specialize in the futures markets, with a much shorter time horizon, like to employ a 40-day average. The 20-day average is also used in another popular indicator that we'll cover later in the chapter. These daily average lines can be translated onto weekly price charts by adjusting the time periods. For example, a 50-day average translates to a 10-week average, while a 200-day line corresponds to a 40-week average.

The trend is considered to be *up* as long as the price of the market is above the moving average line and the line is rising. A close below a moving average line is a warning of a potential price change (see Figure 4.1). If the moving line turns down as well, the negative signal becomes much stronger. A stock is considered to be strong if it is above its 50- and 200-day moving averages. A close below its 50-day average signals a short-term top and a possible drop to the 200-day average (see Figure 4.2). A close below a 200-day average is considered very bearish and hints of a major trend change. Many times prices will drop back to their moving average lines before resuming their uptrend. In these instance, moving average lines act as support levels and function like an up trendline (see Figures 4.3 and 4.4).

During the early stages of an upturn, the minimum requirement for purchase of a stock is usually a close over its 50-day (10-week) average. More conservative investors often require a close above the 200-day (or 40-week) line as further proof of a bullish trend change before committing funds to a stock. Most analysts employ a combination of averages.

MOVING AVERAGE COMBINATIONS

Two moving averages are commonly used to analyze market trends. How the two averages relate to each other tells a lot about the strength or weakness of a trend. Two commonly employed numbers among stock investors are the 50-day (10-week) and the 200-day (40-week) combination. The trend is considered bullish (upward) as long as the shorter average is above the longer (see Figures 4.5 and 4.6). Any crossing by the shorter average below the longer is considered negative. Some analysts use a 10-week and a 30-week average for the same purpose. In that case, a bullish case requires that the 10-week average crosses and stays above the 30-week average.

Short-term traders, particularly in the futures pits, use a 10- and 40-day combination or a 9- and 18-day pairing (see Figures 4.7 and 4.8). Whichever combinations are employed, the principle is always the same. *The shorter moving average must be above the longer to justify a bullish case.* Crossover *buy* and *sell* signals are given when the shorter average crosses above or below the longer moving average line, respectively.

Figure 4.1   An example of how to use a 50-day moving average for trend signals. A price rise above the average at point A gave a buy signal while a drop below the average at point B gave a sell signal. *(MetaStock, Equis International, Inc.)*

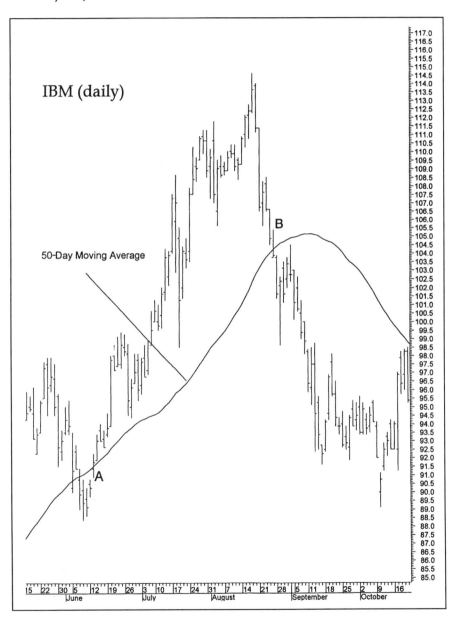

Figure 4.2   An example of a downside violation of the 50-day average at point A leading to a retest of the 200-day average at point B. *(MetaStock, Equis International, Inc.)*

Figure 4.3   Example of how to use a 40-week moving average for longer-term signals. A sell signal at point A was followed by a buy signal at point B. (*MetaStock, Equis International, Inc.*)

Figure 4.4   In this example, the 40-week average acts as a curving trendline and provides support during price corrections. *(MetaStock, Equis International, Inc.)*

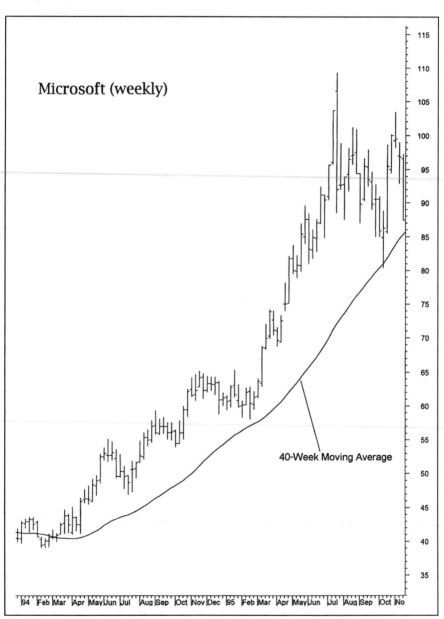

Microsoft (weekly)

40-Week Moving Average

Figure 4.5   Trading signals can be given by moving average crossovers. A sell signal was given at point A when the 10-week average crossed below the 40-week average. The last signal given was a buy at point B when the 10-week average crossed above the 40-week average. *(SuperCharts, Omega Research)*

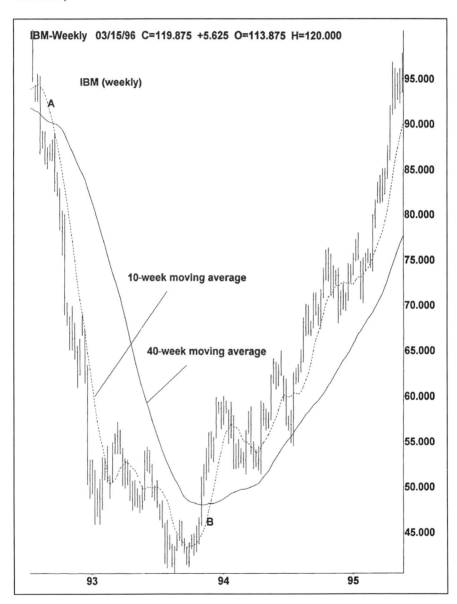

IBM-Weekly 03/15/96 C=119.875 +5.625 O=113.875 H=120.000

IBM (weekly)

A

95.000

90.000

85.000

80.000

75.000

10-week moving average

70.000

40-week moving average

65.000

60.000

55.000

50.000

B

45.000

93   94   95

Figure 4.6   Example of using the 10- and 40-week moving averages together. A bullish signal given at A remains in effect until the shorter average (10-week) crosses below the longer average (40-week). *(SuperCharts, Omega Research)*

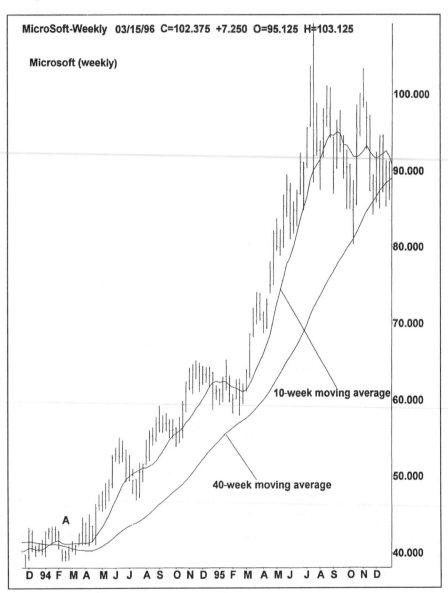

MicroSoft-Weekly 03/15/96 C=102.375 +7.250 O=95.125 H=103.125

Microsoft (weekly)

100.000

90.000

80.000

70.000

10-week moving average
60.000

40-week moving average
50.000

A

40.000

D 94 F M A M J J A S O N D 95 F M A M J J A S O N D

Figure 4.7   Short-term signals can be given by crossovers of the 10- and 40-day averages. On this Treasury bond chart, note the sell at A and the buy signal at B. *(SuperCharts, Omega Research)*

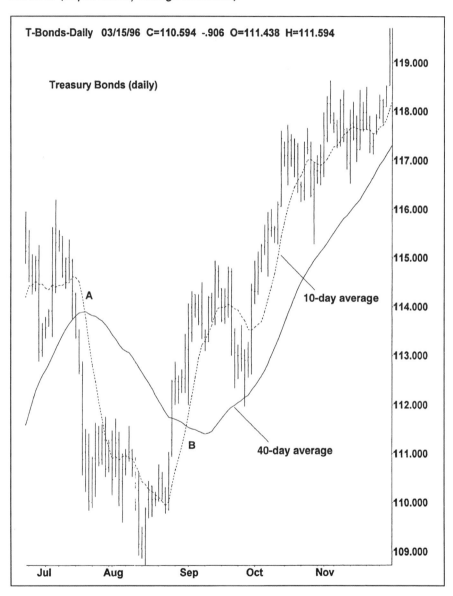

Figure 4.8   Short-term futures traders got a buy signal at A and a sell signal at B on crossovers of the sensitive 9- and 18-day average combination. *(SuperCharts, Omega Research)*

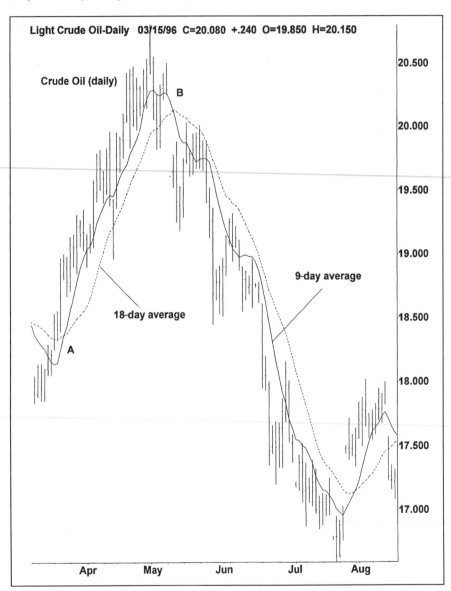

Since moving average lines are trend-following indicators, *they do best in a trending environment.* During an extended uptrend, for example, moving averages will get you aboard and keep you aboard the market trend until it exhausts itself. By the same token, moving averages can act as a valuable filter to keep you from buying stocks in a downtrend. Moving averages, however, are not that helpful in an extended trading range or a period of sideways price action. They need a trend to function well.

Computers also allow you to plot the *difference* between the two averages. During a strong uptrend, for example, the shorter moving average rises faster than the longer average. The spread between the two averages will widen. When the spread between the two averages begins to narrow, that is usually an early warning that the uptrend is losing some momentum.

Put Envelopes around the Average

There are other ways to use the moving average to help monitor support and resistance levels and to determine market extremes. *Trading envelopes* is one example. This technique plots lines, called *envelopes,* at predetermined percentage amounts above and below a moving average line. The percentages may vary, depending on which trend and which market is being studied. Short-term traders, for example, often plot envelopes 3 percent above and 3 percent below a 21-day moving average (see Figure 4.9). Prices will often stall at the upper and lower envelope lines before correcting back to the moving average line in the middle. A longer-term version might entail plotting envelopes 3 percent or 5 percent around a 10-week average and 10 percent or 20 percent envelopes around a 40-week average (see Figures 4.10 and 4.11). A price move outside the envelopes warns that a market has reached a dangerous extreme and is vulnerable to a retracement in the other direction. Some experimentation is needed to tailor this technique to the market you're following and to the appropriate time span to suit your purposes.

Or Put Bands around It

Bollinger bands, developed by John Bollinger, blend a statistical concept with the envelope technique. Two bands are placed above and below the centered moving average, as with envelopes; but instead of using fixed percentage amounts (such as 5 percent or 10 percent) around the moving average line, Bollinger bands are plotted *two standard deviations* above

Figure 4.9   Example of 3 percent envelopes around a 21-day average during 1995 for shorter-term trading purposes. During an uptrend, the prices will have an upward bias and may not reach the lower envelope. *(Super-Charts, Omega Research)*

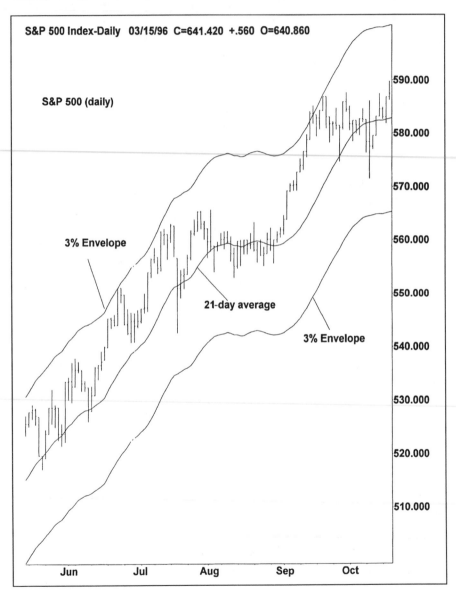

Figure 4.10   During the sideways stock market of 1994, 3 percent envelopes above and below a 10-week average contained most of the price action. Moves outside the envelopes provided short-term trading opportunities. *(MetaStock, Equis International, Inc.)*

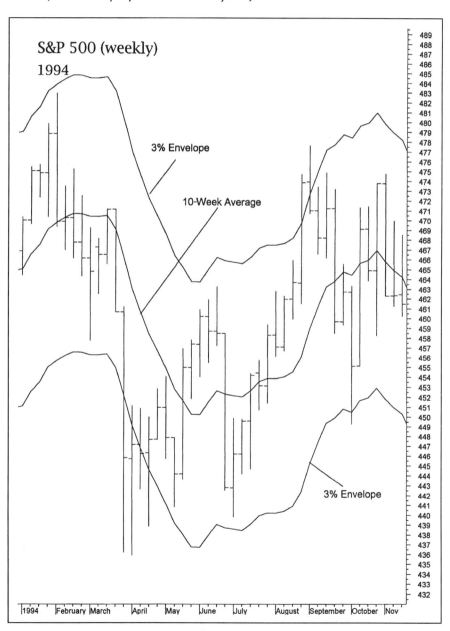

Figure 4.11   For longer-range analysis, 10 percent envelopes plotted over and under a 40-week average can help identify market extremes. *(MetaStock, Equis International, Inc.)*

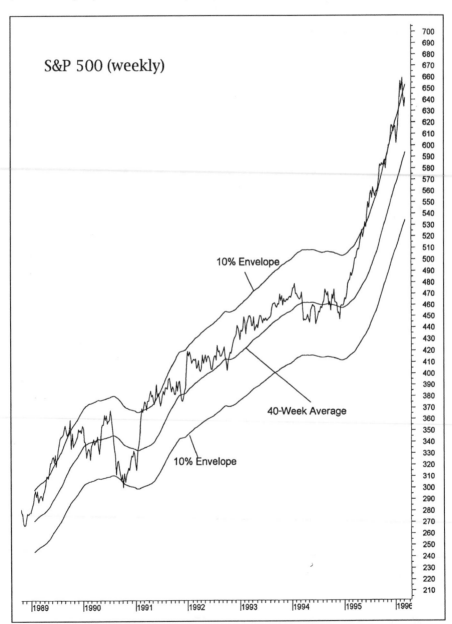

and below a moving average line, which is usually 20 periods (see Figure 4.12). Bollinger bands also contract and expand depending on the market's degree of volatility.

Standard deviation is a statistical concept that describes how a set of data (prices) is dispersed (spread) around an average value. The concept of standard deviation has a very specific value in statistics. That is because 68 percent of the data values differ from the middle average by less than one standard deviation. *Ninety-five percent of the data values differ from the middle average by less than two standard deviations.* Since the Bollinger bands are placed two standard deviations above and below the 20-period moving average, 95 percent of all price action should be contained by the two bands.

The interpretation is the same, however. Prices will usually meet resistance at the upper band and support at the lower band. As in the case of envelopes, three lines are overlaid on the price chart. On a daily chart, the middle line is usually a 20-day average. In a bullish environment, prices will rise above and stay above the 20-day line, which acts as support. However, upward price surges will usually stall at the upper band. The opposite is true in a downtrend. Prices will usually trade below the 20-day average, which will function as resistance to price advances. Prices will usually bounce off the lower band. The simplest way to interpret Bollinger bands is that the upper band represents overhead resistance, while the lower band represents support below.

These bands are also helpful in determining price objectives. During a downward price correction, for example, prices can be expected to find support either at the 20-day average or at the lower band if prices fall below the 20-day average line.

Band Width Is Important, Too

There is another important distinction between trading envelopes and Bollinger bands: The width of the envelopes stays constant at all times. For example, in the case of 3 percent envelopes, the two envelopes will always be 6 percent apart (3 percent above and 3 percent below the moving average line). The Bollinger bands, by contrast, are constantly contracting and expanding in order to adjust to market volatility. *Volatility* refers to the degree of movement in prices. The bands will contract during periods of low volatility and expand during periods of high volatility. You can track the width of the bands to determine market volatility. Unusually narrow bands (reflecting low volatility and a quiet market) are usually followed by

Figure 4.12   Notice how prices tend to back off the upper Bollinger band and bounce off the lower band. *(MetaStock, Equis International, Inc.)*

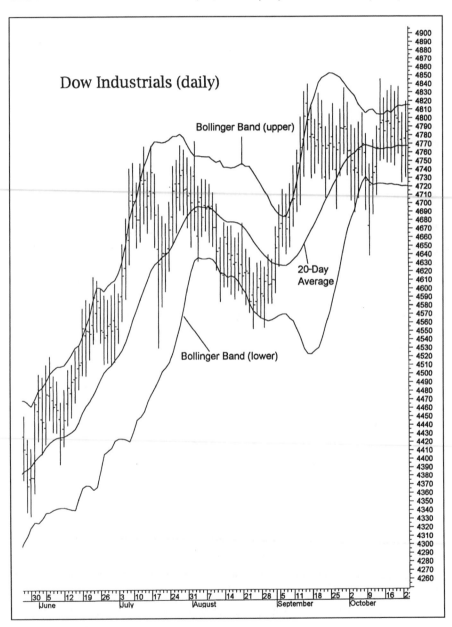

Dow Industrials (daily)

Bollinger Band (upper)

20-Day Average

Bollinger Band (lower)

Figure 4.13   Bollinger bands expand and contract to market volatility as shown here. Widening bands signal a strong trend, while narrowing bands (upper right) hint at a weakening trend. Note that the selloff to the right has stopped at the lower Bollinger Band. *(SuperCharts, Omega Research)*

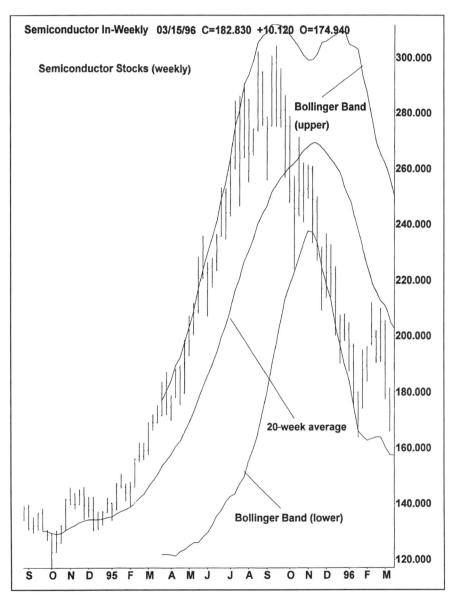

Semiconductor In-Weekly   03/15/96 C=182.830 +10.120 O=174.940

Semiconductor Stocks (weekly)

300.000

Bollinger Band
(upper)

280.000

260.000

240.000

220.000

200.000

180.000

20-week average

160.000

140.000

Bollinger Band (lower)

120.000

S   O   N   D   95   F   M   A   M   J   J   A   S   O   N   D   96   F   M

Figure 4.14   Bollinger bands can be applied to weekly charts. During the sideways action of 1994, most price movement was contained by the upper and lower bands. During the uptrend of 1995, prices traded between the upper band and the 20-week average. *(SuperCharts, Omega Research)*

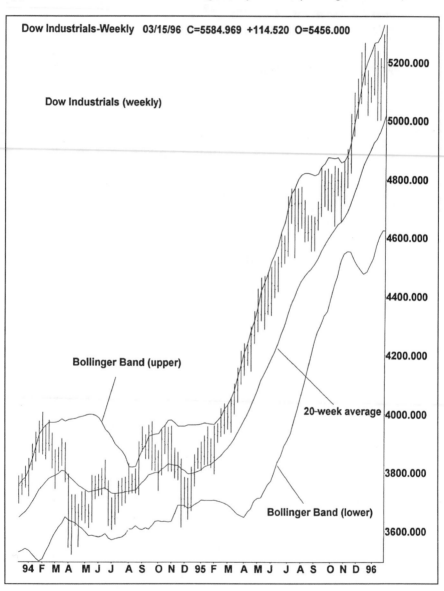

a period of high volatility (rapid and substantial price moves). Conversely, unusually wide bands (reflecting high volatility and a strong trend) usually warn of a possible slowing in the existing trend (or a return to a trading range environment [see Figure 4.13]).

Bands Work on Weekly Charts

While many traders apply Bollinger bands to daily charts, they work equally well on weekly charts for longer-term perspective. All you have to do is to switch from a 20-day to a 20-week moving average. In the case of the weekly chart, the 20-week moving average usually functions as support during an uptrend or resistance in a downtrend. The *weekly* bands also help to identify price targets and market extremes in the same way that they do on *daily* charts. The weekly bands also carry much more significance than the bands on the daily chart, which measure only shorter-term market swings (see Figures 4.13 and 4.14).

SUMMARY

Like trendlines, *moving averages* help identify potential support and resistance levels and alert us when a trend change is taking place. It is important to tailor the *length* of the average to the length of the trend being followed. Moving averages can be used by themselves or in combination to generate trading signals. Trading *envelopes* and *bands* determine market extremes by measuring how far prices have traveled from a moving average centerline. Moving averages work best in trending markets and usually lag the price action. In the next chapter, we show some indicators that can anticipate market turns and that also work well in a less trendy and more choppy market environment.

5

Is It Overbought or Oversold?

MEASURING OVERBOUGHT AND OVERSOLD CONDITIONS

There are several ways to determine when a market is overbought or oversold. The most effective way is to use an indicator called an *oscillator*. Oscillators tell us when a market has reached an extreme in either direction, which makes it vulnerable to a countertrend correction. When a stock has gone up too far, analysts will often say that the stock is *overbought*. That simply means that the stock may have to pause for a while to digest those gains, or possibly have to correct downward before resuming its uptrend. At a stock's most extreme highpoint, some traders will take profits and temporarily halt the advance. Other buyers will reemerge during the ensuing price setback, and the stock will eventually be pushed higher. An *oversold* condition is just the opposite, and implies that a stock has fallen too far and is probably due for a short term bounce. It's generally better to buy a market when it's oversold and sell when it's overbought.

DIVERGENCES

There's a second element in oscillator analysis that is extremely valuable. Not only do oscillators help us determine when a market is overbought or oversold, but they also warn us in advance when a *divergence* is building up in a stock. Divergences usually warn of an impending trend reversal. We've encountered the idea of divergence in our discussion of on-balance volume in Chapter 3. In other words, we study two lines that usually trend in the same direction. When they start to diverge from one another, the analyst begins to suspect that the trend is losing momentum. Oscillators are especially helpful for this purpose. There are two elements, then, to oscillator analysis: One is to spot when a market has reached a dangerous extreme (either overbought or oversold) and the other is to identify divergences while prices are in that extreme oscillator range. We'll show you how this is done.

MOMENTUM

This is the most basic concept in oscillator analysis. A price chart tells us whether prices are rising or falling. An oscillator chart tells us more about the *momentum,* or pace, of a market. An oscillator tells us the *rate* (also called *rate of change*) at which a market is rising or falling. This type of oscillator tells us whether the current trend is gaining or losing its momentum. In the latter stages of an advance, the momentum of the advance (or the rate of change) usually begins to slow. That slowing in the momentum may not show up on the price chart, but will usually be seen on the oscillator that accompanies the price chart. Oscillators that measure momentum and rate of change are the most basic kind. There are other more sophisticated oscillators, which we'll deal with a bit later in this chapter. But let's begin with the basics.

Momentum or Rate of Change Oscillators

There are various ways to construct these two oscillators, but their interpretation is basically the same. The trader is comparing the latest closing price to a price in the past. Depending on which variation is chosen, the computer will either take the *difference* between the latest price and the price in the past or a *ratio* of the two. Let's use a 10-day period as an example. In the first case, the computer subtracts the price 10 days ago from the latest price. If the latest price is higher than the old price, the oscillator value will be positive. If the latest price is lower, the oscillator value will be negative. Using that construction, the oscillator will fluctuate above and below a midpoint line which is called a *zero line* (see Figure 5.1).

Figure 5.1   A 10-day momentum chart plotted around a zero line.
(MetaStock, Equis International, Inc.)

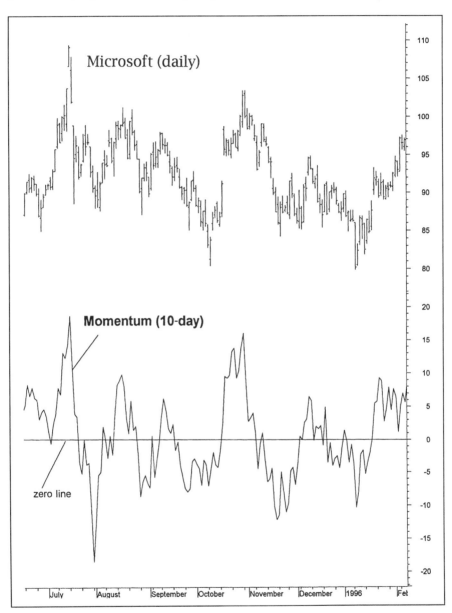

Using the *ratio* method, the computer *divides* the latest price by the price 10 days ago. In that case, prices will fluctuate above and below 100, which serves as the midpoint line. It matters little which formula is used, because both charts look exactly alike and are interpreted in the same way (Figure 5.2). Software programs sometimes differ in the way these two oscillators are named and constructed, even though the basic principles are always the same. To prevent any confusion, read the user manual for the software package that you are using to make sure that you know exactly how your software defines and constructs *momentum* and *rate of change (ROC)* oscillators.

Interpretation of Momentum and Rate of Change

The midpoint line (either 0 or 100) is the key to this type of oscillator. A crossing above the midline is considered to be positive (a buy signal). A crossing below the midline is negative (a sell signal). Many analysts use these oscillators just to generate that type of buy and sell signal. However, they can also be used to spot market extremes. When the oscillator line has traveled too far above or too far below the midline, the market is considered to be overbought (above) or oversold (below). If the oscillator line starts to move back toward the midline, it is an early signal that the current trend is losing momentum.

Longer-Range Momentum

The 10-day period used in the prior example would only be useful for very short term trading purposes. Analysts generally employ longer time spans for longer-range momentum analysis. For example, the analyst might compare the last closing price to the price 13 weeks, 26 weeks, or even 52 weeks in the past (see Figure 5.3). Naturally, the longer the time span used, the more significant the signals will be, although they will be much fewer. This oscillator does have one drawback.

Market Extremes Are Too Subjective

By studying the historical pattern of momentum oscillators, it is possible to estimate what values marked overbought or oversold extremes in the past. However, there are no *preset* values that can be used universally. For that reason, many analysts prefer other types of oscillators that preserve the benefits of the momentum and rate of change lines but solve the problem just mentioned. One of the most popular is the *relative strength index (RSI)*.

Figure 5.2   Momentum and rate of change are, essentially, the same indicator. Note how rate of change oscillates around a base line of 100. Note how momentum oscillates around a base line of zero. *(MetaStock, Equis International, Inc.)*

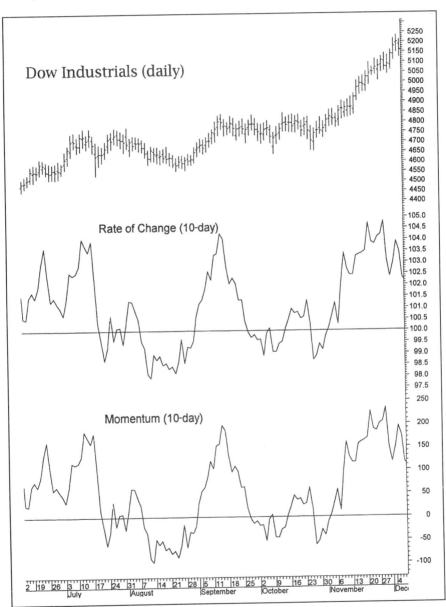

Figure 5.3   Crossings above and below zero line on 52-week momentum chart (see arrow) can help determine major trend of market and which side to trade from. *(MetaStock, Equis International, Inc.)*

WELLES WILDER'S RELATIVE STRENGTH INDEX (RSI)

This popular oscillator was first described by J. Welles Wilder, Jr., in his 1978 book, *New Concepts in Technical Trading Systems*. The main value of this oscillator is that it presents the analyst with upper and lower boundaries to determine overbought and oversold conditions. The values of the RSI oscillator range from 0 to 100. Readings over 70 are considered to be overbought. Readings below 30 are considered to be oversold. Applying those two boundaries to any market environment greatly simplifies the search for markets that have reached dangerous extremes. It's also worth nothing that the midpoint value of 50 can serve the same purpose as the zero line in the momentum oscillator, and crossings above and below that value can generate trend signals. (Figure 5.4 shows an example of 70 and 30 lines on the RSI, and also suggests one way to combine the RSI oscillator with the momentum chart from Figure 5.3.)

Which Time Spans to Use for the RSI

The two values most commonly used for the relative strength index are 14 and 9. Most software programs offer one of those numbers as the default value. (*Default value* simply means that the software program will suggest the most commonly used value for an indicator.) A daily RSI will be based on price data covering the last 9 or 14 days. A weekly chart will include the past 9 or 14 weeks. Since the computer does the calculation for you, it's not necessary to memorize the formula. Still, it's always helpful to know what you're studying.

The relative strength index (RSI) uses a ratio of the average points gained on *up* days during the past *x* number of days (usually 9 or 14) divided by the average points lost on *down* days over the same time span. That value (RS) is then inserted into a formula.

$$RSI = 100 - \frac{100}{1 + RS}$$

$$RS = \frac{\text{Average of } x \text{ days' up closes}}{\text{Average of } x \text{ days' down closes}}$$

$$x = \text{Usually 9 or 14 periods}$$

The fact that 9 or 14 are most commonly used doesn't limit you to those values. But they do provide a good starting point as you learn to use this indicator. Later on, you may choose to experiment with other values.

Figure 5.4   The value of having preset value extremes over 70 and under 30 can be seen. When the 52-week momentum (see Figure 5.3) is above zero, buy signals (up arrows) are more valuable than sell signals (down arrows). *(MetaStock, Equis International, Inc.)*

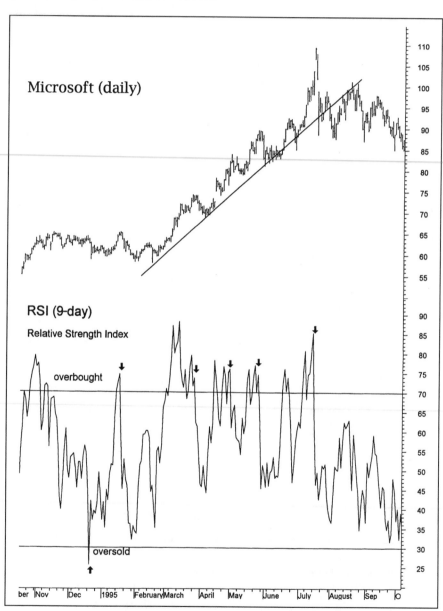

Most software packages allow you to *optimize* values for all indicators by testing for best time span to use in each market. However, the benefit of starting with the default value is that it provides a number you can apply universally to all markets. Also keep in mind that whether you are using daily, weekly, or monthly charts, it's a good idea to use the same numbers. For example, use a 9-day, a 9-week, and a 9-month value.

Modifying Values to Suit Market

The main value of the RSI oscillator is to determine when a given market has reached an overbought (over 70) or an oversold (below 30) region. In a very quiet market with low volatility (movement), you may notice that the swings in the RSI line stay between 70 and 30. In that case, the RSI line has little value. You might want to try increasing its amplitude (wideness) by *shortening* the time span. Try a 7-day RSI line, for example. The idea is to widen the fluctuations in the RSI line to the point that it moves either above 70 or below 30. The way to do that is to shorten the time span.

The opposite case involves a situation where the RSI line is *too* volatile. In a very active market, the RSI line may be too sensitive. Frequent moves above 70 and below 30 become less meaningful. It's hard to distinguish between the valid signals and market noise. In that case, it's necessary to reduce the amplitude of the RSI line by *lengthening* the number of days used. Try 21 days, for example. That will eliminate many of the meaningless moves and help identify those that really matter. Fortunately, the computer lets you vary the time span with a keystroke.

RSI Divergences

The fact that a market has reached an overbought or oversold extreme in any oscillator does not necessarily mean that a trend reversal is imminent. It just alerts you to the fact that prices have entered a *potentially* dangerous area. During a strong uptrend, for example, prices may signal an overbought reading by moving above 70 on the RSI line and stay above 70 for some time. Sale of a rising stock at that point could prove to be premature. This brings us to the second necessary ingredient in oscillator analysis— the existence of divergence.

Quite often, prices will hit a new high accompanied by a value in the RSI line above 70. Prices will then consolidate for a while or experience a short downward correction, before setting a new high. Meanwhile, the RSI line will fail to rise above its prior peak (still above 70). The presence of a double top in the RSI line (above 70) or a pattern of descending RSI peaks while a stock is at a new high is a warning of a possible negative divergence. But there's more.

At that point, the RSI line has two peaks and a trough in between those peaks. If the RSI line then drops below the trough, a *failure swing* has been given. In other words, when the RSI line forms its own double top (above 70) and starts to fall, a potential sell signal is given—even though the stock may still be rising. Many times the sell signal will coincide with an RSI drop back below the 70 line. At a bottom, the situation is reversed. A double bottom in the RSI line (below 30) followed by an upward penetration of the prior peak (or a move back above the 30 line) usually signals a potential buying situation, even if the stock continues to drop. (See Figure 5.5 for examples of bullish and bearish divergence.)

There's More Value in the 70 and 30 Lines

The crossings of the 70 and 30 lines should always be watched closely. During a strong uptrend, it's not unusual for an RSI oscillator line to rise above 70 and stay there. That is usually the sign of a strong uptrend. Prices may stay above the 70 line for weeks. In such instances, it's probably best to ignore the oscillator for the time being, as long as it stays above 70. A crossing below 70, especially if it happens after a long period of time, often signals a change in trend. Many traders treat a crossing below the 70 line as a sell signal and a crossing above the 30 line as a buy signal (see Figure 5.6).

Crossings of the 50 Line Are Important, Too

Although most of the attention in the RSI oscillator is focused on the 70 and 30 lines, the 50 line is also important. Since it is the *midpoint* value on the RSI line (which ranges from 0 to 100), the 50 line often serves the same function as the zero line in the momentum oscillator. In that case, buy and sell signals are often given by crossings above and below the midpoint line. You'll notice, for example, that during a correction in an uptrend, the RSI line will often find support at the 50 line before turning back up again. During a downtrend, bounces in the RSI line will halt near the 50 line. Crossings of the 50 line, therefore, do carry some significance and should be monitored (see Figure 5.7).

Use Weekly and Monthly Charts

We've been talking mainly about daily charts. It's important, however, to monitor the RSI line on weekly charts as well. Daily charts tend to be the

Figure 5.5   A nine-day RSI applied to IBM showing both a bearish and a bullish divergence. *(MetaStock, Equis International, Inc.)*

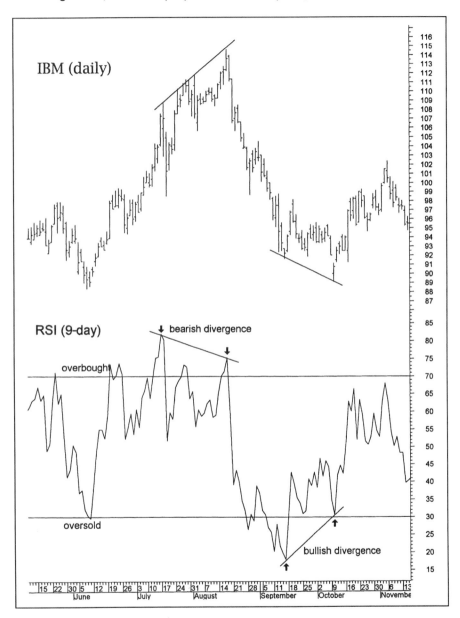

Figure 5.6   Using crossings above the 30 line to generate buy signals (up arrow) and crossings under the 70 line (down arrow) for sales. *(MetaStock, Equis International, Inc.)*

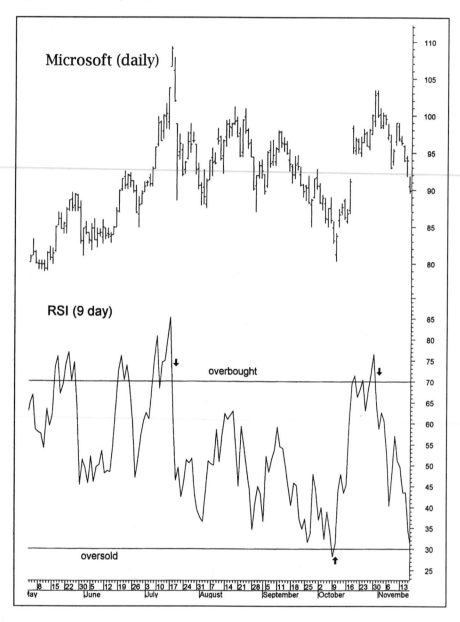

Figure 5.7   Example of using the crossings of the midpoint 50 line to generate buy and sell signals. *(MetaStock, Equis International, Inc.)*

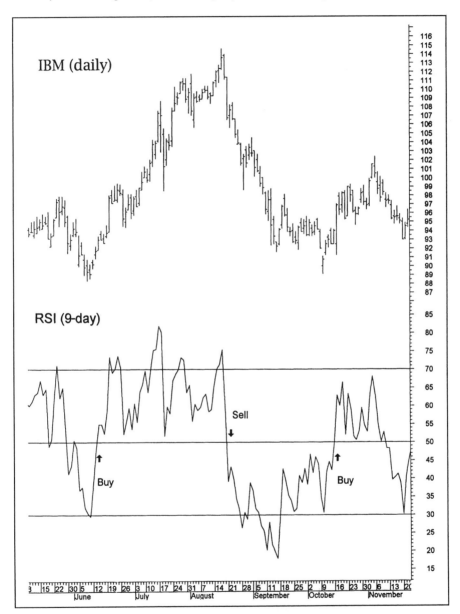

most volatile and are geared for short-term timing purposes. Weekly charts carry much more significance and should always be used as a filter on the daily charts. The most potent buy signals, for example, are given when both the daily and weekly lines are turning up from below 30. If the daily RSI line turns up while the weekly RSI line is dropping, the buy signal is much weaker and is probably not very trustworthy. It's preferable to use the weekly chart for *major trend* analysis and the daily chart for *timing* purposes.

Monthly charts are also valuable, but only for very long term analysis. Once you have asked the computer to show you a 14-day RSI oscillator on a stock chart, for example, a simple keystroke switches you to a 14-week oscillator. Another keystroke switches you to a 14-month oscillator. Short-term traders, utilizing intraday data, can shorten the time span to a 14-minute or 14-hour RSI for day-trading purposes. Although oscillators are generally placed along the bottom of the chart for comparison with the prices located in the upper half of the chart, most charting programs allow you to overlay the RSI line right on top of the price action for easier comparison. Doing that makes divergence analysis a good deal easier.

Let's take a look at another popular oscillator that can be used along with the relative strength index.

THE STOCHASTICS OSCILLATOR

This oscillator, popularized by George Lane, has many of the same features as the RSI line. The time span for both indicators is usually 9 or 14. *Stochastics* is also plotted on a scale from 0 to 100. However, its overbought and oversold boundaries are slightly wider than the RSI in the sense that stochastic readings above 80 are overbought and below 20 are oversold. This is because the stochastic oscillator is more volatile than the RSI. The other major difference is that the stochastics oscillator utilizes two lines instead of one. The slower *%D line* is a moving average of the faster *%K line*. It is the presence of two lines instead of one that distinguishes the stochastics from the RSI line and gives the former greater value in the eyes of many traders. That is because precise trading signals on the stochastics oscillator are given *when the two lines cross* and when their value is above 80 or below 20 (see Figure 5.8).

What Does Stochastics Mean?

The American College Dictionary defines *stochastic* as an adjective "based on one item in the probability distribution of an ordered set of observations." The use of the term as a market indicator has a much more specific

Figure 5.8   These three crossover signals (see arrows) during 1995 demonstrate the value of using weekly stochastics. Moves over 80 or below 20 on
weekly charts provide stronger signals. *(MetaStock, Equis International, Inc.)*

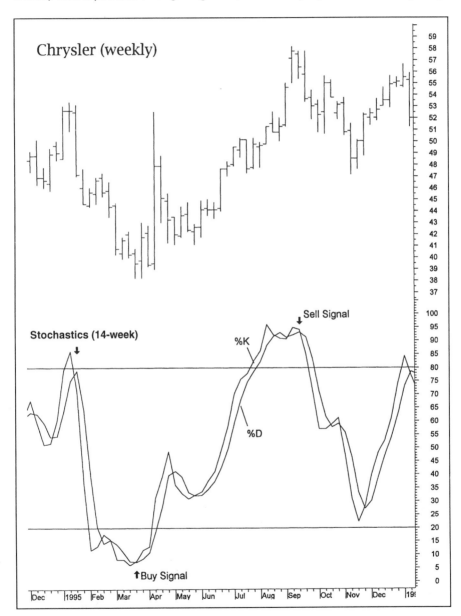

meaning, which may be a loose adaptation of the true meaning of the word. In the way that we are using it here, *stochastics* refers to the location of a current stock price in relation to its range over a set period of time. The time span most often used is 14 days. The stochastics oscillator determines where the current price is located on a percentage scale from 0 to 100, in relation to its price range over the past 14 days. The formula for stochastics is quite simple:

Fast line (%K) = 100 [(close – low$_{14}$) / (high$_{14}$ – low$_{14}$)]
Slow line (%D) = 3-day average of %K

where *Close* represents the latest closing price and *high* and *low* are the respective highest and lowest values for the past 14 days. The slower %D line is a 3-day moving average of the faster %K line.

Fast Versus Slow Stochastics

The formula just described is referred to as *fast stochastics*. If plotted on a chart, the two lines will look very jagged. As a result, most traders employ a smoother version of this indicator, referred to as *slow stochastics*. The slow stochastics formula simply takes the slower %D line and smooths it one more time. The result is three lines. Fast stochastics uses the two faster lines while slow stochastics uses the two slower (smoother) lines. It is recommended that you utilize slow stochastics. The default values for slow stochastics are 14, 3, and 3. You'll find the slower stochastic lines much smoother and more reliable.

Stochastic Line Crossings

The interpretation of stochastics is similar to that of the RSI line. Look for overbought and oversold situations (in this case, however, the values are 80 and 20). Then look for potential divergences, as with the RSI. What distinguishes stochastics is the *crossing* of the two lines, which adds a valuable ingredient to this oscillator. Given an oversold condition (below 20), especially where a positive divergence exists, a crossing by the faster %K line above the slower %D line constitutes a buy signal. In an overbought condition (above 80), any crossing by the faster %K line below the slower %D line constitutes a sell signal. Therefore, the stochastics oscillator provides not only a warning of a dangerously extended market, but provides an action signal as well. (Study Figures 5.8 through 5.10 for examples of crossover signals.)

Figure 5.9   Compare this weekly version with the daily signals for the same time span in Figure 5.10. You'll see why it's better to use the weekly signals as a filter on the more volatile daily signals. *(MetaStock, Equis International, Inc.)*

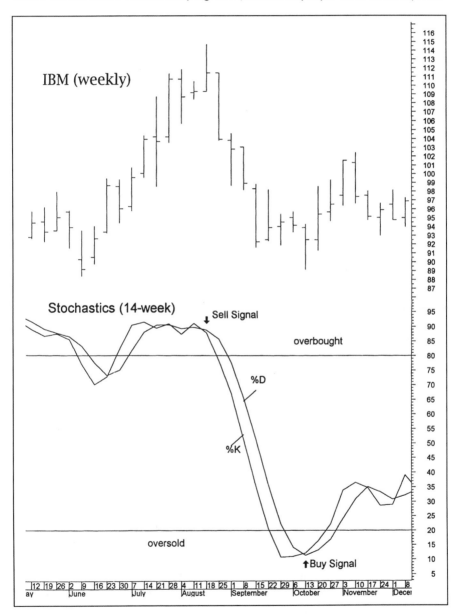

Figure 5.10   Stochastic buy and sell signals on daily charts are too frequent and should not be used alone. *(MetaStock, Equis International, Inc.)*

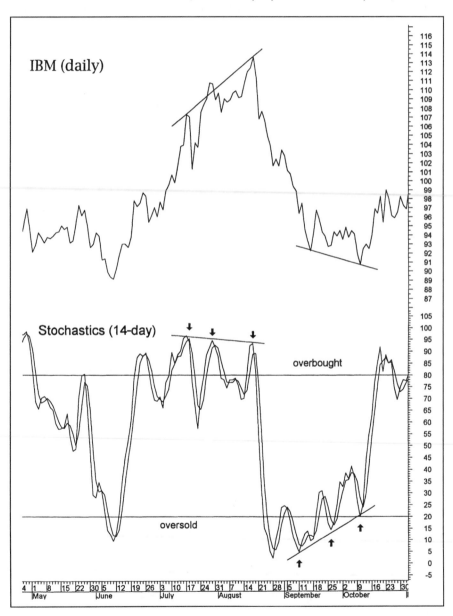

What About Running Markets?

As discussed previously, a strong uptrend will often provide stochastic readings that rise above 80 and stay there. In those cases, it's usually best to wait for the stochastic lines to drop below 80 to give a sell signal. There are going to be periods during strong trending markets when this oscillator is not very helpful. That is why some judgment is always involved, and why it's important to use this and all oscillators in conjunction with other indicators. It's foolish to slavishly follow all buy and sell crossings in this indicator without consideration of the overall trend of the market. Which brings us to our final point—the use of longer-range signals.

Weekly Signals Determine Position

Perhaps the greatest weakness in the oscillator approach is the absence of a *trend filter*. Daily stochastics charts fluctuate endlessly from overbought to oversold and back to overbought again. Successive buy and sell signals are given. It's silly to attempt to follow each signal. For example, during an uptrend, buy signals are much more important than sell signals. During a downtrend, sell signals are much more important than buy signals. The overall trend of the market must always be taken into consideration. Why would you want to sell a stock that is in an uptrend or buy a stock in a downtrend? One way to get around this problem is to employ other trend-following techniques, such as the moving average, to determine the direction of the market. Another is to employ a weekly stochastics chart as a trend filter on the daily stochastic chart.

Use the weekly stochastic indicator to determine the trend of the market and which side of that market you will be trading from. As long as the weekly stochastic lines are positive (the faster %K line above the slower %D), operate only from the buy side. Utilize oversold readings on the daily chart for buying opportunities while ignoring the short-term sell signals. When the weekly stochastics lines are negative (faster line below the slower), ignore buy signals on the daily chart and utilize short-term overbought readings for selling purposes. What you're doing then is buying dips in uptrends and selling rallies in downtrends. (Figures 5.9 and 5.10 show why it's better to combine weekly and daily signals.)

Time Filter Signals

Monthly stochastics charts are also recommended for longer-range analysis and confirmation. At the other extreme, short-term traders often utilize 14-hour charts and 14-minute stochastic charts for day-trading purposes.

Whatever time period you are trading (14 hours, 14 days, or 14 weeks), always use the *next longer* time period to determine the direction of the market you will be trading from. If you are trading 14-hour stochastics, use 14 *days* to determine the trend. If you are trading 14-day stochastics, use 14 *weeks* as a trend filter. Why not use the 14-month stochastics as a filter on the 14-week chart as well?

It's also a good idea to use the same time span on all of your charts. For example, if you use 14 on your dailies, use 14 on your weeklies and monthlies as well.

COMBINE RSI AND STOCHASTICS

It's always best to combine indicators. Each of these oscillators can be used by itself, but their value is enhanced when they are used together. For one thing, the stochastics oscillator (being more volatile) tends to reach overbought and oversold areas much faster than the RSI line. Stochastics also tends to provide many more divergences than the RSI line. As a result, the stochastics signals are earlier, but often less reliable than those given by the relative strength index. I like to keep both oscillators on the bottom of the chart. When the stochastics lines are giving overbought or oversold readings, I generally like to wait for the slower RSI line to confirm the stochastic reading by moving above 70 or below 30. I find that the most reliable signals are given when both oscillators are in overbought or oversold territory simultaneously. Then one can switch to the stochastic lines to generate the actual buy or sell signal with much more confidence (see Figure 5.11).

Combine Other Indicators

The best way to enhance the value of any indicator is to combine it with other indicators. You could combine RSI with Bollinger bands (see Figure 5.12). Signals on oscillators take on greater meaning if prices are also touching one of the trading bands. Another possibility is to combine oscillators with moving averages. Why not use a 40-week moving average to determine whether you wish to emphasize buy or sell signals on the oscillator charts? (See Figure 5.13.) The possibilities are endless. Use your computer power to combine indicators for better results.

SUMMARY

Charting programs offer many types of oscillators to help determine market extremes and potential turning points. The most basic are *momentum*

Figure 5.11   Notice how the smoother and less frequent RSI signals help filter premature stochastic signals. *(MetaStock, Equis International, Inc.)*

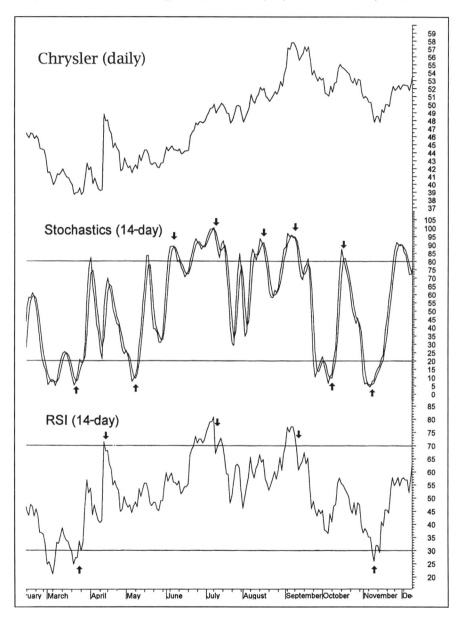

Figure 5.12   Combining RSI signals with Bollinger band extremes.
(MetaStock, Equis International, Inc.)

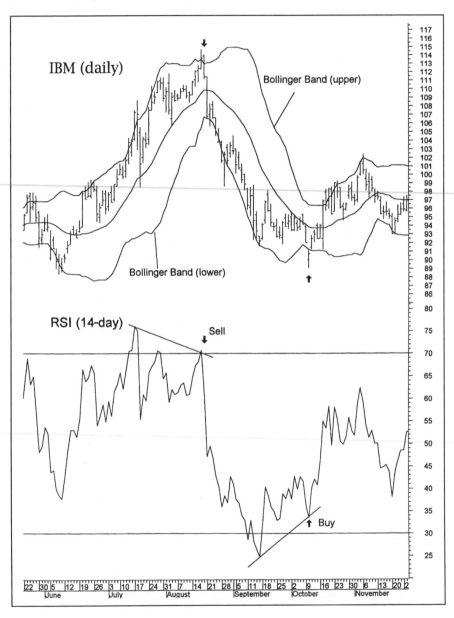

Figure 5.13   How to combine moving average and oscillator analysis. During bull markets (prices over the 40-week average), major buy signals are given with stochastics under 20. *(MetaStock, Equis International, Inc.)*

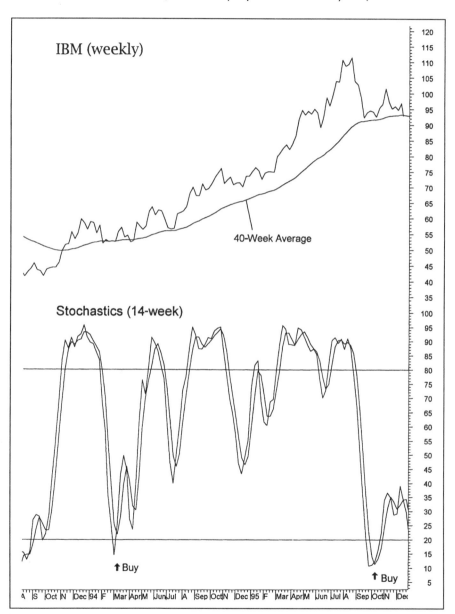

and *rate of change* indicators. The two most popular, and probably most valuable, are the *relative strength index* and *stochastics*. This type of indicator is most useful during choppy market periods and when a trend is nearing completion. They are much less valuable in the middle of a strong trend. Therefore, oscillators should not be overused and should be deemphasized during strong trending markets. For example, a moving average is more helpful during a strong trend. There are some indicators that combine the trend-following properties of a moving average system with the overbought/oversold properties of an oscillator. The next chapter discusses one of the better ones.

6

How to Have the Best of Both Worlds

The most critical problem facing the visual investor is knowing when to emphasize each class of indicator. During a strong trending period, moving averages will outperform most other indicators. During choppy market periods, when prices swing back and forth in an essentially trendless manner, oscillators are much better than moving averages. Fortunately, there is one indicator that combines the best of both worlds in the sense that it is both a trend-following system and an oscillator. It employs moving averages to generate trend-following signals, but also helps to determine when a trend is overbought or oversold. It is also helpful in spotting divergences, one of the greatest strengths of an oscillator. After showing you how to use it, we'll show you an even better way to use it. We're speaking of the *moving average convergence divergence* (*MACD*) indicator.

MACD CONSTRUCTION

This indicator, developed by Gerald Appel, utilizes three moving averages in its construction although only two lines are shown on the chart. The first line (called the *MACD line*) is the difference between two *exponentially smoothed* moving averages of the price (usually 12 and 26 periods). The computer subtracts the longer average (26) from the shorter (12) to obtain the MACD line. A moving average (usually 9 periods) is then used to smooth the MACD line to form a second (signal) line. The result is that two lines are shown on the chart, the faster *MACD line* and the slower *signal line* (see Figure 6.1). Some analysts prefer to use the preceding moving average values for buy signals and another set of values for sell signals, as Appel originally recommended. The problem with doing that is that you need to construct two different MACD indicators with two different sets of numbers. Perhaps for this reason, or for purposes of simplicity, most analysts seem content to employ the previously mentioned default values (9, 12, and 26) in all situations. By doing it that way, the same moving average values can be used for buy and sell signals on all markets, as well as on daily, weekly, and monthly charts.

MACD AS TREND-FOLLOWING INDICATOR

Interpretation of the two lines in the MACD system is relatively straightforward and is similar to the *crossover* technique described in the discussion of moving averages in Chapter 4. In other words, buy signals are registered when the faster MACD line crosses *above* the slower signal line. Sell signals occur when the faster line crosses *below* the slower. By using it in that fashion, valuable trading signals are given that will keep you on the right side of a trend (i.e., on the *long* side during uptrends, and on the *short* side or out of the market during downtrends). Naturally, signals given on daily charts are more frequent and of shorter duration than those given on weekly charts. That is why it is best to place more reliance on the MACD crossover signals given on weekly charts, and to utilize the daily charts for timing purposes or for shorter-term trading signals (see Figure 6.2).

MACD AS AN OSCILLATOR

Being able to use this same indicator to determine overbought and oversold conditions gives it a particularly unique quality. This is possible because the MACD and signal lines fluctuate above and below a zero line, just like the momentum oscillator described in Chapter 5. The best buy signals are given when the two lines are below the zero line (oversold) and the best sell signals when the two lines are above the zero line (overbought). Some analysts use crossings above and below the zero line as an additional way to find buy and sell signals. A bullish crossing of the MACD lines that takes place below the zero line, for example, would be confirmed when both lines cross above the zero line themselves.

Figure 6.1   Short-term signals are given on line crossings. *(MetaStock, Equis International, Inc.)*

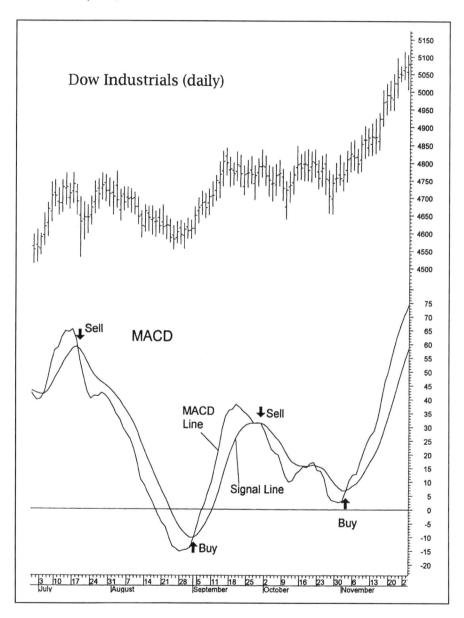

Figure 6.2   The weekly MACD line stayed bullish from January to August in 1995. *(MetaStock, Equis International, Inc.)*

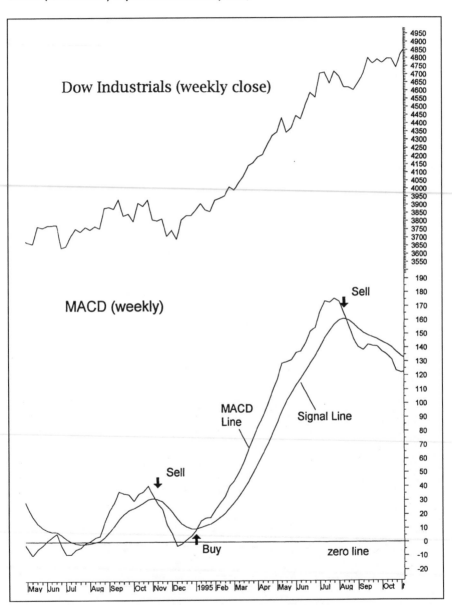

Studying the MACD system, you will observe that when the lines rise too far above the zero line, a potential *overbought* signal is given. Conversely, when the lines drop too far below the zero line, a possible *oversold* condition is signaled. Unfortunately, the MACD lines have no predetermined overbought and oversold levels as exist with the relative strength index (70 and 30) or stochastics (80 and 20). It is up to the user to compare where the MACD lines are presently located to their extreme upper and lower boundaries in the past. In this way, the MACD system can be used much the same as an oscillator to determine when markets have risen or fallen too far. But there's another way in which this indicator resembles an oscillator.

MACD DIVERGENCES

The previous chapter discussed how to spot divergences on oscillator charts. This can also be done with the MACD system. You will notice that after the MACD lines have risen far enough above the zero line, they will begin to diverge from the price action. In other words, prices will continue to advance while the MACD lines form a double top or a series of declining peaks. This is an early warning that the uptrend is losing momentum. A sell signal given when the MACD lines are stretched too far above the zero line and after a negative divergence has been formed is usually worth paying attention to (see Figure 6.3). The situation is reversed at bottoms. A double bottom in the MACD lines while they are too far below the zero line warns that prices may be nearing a trough. This potentially bullish warning is confirmed by a bullish crossing of the two lines from that oversold placement. Here again, weekly signals carry much more weight than daily signals (see Figure 6.4).

HOW TO BLEND DAILY AND WEEKLY SIGNALS

Signals given on weekly charts always carry more trend significance than those given on daily charts. It also follows that signals on weekly charts are less important than those on monthly charts, while signals on daily charts carry more significance than those on hourly charts. The universal guiding price in all market analysis is that a longer-range chart is always more significant than a shorter-time chart. Our primary concern here is how to blend weekly and daily signals. Let's say that your computer flashes a bullish crossing of the MACD lines from below the zero line on a daily chart. Do you jump in and buy the stock in question? Not necessarily.

Figure 6.3   A bearish divergence is seen between MACD and Motorola from above the zero line. In such cases, the second signal (C) is the key. The buy signal is given from below the zero line at point A. *(MetaStock, Equis International, Inc.)*

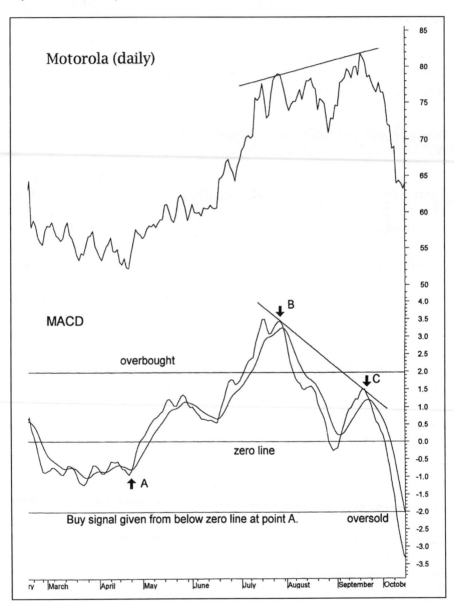

Figure 6.4   Weekly MACD signals are less frequent and more reliable. The May 1995 buy signal lasted five months. Weekly signals should filter daily signals. The sell signal on this chart confirms a bearish divergence during September on the daily chart (see Figure 6.3). (*MetaStock, Equis International, Inc.*)

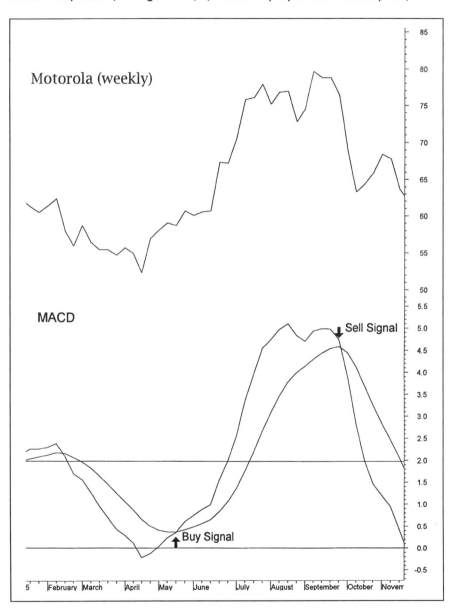

You should always check to see what the weekly indicator looks like. If that is also in an oversold condition (or already in a bullish alignment), then the buy signal on the daily chart may provide a good entry point. If the weekly chart is too far above the zero line (or in a bearish alignment), then it's probably best to ignore the buy signal on the daily chart. It's generally best to start with the weekly chart to determine major buying and selling zones. The daily chart can be used for earlier trend warnings and to fine-tune entry and exit points.

HOW TO MAKE MACD EVEN BETTER—THE HISTOGRAM

As good as the MACD indicator is in the form just described, there's a way to make it even better. That technique is called the *MACD histogram*. The MACD histogram will provide even earlier warnings of potential trend changes and greatly enhances the value of the indicator. Since the histogram shows the MACD crossover signals (in a slightly different way), nothing is lost in its use. What is gained is a way to generate action signals much sooner. The histogram simply plots the *difference* between the MACD line and the signal line. It's called a *histogram* because vertical bars are used to show the difference between the two lines (see Figure 6.5).

The MACD histogram fluctuates above and below a zero line of its own. When the histogram value is above the zero line, it simply means that the two MACD lines are in bullish alignment (MACD over signal line). As long as the histogram value is above its zero line, the MACD signals are still bullish. When the faster MACD line crosses below the slower signal line (registering a sell signal), the histogram value falls below its zero line as well. Crossings above and below the zero line by the histogram always coincide with bullish and bearish crossings by the two MACD lines themselves. As stated earlier, this is just another way of viewing the same system. Here's where the advantage of the histogram comes in.

If the histogram is above its zero line (bullish), but begins to drop toward the zero line, that tells us that the positive relationship (or spread) between the two MACD lines, although still positive, is beginning to weaken. Remember that the histogram measures the *difference* between the two MACD lines. The plus or minus value of the histogram (above or below its zero line) tells us if the MACD lines are bullish or bearish. The *direction* of the histogram tells us whether that bullish or bearish relationship is gaining or losing momentum.

Let's take a market in a downtrend. The histogram is below zero, which means that the MACD line is below its signal line. In other words, the stock

Figure 6.5   MACD crossover signals coincide with zero line crossings on
MACD histogram (see circles). Turns in histogram precede crossover signals
(see lines). *(MetaStock, Equis International, Inc.)*

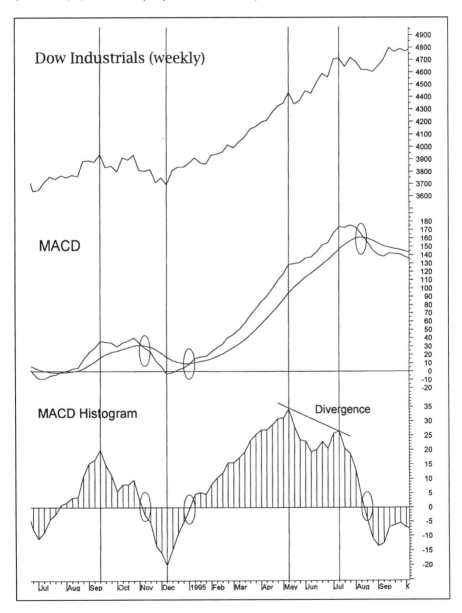

is in a downtrend. For a while, the histogram is also dropping. Suddenly, the histogram lines start to rise toward the zero line. This tells us that although the MACD system is still negative (no buy signal yet), the downtrend is losing momentum. Many traders will cover short positions in this instance. An actual buy signal to initiate a long position doesn't take place until the histogram moves above its zero line. The pattern is just the opposite in an uptrend.

During an uptrend, a positive histogram reflects a bullish MACD alignment. For a while, the histogram will be above its zero line and rising. At some point, however, the histogram will begin dropping toward its zero line. Traders will often use the decline in the histogram as an early signal to begin taking some profits in the rising stock. No actual sell signal is given, however, unless and until the histogram actually drops below the zero line.

The signals can be applied to the both weekly and daily charts, although the latter has less reliability. Weekly charts are preferable. But, here again, it's important to blend the two. The first buy and sell signals are always given on the daily chart, since it's the more sensitive. Check to see what the weekly chart is doing. If the daily MACD histogram is giving a buy signal while the weekly MACD histogram is beginning to rise toward its zero line (or already above it), the daily buy signal is probably a good one. It's always good to have the daily and weekly charts agree with each other (see Figure 6.6).

USING MACD WITH STOCHASTICS

Blending indicators is always a good idea. In the previous chapter, we discussed the value of combining RSI with stochastics. Signals generated by the stochastics lines are often too frequent and unreliable when used by themselves. MACD crossovers are less frequent and more reliable (although usually slower). One way to enhance the value of both indicators is to combine them. Why not use the trend-following characteristics of the MACD system as a filter on stochastics, for example? In other words, follow buy signals on stochastic crossovers only when the MACD lines are in positive alignment (see Figure 6.7).

Or how about using weekly MACD histogram signals as a filter on *daily* stochastic signals? You would use buy signals on the daily stochastic chart for entry on the buy side only when the weekly MACD histogram is positive or rising. In that bullish environment, you would ignore short-term sell signals on the more sensitive stochastics system. Each indicator

Figure 6.6   Notice how the histogram started to weaken 10 weeks before actual sell signal crossing. *(MetaStock, Equis International, Inc.)*

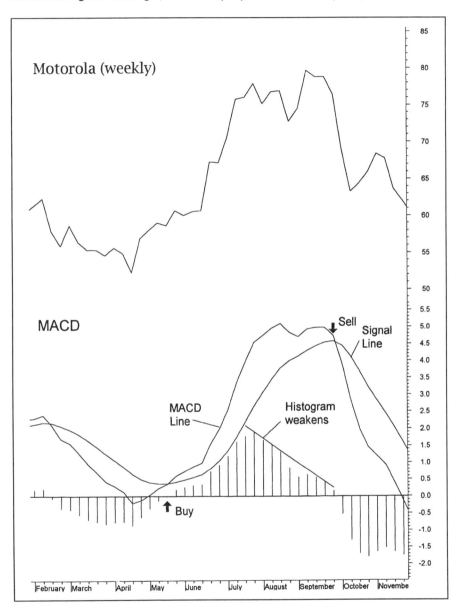

Figure 6.7   Using smoother MACD lines (even with trend lines) can help filter out noise on the more volatile stochastics oscillator. *(MetaStock, Equis
International, Inc.)*

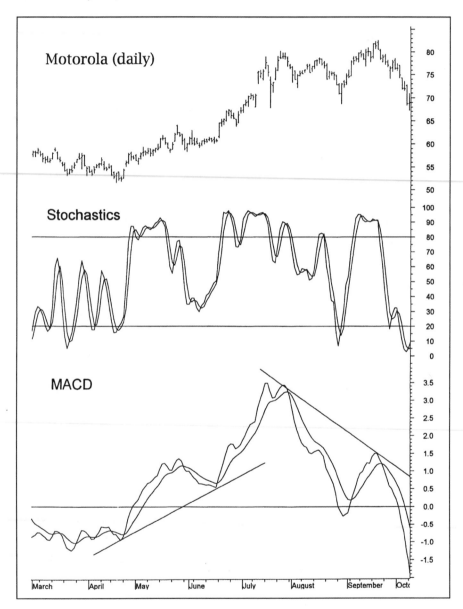

has its own strength and weakness. The computer lets you put as many indicators as you want on your price chart. Try combining them.

HOW TO KNOW WHICH INDICATORS TO USE

There is one more critical problem that still hasn't been resolved. How do you know when to employ a trend-following indicator (like a moving average), or an overbought/oversold oscillator like stochastics? Moving averages are your friend during a trend, but can be cruel to your bottom line during a trading range environment like the one in 1994, when most stock market averages moved sideways for a year.

Oscillators work especially well in choppy market environments (like 1994) and at important turning points when a trend is losing momentum. During a strong uptrend in the stock market, like the one in 1995, oscillators can be more harmful than helpful. Fortunately, there is an indicator that can help resolve this dilemma.

THE AVERAGE DIRECTIONAL MOVEMENT (ADX) LINE

This line is part of a more complex trading system, also developed by Welles Wilder, called *directional movement*. We're only introducing this trading system here to alert you to how it might help solve the previously mentioned problem. You can check your software user's manual for a more in-depth explanation of the entire system. The idea behind directional movement is to determine whether a market is in a *trending* or *nontrending* mode.

First, two lines that measure buying and selling pressure are generated. They are called +DI (positive directional indicator) and –DI (negative directional indicator). A bullish environment exists when the +DI line is greater than the –DI line. From these two lines, a third line is generated, called the *average directional movement (ADX) line.*

A rising ADX line tells us that a market is in a trending mode. A falling or flat ADX line reflects a trading range environment. An ADX line fluctuates from below 20 to above 40. An ADX line which has fallen below 20 implies low volatility and the absence of any trend (favoring a nontrending approach). An ADX line that suddenly rises above 20 often signals the beginning of an important trend (and the application of trend-following techniques). An ADX that has risen too far above 40 and starts to drop usually signals that the trend has exhausted itself and that it may be time to switch from a trend-following system back to one which emphasizes a more volatile market environment.

Figure 6.8   (B) Rising ADX shows trending market favoring use of moving averages. (A) Falling ADX line suggests trendless market and use of oscillator approach. *(MetaStock, Equis International, Inc.)*

Try using the average directional movement line as an overall filter to help determine which type of indicator is most suitable in the current market environment. A rising ADX line favors moving averages; a falling ADX line favors oscillators. The ADX line can be used on daily and weekly charts, although weekly signals are more significant (see Figure 6.8).

SUMMARY

The *moving average convergence divergence (MACD)* indicator combines the best features of a moving average crossover system with the ability to determine overbought and oversold conditions like an oscillator. Employing a *histogram* greatly enhances the value of the MACD lines by enabling the trader to anticipate signals even before they happen. Although these signals can be used on daily and weekly charts, the latter are considered to be more important. As in the case of other computerized indicators, it is suggested that you begin with the default values of 12, 26, and 9. As you gain more experience with this and other indicators, you can begin experimenting with other numbers. The *average directional movement (ADX) line* can be helpful in determining which set of indicators to employ at a given time—trend-following (moving averages) or countertrend (oscillators). It's generally a good idea to combine various indicators to enhance their value. Combine *MACD* lines with *RSI* and *stochastics,* for example. Be creative. No indicator is perfect. Combining some of the better ones and ensuring that they agree with one another will greatly improve your chances for success.

SECTION 3

———

Linkage

7
Market Linkages

INTRODUCTION

The visual (charting) approach to investing has traditionally emphasized a *single market* approach. A stock trader would study the price charts of the stock market or individual common stocks with little consideration of outside market influences. It was sufficient to study the price charts of the market in question along with its own set of internal indicators. That is no longer the case. Chart analysis has taken a major evolutionary step over the past decade by emphasizing a more universal intermarket approach. I like to think that my book, *Intermarket Technical Analysis* (John Wiley & Sons, 1991), made a major contribution in that direction. This chapter provides an overview of *intermarket analysis* to show why it's so important to understand how markets interact with and influence one another.

An understanding of intermarket principles is critical to knowing how bond prices and interest rates relate to the stock market. You'll see why interest rate–sensitive stock groups usually lead the general stock market, and what that tells us about where we are in the *business cycle*. You'll come to understand that the stock market is composed of dozens of stock groups that behave differently in shifting economic climates. The question of whether to be in stocks gives way to the more important question of where in the market to concentrate one's money. A greater appreciation of *sector analysis* should be the likely result. The logical extension of sector analysis finds its application in mutual funds, which have become increasingly segmented. Intermarket analysis leads logically into sector and mutual fund investing. This analysis isn't limited to domestic U.S. markets. The same principles of intermarket analysis will be applied to the problem of global investing through mutual funds.

HOW THREE ASSET CLASSES INTERACT

Our introduction to intermarket analysis focuses primarily on the interaction between the three major asset classes—*commodities, bonds,* and *stocks.* Most investors are intuitively aware of the important interaction between bonds and stocks. Important as that relationship is, however, it excludes consideration of commodity markets as a separate asset class, and the important influence commodity markets have on large sectors of the stock market. You'll see why commodity markets are so important to the intermarket picture and why they shouldn't be ignored. The U.S. dollar and the foreign exchange markets also play a role in these market linkages, but their impact is more indirect. Although the impact of currency trading is not central to our discussion here, its impact will be mentioned where it is relevant.

THE IMPORTANCE OF COMMODITY PRICES

This may be the most important and yet least understood link in the intermarket chain. Only in recent years have commodity prices been given the attention they deserve by market analysts and economists. Even if you have no interest in *trading* commodity markets, you would be well advised to monitor their movements. Trends in commodity markets tells us a lot about the strength of the *economy,* which way *inflation* is heading, and the direction of *interest rates.* Individual commodity markets—such as gold, crude oil, and copper—also have a direct bearing on the stock market sectors that are tied to those commodities. You should know what is happening in those commodities before committing your funds to their related stock sectors. But before we consider the question of stock sectors and individual commodities, let's begin on a more macro level by comparing the general commodity price level to bond prices.

The Link between Commodity and Bond Prices

Commodity prices trend in the *opposite* direction of bond prices. That makes economic sense. Bond prices are extremely sensitive to the direction of inflation. Rising commodity prices (higher inflation) are generally indicative of economic strength, which results in higher interest rates and lower bond prices. Falling commodity prices (lower inflation) usually coincides with periods of slower economic growth (often a recession), which are characterized by falling interest rates and rising bond prices. Since commodity markets represent prices in their *raw material* stage, important turns in that sector usually precede turns in broader gauges of inflation, such as the *Consumer Price Index* and the *Producer Price Index*. For that reason, bond traders keep a close eye on the direction of commodities.

Commodity Research Bureau (CRB) Futures Price Index

This index of commodity markets is the most widely followed measure of commodity price direction. Changes to the index in late 1995 reduced the number of commodity markets from 21 to 17. However, it still represents the main universe of commodity sectors, including precious metals, energy, grain, livestock, industrial, and tropical commodities. Any longer-range chart that compares the CRB Index to Treasury bond prices will see that they generally trend in opposite directions. Figure 7.1 shows that inverse relationship during 1993 and illustrates how one asset class warned of trouble in another.

Heading into 1993, commodity prices were falling while bond prices were rising. Early in 1993, however, the CRB Index turned higher and rose through the balance of that year. Commodity and bond prices rose together for several months until the fourth quarter of 1993, when bond prices suffered their worst collapse in half a century. Since the two markets generally trend in opposite directions, the rise in the CRB Index provided a warning that the uptrend in bonds was unsustainable. The interplay between commodities and bonds during 1993 showed how activity in one asset class can affect another. How could one have dealt with that unusually long lead time between the upturn in the CRB Index and the peak in bonds?

WATCH INDUSTRIAL PRICES

Although the inverse relationship between the CRB Index and bond prices holds up very well over time, turns in the CRB Index often *lead* turns in the bond market. For that reason, it's wise to consult other measures of general commodity price trends and certain sectors in particular, such as industrial metals. Industrial metals such as *copper* and *aluminum* are especially sensitive to economic trends, since they are used in the building of

Figure 7.1   Commodity Research Bureau Index of 17 commodity markets.
The rise in commodity prices that started in early 1993 (point A) eventually
caused the bond market peak at point B. Bond and commodity prices usually trend in opposite directions. *(MetaStock, Equis International, Inc.)*

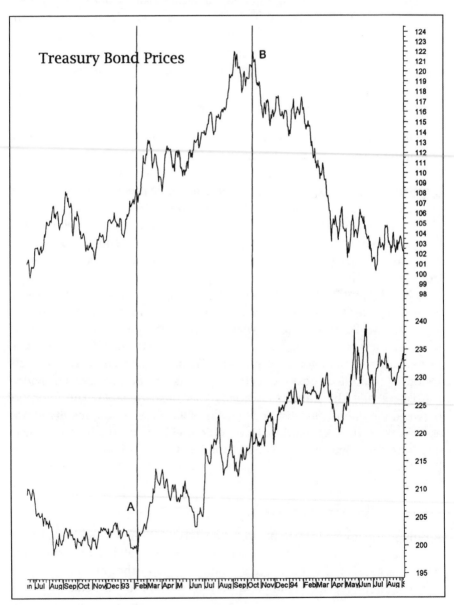

autos and homes. For this reason, these markets often have a much closer correlation to bond prices than other commodities that are more weather-related, such as the food and grain markets (see Figure 7.2).

Figure 7.2 shows a closer inverse relationship between copper and Treasury bond prices from 1992 to 1994. Note that the upturn in copper during the fourth quarter of 1993 coincided exactly with the bond market peak. Note also how the break of a down trendline in copper was confirmed by an up trendline violation in bonds, showing how traditional chart analysis can be blended with intermarket analysis. Figure 7.3 shows the same two markets overlaid on one another, which is a more useful way to perform intermarket analysis. Not only did the copper bottom coincide with the bond top in late 1993, but the bulk of 1994 saw falling bond prices accompanied by surging copper. The rise in copper was symptomatic of economic strength which, in turn, pushed bond prices lower and interest rates higher. We'll come back to the bullish effect the copper uptrend had on *nonferrous metal* shares later in the chapter.

GOLD AND OIL ARE ALSO IMPORTANT

In addition to industrial metals, two other sectors that should be watched closely are the *gold* and *oil* markets. Gold is viewed as a traditional leading indicator of inflation and carries important psychological weight. Investors may not be that concerned by rising soybean prices, but a jump in the price of gold makes immediate headlines. The Federal Reserve Board also watches gold prices carefully to help determine if monetary policy is on course. Gold price direction also has a major influence on the trend of *gold-mining* shares, which we deal with in the next chapter.

The price of energy has more than a psychological effect on the inflation picture. A rise in the price of oil has a rippling inflationary effect throughout the global economy. Oil-related stocks are also dependent to a large extent on the trend of oil.

A sharp rise in either of these key commodities sends an immediate warning to bond traders. A rise in both commodities can cause nightmares for bond bulls. As long as these two commodities remain weak, however, bond bulls usually sleep a lot better.

JOURNAL OF COMMERCE (JOC) INDEX

Another commodity index that has gained popularity in recent years is the *Journal of Commerce (JOC) Index* of spot industrial material prices.

Figure 7.2 The bond price peak in late 1993 coincided with a major bottom in copper. Falling copper prices imply economic weakness which is bullish for bond prices. The dramatic rally in copper that began in late 1993 helped push bond prices lower. *(MetaStock, Equis International, Inc.)*

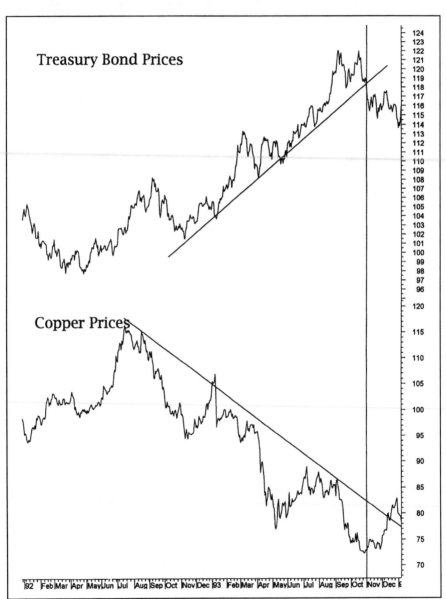

Figure 7.3   Bond and copper prices usually trend in opposite directions.
The 1993 bond peak coincided with a major bottom in copper. *(MetaStock,
Equis International, Inc.)*

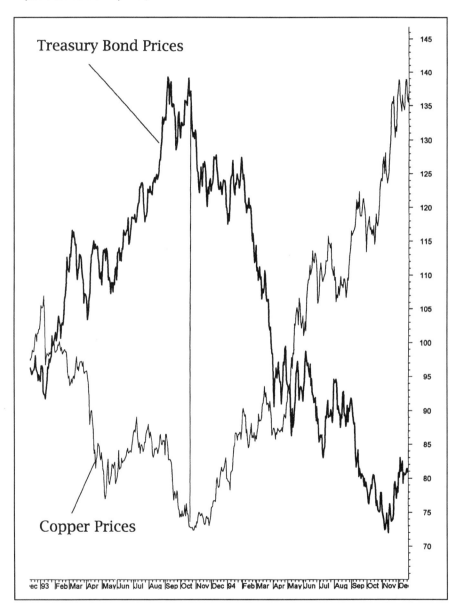

This index was created by the Center for International Business Cycle Research at Columbia University. The JOC Index comprises 17 industrial commodities that are sensitive to turns in the business cycle and have good records at anticipating turns in the rate of inflation. What distinguishes the JOC Index from the CRB Index is that the former does not include any food or agricultural commodities. Therefore, the JOC Index is believed to have a more direct bearing on the direction of interest rates (see Figure 7.4).

The JOC Index has a heavy weighting of industrial metals such as steel, copper, aluminum, zinc, lead, and tin, many of which are traded on the London Metals Exchange. The JOC Index is also comprised of *spot* or *cash* prices as opposed to *futures* prices. Therefore, the JOC Index is calculated at the end of each trading day. The CRB Index, by contrast, is

---

Figure 7.4 The upturn in the JOC Index of Industrial Material Prices coincided exactly with the major bottom in bond yields in late 1993. *(Knight-Ridder Tradecenter, a trademark of Knight-Ridder's Financial Information)*

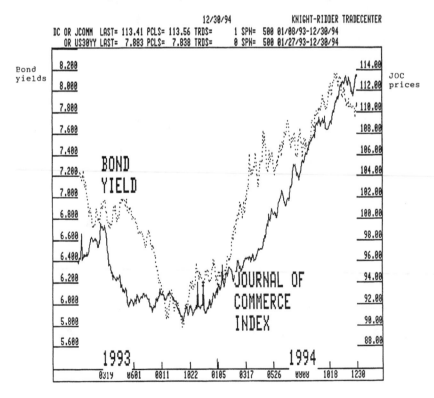

comprised of actively traded commodity markets and is updated during the trading day. A futures contract exists on the CRB Index for trading and hedging purposes. (A chart of the JOC Index can be seen each week on the commodity pages of *BARRON'S* along with a chart of the CRB Index.)

GOLDMAN SACHS COMMODITY INDEX

This is the newest of the commodity indexes. It includes pretty much the same commodity markets as the CRB Index; but it is a trade-weighted index. In other words, it *weights* the various commodities according to their importance in the world trade picture. As a result, energy prices comprise almost half of its weighting. For this reason, it's not as useful in measuring overall price trends, but is helpful in monitoring the impact of energy prices on the overall commodity price trend (see Figure 7.5). The Goldman Sachs Commodity Index is also traded as a futures contract.

Since none of these commodity indexes is perfect, it's a good idea to keep an eye on all of them. The most convincing evidence of the direction of commodity price trends occurs when all three of these commodity indexes are trending in the same direction.

THE IMPACT OF BONDS ON STOCKS

We've seen that commodity prices affect the direction of bond prices. Bond prices, in turn, affect the direction of stock prices. Rising bond prices (falling bond yields) are positive for equity prices. Falling bond prices (rising bond yields) are negative for equities. However, it's important to recognize that turns in the bond market often *precede* similar turns in the stock market by several months. That being the case, important turns in the direction of bond prices can provide an early warning of an impending turn in stocks.

We've shown that the upturn in commodity prices warned of the downturn in bonds in September 1993. Figure 7.6 shows that the bond peak preceded a stock market peak approximately five months later, in February 1994. Although the stock market resumed its climb a year later, the collapse in bond prices caused a nearly 10-percent loss in most major averages, with certain sectors of the market experiencing losses in excess of 20 percent—thereby qualifying 1994 as what has come to be called a *stealth* bear market.

Figure 7.5   A bullish breakout in late 1995 by this energy-dominated index signaled higher energy inflation. *(MetaStock, Equis International, Inc.)*

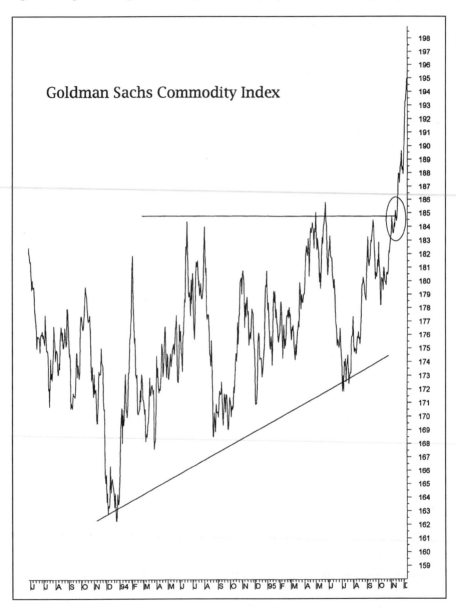

Goldman Sachs Commodity Index

Figure 7.6   Bond prices usually lead stock prices. The bond market top in late 1993 (point A) warned of a stock market top within six months (point B). *(MetaStock, Equis International, Inc.)*

UTILITIES' LOSS WAS METALS' GAIN

Besides the negative macro effect that rising commodity and falling bond prices have on the overall stock market, it's important to consider the dynamic rotation that is caused within certain stock *sectors*. This consideration leads to an extremely important element in intermarket analysis, that is, how the interplay between the three asset classes helps explain the *rotation* within the stock market from sector to sector. That insight will help you determine which sectors of the stock market to emphasize at certain times to ensure that you are always in the sector that is outperforming the general market. Figures 7.7 and 7.8 show how the events of late 1993 and most of 1994 had a dramatically different effect on two stock market sectors.

Utility stocks are considered to be interest rate driven and, as a result, track bond prices very closely. Note in Figure 7.7 how the utilities peaked along with bonds in late 1993 and then suffered a devastating loss of 30 percent during 1994. In a climate of falling bond prices, utility stocks are among the stocks that suffer the greatest damage. Where does one put one's money when bond prices are falling and commodity prices are rising? A glance at Figure 7.8 should answer that question. With copper and most base metal prices rising, their related stocks also did quite well during 1994. Copper and aluminum stocks were among the strongest sectors of the stock market during an otherwise dismal 1994. We discuss the implications for sector rotation using intermarket principles more fully in Chapters 8 and 9.

1995 MARKETS REVERSE INTERMARKET PICTURE

The general rotation among the three asset classes is this—commodities turn first, bonds turn second, and stocks turn last. A general rise in commodities during 1993 preceded the downturn in bonds (with copper prices turning at about the same time as bonds). Stocks turned down several months later. The intermarket rotation that unfolded in late 1994 and early 1995 followed the same order described previously but in the opposite direction, as shown in Figures 7.9 and 7.10. Copper prices peaked in early 1995 (see Figure 7.9), which roughly coincided with a major bottom in bond prices (the CRB Index had actually peaked six months earlier during the summer of 1994). Not surprisingly, utilities also turned up around the same time that bonds did, while metal stocks peaked.

That reversed the bearish intermarket alignment of a year earlier and set the stage for a bullish advance in the stock market throughout 1995. Figure 7.10 shows that the bottom in bond prices in late 1994 was a major

Figure 7.7   Bond prices and utility stocks usually trend in the same direction. They peaked together in late 1993 and bottomed together in late
1994. *(MetaStock, Equis International, Inc.)*

Figure 7.8 The bottom in copper prices may have been bearish for bonds and utilities, but was bullish for related metal stocks. *(MetaStock, Equis International, Inc.)*

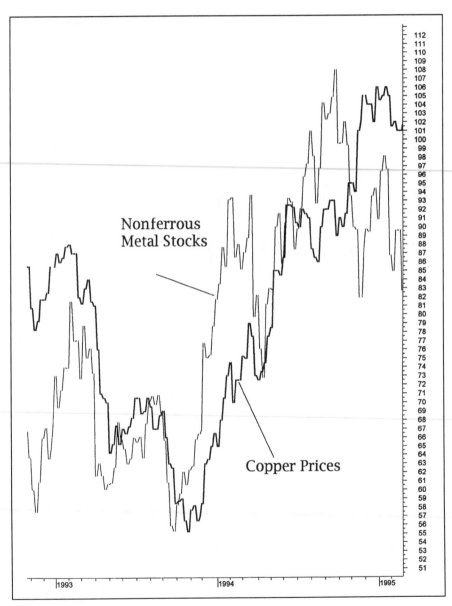

Figure 7.9   At the start of 1995, the peak in copper prices coincided with
an important bottom in bond prices. *(MetaStock, Equis International, Inc.)*

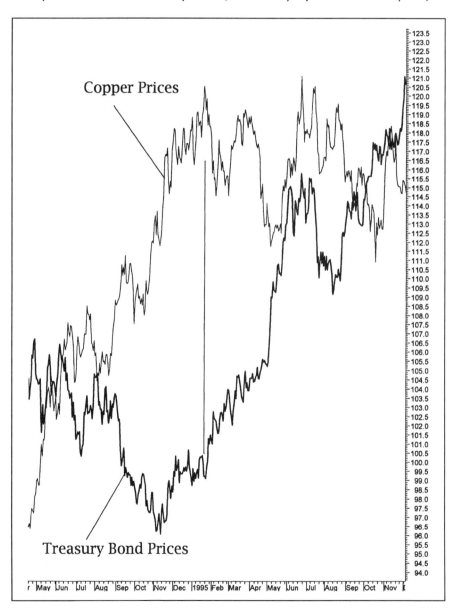

Figure 7.10   Weakness in bond prices during 1994 caused a 10 percent correction in stock prices and a year of consolidation. The late 1994 bottom in bonds helped launch another bull leg in stocks. *(MetaStock, Equis International, Inc.)*

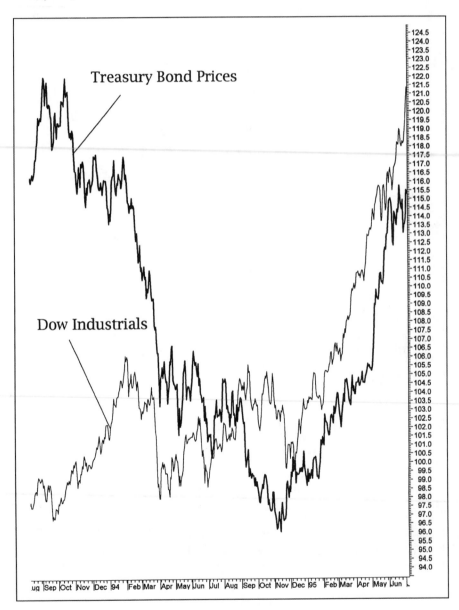

contributing factor that helped launch the spectacular bull run in both markets for the following year. But the general rotation was maintained. Commodity prices measured by the CRB Index peaked first (in mid-1994), the peak in copper coming six months later when bonds troughed. Stocks turned up a couple of weeks after bonds.

The lead and lag times do tend to vary, and it's not realistic to expect a *rigid* application of the intermarket rotation just described. However, it seems safe to say that an understanding of how these three asset classes— commodities, bonds, and stocks—interact with each other does explain a lot about market direction and also sheds important light on the question of sector rotation.

There is another simple indicator that is especially helpful in determining the health of the overall stock market and helps to determine whether one's portfolio should be emphasizing *inflation-* or *interest rate–sensitive* stocks.

THE CRB INDEX/TREASURY BOND RATIO

This simple ratio divides the price of the CRB Index (as a proxy for commodity prices) by the price of Treasury bonds. The ratio is a measure of *relative strength,* a concept that we explore more fully in Chapter 9. When the ratio is rising, commodity prices are outperforming bond prices. In that climate, commodity markets or commodity-related stocks should be emphasized. That would include natural resource stock sectors that tend to benefit from rising commodity prices, such as copper and aluminum, energy, and gold-mining stocks, to name a few. These are sectors that tend to outperform the general market during periods of rising inflation and economic strength.

Figure 7.11 shows the *CRB Index/Treasury bond ratio* turning up in late 1993 and rising for about a year to the fourth quarter of 1994. Remember that copper stocks did especially well during that time period, while utility stocks lost 30 percent. A rising CRB Index/Treasury bond ratio is generally negative for the overall stock market, since it signals rising inflation and higher interest rates. Remember also that 1994 was a difficult year for the overall stock market, in particular for interest sensitive stocks and bonds. The peak in the CRB Index/Treasury bond ratio in November 1994 signaled a shift in the asset allocation mix, away from commodity-type stocks and back to financial stocks, which lasted through most of 1995. The falling ratio also paved the way for a strong stock market during 1995.

Figure 7.11 A rising ratio signals inflationary pressure, which is generally negative for stocks (1994). The peak in the ratio in early 1995 was negative for commodities, but bullish for both bonds and stocks. *(MetaStock, Equis International, Inc.)*

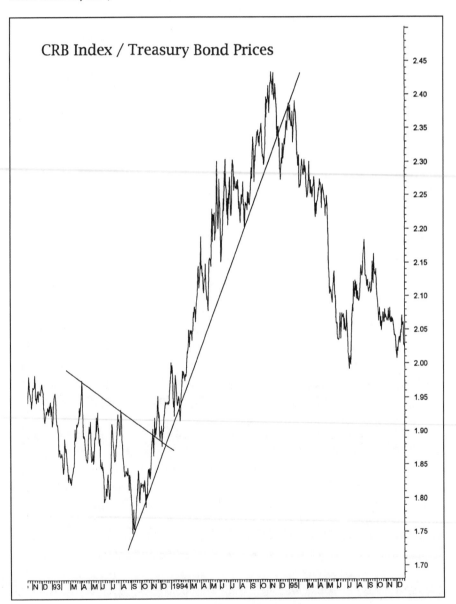

CRB Index / Treasury Bond Prices

THE INTERNATIONAL DIMENSION

The question of where to invest one's assets has taken on an important *international* dimension. Investors not only have to decide how to allocate their funds among their own domestic asset classes, but how to allocate funds globally as well. The principle of diversification is based on the idea that investors shouldn't put all of their eggs in one basket. By spreading funds among different types of assets, an optimal mix is achieved that should balance the search for superior returns with the desire to reduce risk. One way to achieve this happy result is to invest some funds overseas. If an American is willing to buy a Japanese car because he or she believes it is superior to an American car, why not buy a Japanese automobile stock as well?

Mutual funds have made it especially easy for American investors to invest globally. *Open-* and *closed-end* mutual funds make it possible to invest in individual countries, as well as geographic regions, such as the Pacific Rim and Latin America. *American depository receipts (ADRs)* of individual foreign stocks are traded right on the New York Stock Exchange. We deal with the subject of global investing in Chapter 12. Our purpose here is to make you aware that international markets also play an important role in intermarket analysis.

Intermarket linkages exist among the world's major markets in both bonds and stocks. Global bond and stock markets generally rise and fall together. Some are more closely linked than others, however. Figure 7.12 shows two global stock markets that generally correlate closely with each other—the British and American stock markets. For that reason, it's generally a good idea to know what's happening in Britain. The American markets influence and, in turn, are influenced by foreign markets. Therefore, analysis of global trends plays an important role in our analysis of the American markets and is crucial if one is looking to put some money overseas. Fortunately, the traditional charting techniques described in the preceding chapters, as well as intermarket analysis, can be used on the international front.

SUMMARY

Intermarket analysis adds an additional dimension to traditional chart analysis. By studying the interplay among various asset classes—such as commodities, bonds, and stocks—investors can obtain a better understanding of economic forces that move each sector and of where to employ

Figure 7.12   Linkages exist between global markets. The British and American stock markets are highly correlated. They both peaked in early 1994
(point A) and troughed together in early 1995 (point B). *(MetaStock, Equis
International, Inc.)*

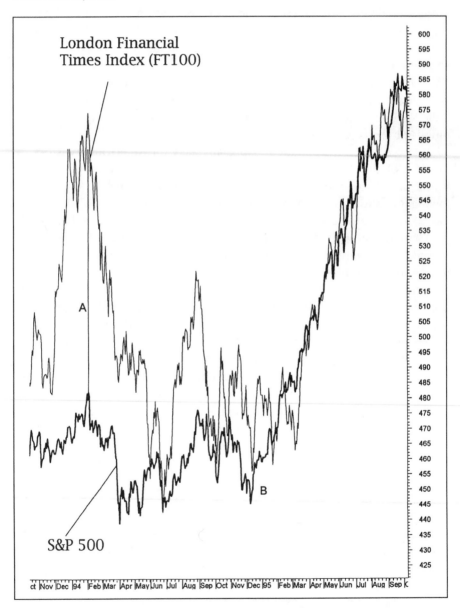

one's funds within the market itself. Commodity price trends influence the trend of bond prices which, in turn, influence stock prices. It's important to monitor the trends of all three categories. By studying the relative strength between bonds and commodities with the *CRB Index/Treasury bond ratio,* the investor is better able to determine whether the environment is positive or negative for the overall stock market. A rising ratio is negative, while a falling ratio is positive. The direction of that ratio also helps one decide whether to emphasize inflation-type stocks or interest-sensitive shares. *International* markets play an important role in the global intermarket picture. Since global markets are linked, it's always a good idea to know what's happening to bond, stock, and currency markets around the globe. (A more in-depth treatment of intermarket analysis can be found in my earlier book, *Intermarket Technical Analysis* [John Wiley & Sons, 1991].)

8

Stock Sectors

INTRODUCTION

The previous chapter emphasized the macro effect that commodity price trends have on interest rates and bonds, and the way bond prices impact on the stock market. For that reason, it's always a good idea to keep track of which way commodity and bond prices are trending in order to assess the bullish or bearish effect on the stock market. The CRB Index/Treasury bond ratio was offered as one way to monitor the *relative strength* of those two important sectors. A rising ratio (such as in 1994) suggests that commodity prices are outperforming bond prices, which is normally negative for the stock market as a whole. A falling CRB Index/Treasury bond ratio (as occurred during 1995) shows that bond prices are the stronger vehicle, which is generally positive for stock prices.

This chapter focuses more on utilizing the futures markets for *sector analysis* of the stock market. For example, when commodity prices are outperforming bonds (a rising CRB/bond ratio), the stronger stock sectors are inflation-sensitive *natural resource* stocks. When bond prices are stronger than commodities (a falling CRB/bond ratio), *interest-sensitive* stocks are the place to be. The simple viewing of how commodity prices are doing relative to bonds can help decide which sectors of the stock market to emphasize in one's portfolio. Natural resource stocks include copper, aluminum, energy, and gold-mining stocks, among others. Interest-sensitive stocks include utilities, banking, and financial stocks.

THE NEW YORK STOCK EXCHANGE (NYSE) ADVANCE-DECLINE LINE

Before we get to those sectors, however, let's take a brief detour to explain how the *advance-decline (AD) line* is used. You'll then see how the AD line is itself affected by a couple of market sectors and why it does what it does. This indicator of market *breadth* is used to help determine the direction of the stock market. It is calculated each day by taking the difference between the number of advancing stocks and the number of declining stocks. If the number of advancing stocks is greater than the declining stocks, that positive difference is added to the previous day's total. If the number of declining stocks is greater, the negative difference is subtracted from the previous day's total. The advance-decline line then is a running cumulative total of the number of advancing stocks minus the number of declining stocks.

A rising AD line implies that most stocks are advancing, which is considered bullish for the market. A falling AD line suggests that most stocks are falling, which is considered to be negative for the market. The AD line can be calculated on a daily or weekly basis. Many analysts prefer to use the weekly version for longer-range analysis and the daily line for shorter-term perspective. (Note: Appendix A contains more detailed information on the advance/decline line along with some additional measures of market breadth, such as the *new highs/new lows* list, the *McClellan oscillator,* and the *McClellan summation index.*)

Advance-Decline Line Divergence

The AD line is compared to the major stock averages, such as the Dow Industrials. Although the Dow Jones Industrial Average is the most widely followed measure of stock market performance, the fact is that it includes only 30 stocks—1 percent of the 3,000 stocks traded on the New York Stock Exchange (NYSE). Even the broader Standard & Poor's (S&P) 500 index includes less than 20 percent of the total number of NYSE stocks. For that reason, market analysts study the trend of the NYSE advance-decline line for a more realistic gauge of what the *entire* market of stocks is doing. As long as the AD line is trending along with the major averages, market breadth is said to be *in gear.* In other words, the AD line *confirms* that most stocks are moving in gear with the narrower market indexes.

It is when the AD line begins to *diverge* from the Dow or the S&P 500 that analysts begin to take note. During an uptrend, a flat or falling AD line (while the major stock averages are still rising) is considered to be an early warning of a possible market top. The problem is that these negative divergences may last for as long as six months before the rally stalls. For that reason, the AD line is considered to be a *leading* indicator of stock market performance.

Bonds versus the AD Line

You may be asking yourself what the AD line has to do with intermarket analysis. The fact is, the AD line has a lot to do with intermarket analysis and with bond prices in particular. Since 38 percent of the stocks traded on the New York Stock Exchange are *interest rate–sensitive* and follow bond prices closely, the direction of bond prices influences over a third of the NYSE stock universe. Since the bond market usually leads the stock market, this largely explains why the AD line also leads the general stock market.

Figure 8.1 compares the Dow Jones Industrial Average to the NYSE advance-decline line during late 1993 through 1994. The AD line actually began to flatten out during the fourth quarter of 1993 while the Dow rose to new highs. That constituted a *bearish divergence*. The rally to 4,000 by the Dow during February 1994 coincided with a double top in the AD line (the first peak occurring about five months earlier). That negative divergence between the Dow and the AD line provided an early warning of a tough 1994 in the making. We'll show shortly what caused the top in the AD line.

Figure 8.1 also shows a remarkable difference between the activity in the Dow (which consolidated during 1994 and lost a little less than 10 percent) and the dramatic fall in the AD line. Many stock sectors suffered losses in excess of 20 percent during that year. The carnage that took place in the broader market during 1994 (which was not evident in the Dow Industrials) explains why the 1994 period has been called a *stealth* bear market. It also shows why it's so important not to rely on a handful of narrow market averages to determine what the "market" is doing.

Figure 8.2 shows what caused the top in the AD line in late 1993 and the ensuing plunge in the AD line during 1994. This is where bond prices come into play. The bond peak in September 1993 coincided with the first peak in the AD line. The second peak in the AD line's double top in February 1994 also coincided with a lower peak in the bond market, which started to fall sharply from that point. It can be argued that the peak in the bond market the prior September and the subsequent decline in bond prices during the first quarter of 1994 was a driving force behind the nega-

Figure 8.1   (a) The Dow decline during 1994 was less than 10 percent. (b) The NYSE AD Line failed to support the Dow rally to new highs in early 1994, creating a negative divergence. The broader market suffered much greater losses during 1994 in a "stealth" bear market. *(MetaStock, Equis International, Inc.)*

tive divergence between the NYSE AD line and the Dow Industrials. Remember that the bond market controls the direction of 38 percent of the stocks included in the AD line. The events of late 1993 and early 1994 also show how the stock market tops in stages, with interest-sensitive stocks usually the first to peak along with bonds. Notice, also, how closely the AD line correlated with the falling bond market during most of 1994.

Bonds Lead 1995 Stock Rally

Figure 8.3 shows the bond market troughing out in November 1994 and rising throughout 1995. The bullish impact of rising bond prices can be seen on the rising AD line. In that instance, bond prices actually turned up a month *before* the AD line, providing an even earlier signal of a stock market bottom. Figure 8.4, which compares the AD line to the Dow itself, shows that both measures turned up at about the same time in December 1994 (a full month after bonds). Figures 8.1 through 8.4 are intended to make two points. One is simply to show how the AD line can be used to confirm or, in some cases, to lead turns in the broader market. The second point is that the trend of bonds has a dramatic impact on a large number of interest-sensitive stocks which, in turn, have a strong impact on the AD line— another reason why it's always a good idea to watch what bond prices are doing. (Note: The charts used in these examples are bond *futures* prices. For purposes of longer-range comparisons, futures prices are easier to obtain and track than *cash* bond prices.)

SMALLER STOCKS AND MARKET BREADTH

Another market sector that has an impact on the AD line and market breadth is the universe of *smaller stocks*. If the Dow Jones Industrial Average and the S&P 500 represent large stocks, the Russell 2000 represents a much broader universe of smaller stocks (the question of large versus small is determined by market *capitalization,* which is the product of the number of shares outstanding times the price of each share). It stands to reason that much of the divergence between the 30 large Dow stocks and the advance-decline line is caused by smaller stocks (after all, there are 2,000 of them in the Russell 2000). As a result, there is a close correlation between the Russell 2000 and the NYSE advance-decline line.

Figure 8.5 gives an example of a short-term negative divergence that developed between September and November of 1995, when the AD line peaked in September while the Dow kept rising. Figure 8.6 shows the close

Figure 8.2 Bond prices have a strong impact on the NYSE AD Line since 38 percent of NYSE stocks are interest-sensitive. The AD Line actually peaked with bonds in late 1993. The double top in the AD Line that lasted until February 1994 was caused by relative weakness in interest-sensitive shares. *(MetaStock, Equis International, Inc.)*

Figure 8.3   At the late 1994 bottom, notice that bond prices troughed a month before the NYSE AD Line, showing its leading tendency. *(MetaStock, Equis International, Inc.)*

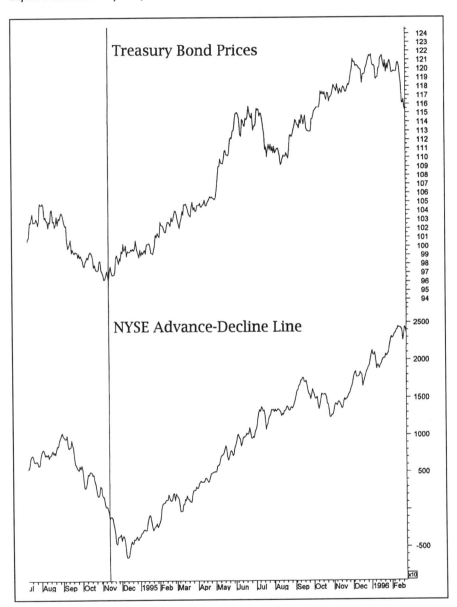

Figure 8.4   The AD Line ended its downtrend in late 1994 and helped support the Dow rally through 1995. *(MetaStock, Equis International, Inc.)*

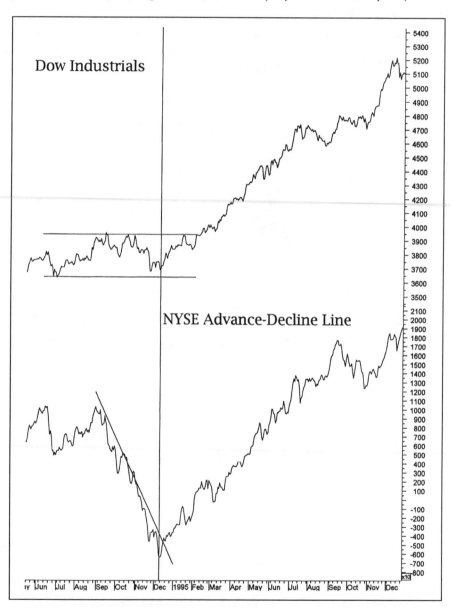

Figure 8.5   The Dow Industrials surged to new highs during late 1995, as did other large-cap stock averages. The AD Line lagged behind (influenced by weaker small and midsize stocks) and formed a short-term negative divergence. *(MetaStock, Equis International, Inc.)*

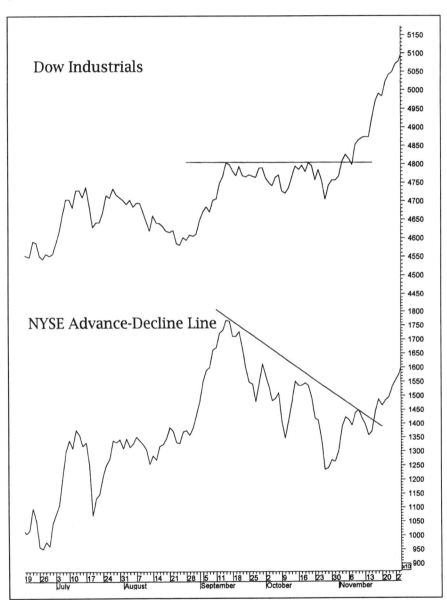

Figure 8.6   The Russell 2000 Index of smaller stocks also has a close correlation to the NYSE Advance-Decline Line. The weakness in the AD Line from
September to November 1995 can be largely explained by weakness in
smaller stocks, as shown below. *(MetaStock, Equis International, Inc.)*

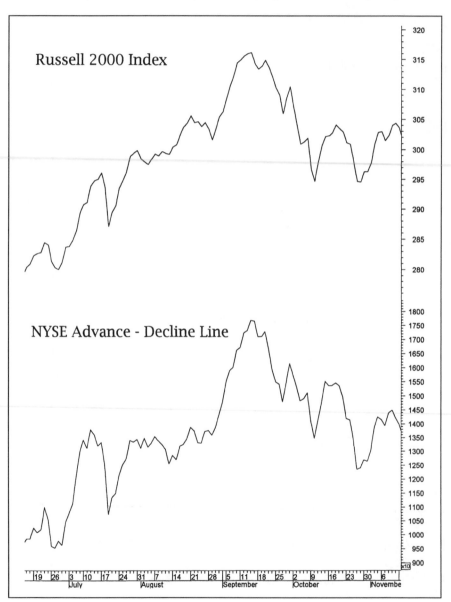

correlation between the AD line and the Russell 2000 index during the same period, suggesting that most of the negative divergence in the AD line came from an underperforming small stock sector. The relative performance between large and small stocks explains a lot about what's happening beneath the surface in the market averages and the AD line. It also shows why it's important to monitor all sectors of the market, not just the large stock averages, and sheds light on the importance of market rotation, which we deal with in the next chapter.

THE DOLLAR'S IMPACT ON SMALLER STOCKS

There's another intermarket feature to consider when measuring the relative performance of small-cap versus large-cap stocks. The large capitalization stocks that reside in the Dow Jones Industrial Average derive much of their revenue from export business. Smaller stocks are usually more dependent on *domestic* American markets. That being the case, the interplay between these two sectors of the markets is often affected by the direction of the *U.S. dollar.* A falling dollar generally favors large stocks over smaller stocks, since it makes American exports more attractive to foreigners. A rising dollar usually favors smaller stocks by making large international stocks less competitive on the international scene. Therefore, when the dollar is rising, smaller stocks tend to outperform larger stocks. When the dollar is weak, larger stocks tend to outperform smaller stocks. Once again, a little knowledge of intermarket forces helps explain much of the rotation that takes place within the various sectors of the stock market.

FINANCIAL STOCKS AND BONDS

Chapter 7 showed the close correlation between bond prices and utilities. Let's widen that universe here to include financial service stocks. Figure 8.7 shows that financial stocks also track bond prices very closely. The S&P Index of financial stocks includes financial service, insurance, and brokerage firms. Bonds and financial stocks peaked together in September 1993 (point A) and troughed together at point B in late 1994 (Figure 8.7). Falling bond prices suggest rotation out of financial stocks, while rising bond prices favor rotation back into financial stocks. Since financial stocks track bonds so closely, and since bonds usually lead stocks, financial stocks also peak and trough ahead of the rest of the stock market. (This also explains why brokerage stocks are considered leading indicators for the rest of the market.)

Figure 8.7   Interest-sensitive stocks, like financials, track the bond market closely. Note the simultaneous peaks at A and troughs at B. *(MetaStock, Equis International, Inc.)*

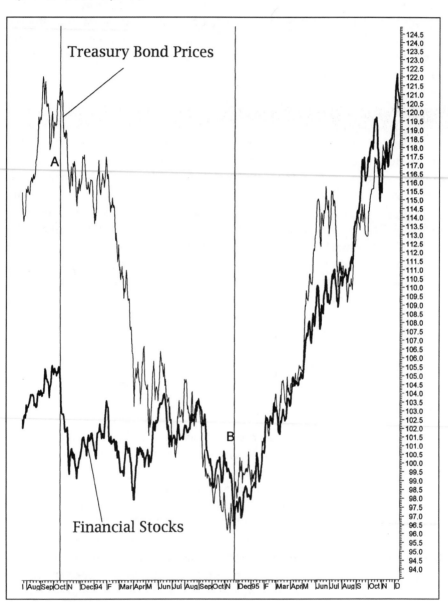

Treasury Bond Prices

A

Financial Stocks

B

During the late stages of a bull market advance, financial stocks tend to peak out ahead of the general market. In the final stages of a bear market decline, financial stocks tend to bottom before the rest of the market. When bond prices are rising (and especially when bonds are rising faster than commodities), one should be rotating into interest-sensitive stocks and away from commodity-related stocks. Remember that over a third of stocks fall into the bond-related, interest-sensitive category. However, as stated in the introduction to intermarket analysis in the preceding chapter, bonds represent only one side of the equation. Let's take a look at the other side.

COMMODITY-RELATED STOCKS

The inverse relationship between commodity and bond prices was covered in the previous chapter. The inverse relationship was also shown between utility stocks (representing the interest-sensitive sector) and copper stocks (representing the commodity sector). During periods of economic weakness with falling inflation, bond-related stocks outperform commodity-related stocks. The opposite occurs during periods of economic strength with rising inflation. One way to measure that relationship is to track the CRB Index/Treasury bond ratio. A rising ratio favors commodity stocks, while a falling ratio favors bond-related stocks. The remaining charts in this chapter are simply intended to show the strong correlation between certain commodity markets and their related stock groups. These are the types of stocks that tend to do well when interest-sensitive stocks are underperforming or falling.

Gold and Mining Stocks

It shouldn't come as a surprise that gold-mining shares are influenced by the price of gold. Rising gold prices are generally bullish for gold-mining shares. Figure 8.8 compares the *Philadelphia Stock Exchange Gold/Silver (XAU) Index* to the price of gold from 1992 through 1995. The best performance by gold-mining shares occurred in early 1993 with a rising gold price. The chart also shows a close correlation between the stocks and the commodity. For this reason, it's necessary for stock market investors to monitor the price of gold. A bullish analysis for gold implies that it's time to rotate some funds into gold-mining shares (see Figure 8.8).

There's also a good reason for gold traders to follow the lead of gold-mining shares: Gold-mining shares usually begin to trend *before* the commodity itself. Rising gold-mining shares often hint at a rise in bullion prices

Figure 8.8   Gold-mining shares are very much influenced by the direction of gold and vice versa. Note the troughs in both gold and mining stocks at points A and C and their peak at point B. *(MetaStock, Equis International, Inc.)*

well before the fact. This tendency for commodity-related stock sectors to lead their underlying commodities is another important element in inter-market sector analysis. We deal with one way to monitor that relationship in the next chapter when we consider how to use *relative strength analysis.*

Oil and Oil Stocks

Not surprisingly, energy stocks are influenced to a great extent by the price of energy. The direction of crude oil prices (along with heating oil and gasoline prices) has a major impact on oil company shares. Rising oil prices are bullish for oil shares, while falling prices are negative. Figure 8.9 compares the price of crude oil futures prices with the *American Stock Exchange Oil Index (XOI)* during the second half of 1995. For most of that period, oil prices were falling and oil shares were generally flat. While the flatness in oil shares may not seem that troublesome, remember that stock prices were soaring in most other sectors. During November 1995, how-ever, crude oil prices turned sharply higher and broke a down trendline. At the exact same time, the XOI rose to a record high.

Figure 8.10 shows that it's also important to keep an eye on natural gas prices. Oil stocks are influenced by trends in natural gas as part of their operations. A rise in gas prices in early 1995 pushed oil stocks higher. The gas peak at midyear coincided with a stock peak. Notice that a sharp rise in natural gas to a new high in November 1995 also contributed to higher oil shares. Not surprisingly, the fourth quarter of 1995 saw the beginning of a rotation toward oil and natural gas pipeline stocks, which benefit from higher energy prices. From a macroeconomic standpoint, ris-ing oil raises the fear of inflation, which often coincides with weaker bond prices and stock market corrections.

SUMMARY

This chapter focuses on how intermarket analysis affects different *sectors* of the stock market. Since a third of stocks are tied to the bond market, they often turn *before* the rest of the market. Interest-sensitive stocks are also heavily represented in the NYSE *advance-decline line* and help explain its tendency to lead the major averages. Smaller stocks included in the *Russell 2000* also have a strong impact on the advance-decline line. A stronger *dollar* favors smaller stocks over larger, while a weaker dollar favors larger stocks. The direction of the *CRB Index/Treasury bond ratio* tells us whether to rotate toward interest-sensitive stocks or commodity

Figure 8.9   (*a*) Crude oil prices have an obvious impact on oil shares.
Declining oil during much of 1995 kept oil shares in check. (*b*) The upturn in
crude oil during the fourth quarter of 1995 pushed oil shares to a new high.
(*MetaStock, Equis International, Inc.*)

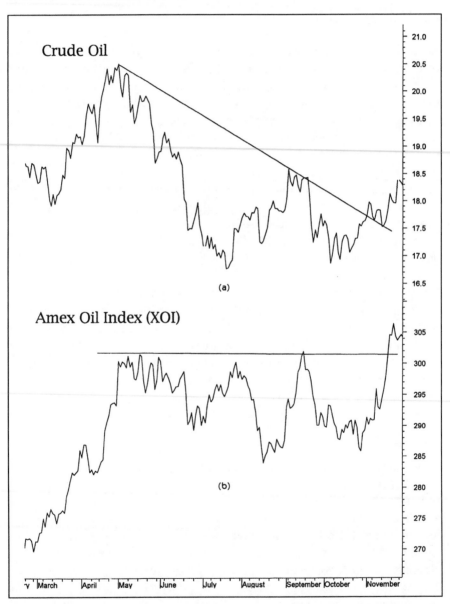

Figure 8.10   The direction of natural gas prices also has an impact on oil
shares. *(MetaStock, Equis International, Inc.)*

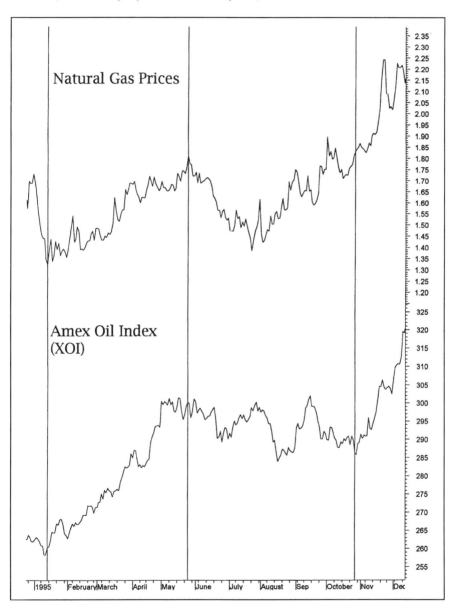

stocks. Large sectors of the stock market are also directly influenced by individual futures markets such as *bonds, copper, gold, oil,* and are indirectly influenced by the *dollar.*

Falling oil prices during the second half of 1995 didn't push oil shares lower, but did cause them to *underperform* the rest of the market. Which leads to a critical point in the study of sector analysis and rotation—that is, the importance of *relative* performance. In the next chapter, you'll learn how to employ *ratio analysis* to help get into the better-performing market sectors and keep out of the laggards.

9
Relative Strength and Rotation

INTRODUCTION

Momentum investing has become a popular buzzword in the investment community. The concept of buying stronger stocks and selling weaker stocks certainly isn't new. What has helped focus so much attention on momentum investing in recent years has been the emergence of *sector mutual funds* that allow investors to rotate easily from one stock market sector to another. As a result, savvy investors have learned to move money into hot sectors and out of those cooling off.

Huge money flows into mutual fund coffers since 1990 in a rising market, combined with pressures on money managers to outperform their mutual fund competitors, has resulted in the practice of putting new money to work right away. The option to raise cash in an overextended market hasn't played well. Those mutual fund managers choosing to cut back on stock market exposure risk being left behind in the ratings battle. This has also contributed in a large way to the *rotation* phenomenon in recent years. Instead of raising cash if a stock sector gets too overextended, the manager simply rotates into a lagging sector that is showing signs of turning up. In this constant search for tomorrow's leaders and laggards, *relative strength* is the driving force.

WHAT IS RELATIVE STRENGTH?

Relative strength is an extremely simple but powerful concept. It compares how one asset is performing relative to another. This is accomplished by constructing a *ratio* between the two competing assets. In other words, one asset is divided by the other. The resulting *relative strength (RS) line* is then plotted along with the respective price charts. In prior chapters, we showed the CRB Index/Treasury bond ratio. By dividing an index of commodity prices by bond prices, the direction of the ratio line tells us which of the two assets is stronger. If the ratio is rising, the *numerator* is the stronger of the two. If the ratio line is falling, the *denominator* is stronger.

Relative strength analysis can be applied to any two assets. One common use is to show a RS line of an individual stock against a benchmark, such as the S&P 500. Most printed chart services show a RS line that divides the stock price by the S&P 500 along the bottom of the chart. You can tell at a glance if the individual stock is doing better or worse than the rest of the market. You want to buy a stock that is *outperforming* the market. Alternatively, you could construct a RS line of an individual stock against its industry benchmark. For example, you could draw a ratio line of Micron Technology against the Philadelphia Stock Exchange Semiconductor Index (SOX). That way, you could tell which stocks are the strongest and the weakest within their own industry groups. Another popular use is to compare stock *sectors* to the general market to determine which sectors are outperforming and underperforming the market.

TOP DOWN ANALYSIS

The easiest way to begin your search for winning stocks is to use a *top down* approach. Begin by choosing those sectors of the market that are showing greater relative strength than the general market. You want to be buying relative strength and avoiding or selling relative weakness. What you want to do is isolate those sectors of the market that display positive trend readings combined with a rising relative strength line. For sector trading through mutual funds, that is as far as you have to go. For individual stock traders, there's another step. Once you've found the sectors that you wish to buy, you then have to find the individual stocks that are strongest in each sector. In other words, you want to buy the strongest stocks in the strongest sectors.

RELATIVE VERSUS ABSOLUTE PERFORMANCE

Before we get into some specific examples, let's see how relative strength analysis differs from traditional chart analysis. Figure 9.1 shows two charts. The top chart is the American Stock Exchange Oil Stock Index (XOI) during the second half of 1995. In the previous chapter, we saw that falling energy prices during that period kept oil shares from rising. A quick study of the XOI chart shows that no serious damage was suffered by oil shares. They simply moved sideways while energy prices were weak. During November, however, oil shares rose to new highs supported by rising oil and natural gas prices.

The bottom chart in Figure 9.1 is a ratio line of the XOI divided by the S&P 500 (the usual stock market benchmark). Here a different picture emerges. From May to November, the ratio line fell, telling us that oil shares were *underperforming* the rest of the market. Why hold an underperforming asset when there's money to be made elsewhere? Although no money was actually lost by holding oil shares during that period, there was an *opportunity cost.* Investors "lost" the opportunity to profit from other sectors of the market that rose during that period. So, in a sense, oil shareholders *did* lose money by holding an underperforming asset. In other words, they were in the wrong sector at the wrong time.

WHY ROTATE AT ALL?

But, you may be asking, what happens when oil shares begin to outperform the market at some point in the future? Isn't it worth holding oil shares during the bad times in hopes of better times in the future? The answer to that depends on you. If you're a long-term investor, then it doesn't make much difference. If you are a more active investor—a trader—then it makes a big difference. The idea behind momentum investing is to hold those sectors that are showing greater relative strength and avoid those showing relative weakness. If you do it right, you won't lose much in the bargain. The reason for that is also shown in Figure 9.1. During November 1995, the ratio line in the bottom chart broke a six-month downtrend line. At that point, the momentum investor would begin to rotate some funds into energy stocks. The point is that there is no need to hold stocks during a relatively bad period, since it so easy to spot when things are improving.

Figure 9.1   (*Top*) Falling energy prices during 1995 kept oil shares flat until November, when oil and gas prices started rising. (*Bottom*) The ratio of oil stocks to the S&P 500 shows the underperformance of oil stocks until late in the year (1995). *(MetaStock, Equis International, Inc.)*

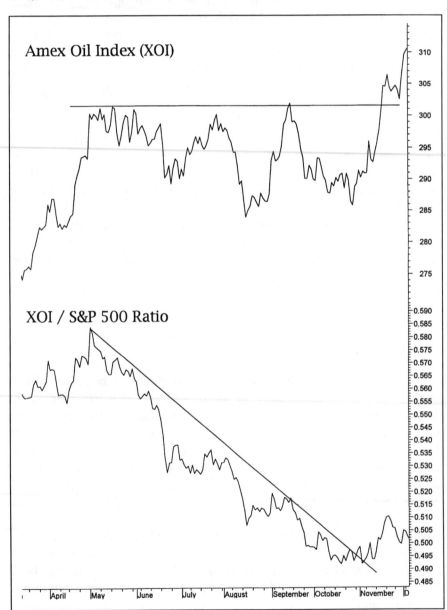

GOLD SHARES AND RELATIVE STRENGTH

Figure 9.2 compares the S&P index of gold shares to the S&P 500. You can see that after a relatively strong 1993, gold shares underperformed in 1994 and 1995. Gold shares were a good place to be in 1993, but not during the ensuing two years. The ratio line would have to break its downtrend line to signal improvement in the gold sector's relative strength and encourage fund rotation toward that sector. One of the advantages of plotting the ratio line right on the price chart is that it adds another dimension to your analysis. Your traditional chart analysis of gold stocks, for example, is now supplemented by a measure of what they are doing relative to the stock market. Even if you were bullish on gold stocks during 1995, the falling relative strength line told you that your funds could be better employed elsewhere. Another advantage is that you can apply simple trendline analysis to the ratio line. Support and resistance levels are also evident on the RS line.

GOLD SHARES VERSUS GOLD BULLION

Another way to utilize ratio analysis is to divide an index of gold shares by the price of gold itself. Gold shares usually rise sooner and faster than the price of bullion. In that sense, gold shares often act as a leading indicator for gold. The best way to monitor that relationship is to use a ratio line. Figure 9.3 compares a gold share/gold ratio in the upper chart and a chart of gold in the lower chart during 1995. Gold shares tried to rally earlier in 1995 but were foiled by the failure of bullion to rise as well.

During November 1995, however, the ratio line broke its downtrend line and started to rise once again. That type of jump in the gold share/gold ratio normally hints that the price of gold is also getting ready to rally. (Gold actually rallied $30 during January 1996 to the highest level in five years.) Stocks often show a tendency to rise or fall before their respective commodities. This can be seen in gold and oil shares, as well as copper and aluminum. That's why it's a good idea to track stocks together with their respective commodities, and it demonstrates another way to use relative strength analysis across asset classes.

SIMPLE ANALYSIS APPLIED TO RELATIVE STRENGTH CHARTS

Figures 9.4 and 9.5 show how traditional chart analysis can be applied to the relative strength lines themselves. Banking shares had an excellent

Figure 9.2   Gold shares outperformed the S&P 500 during 1993, when gold prices were rising. From the beginning of 1994 to the end of 1995, gold shares were weaker than the general market. *(MetaStock, Equis International, Inc.)*

Gold shares / S&P 500

Figure 9.3   Traders were watching to see if the upturn in the gold shares/gold ratio in late 1995 signaled higher gold. *(MetaStock, Equis International, Inc.)*

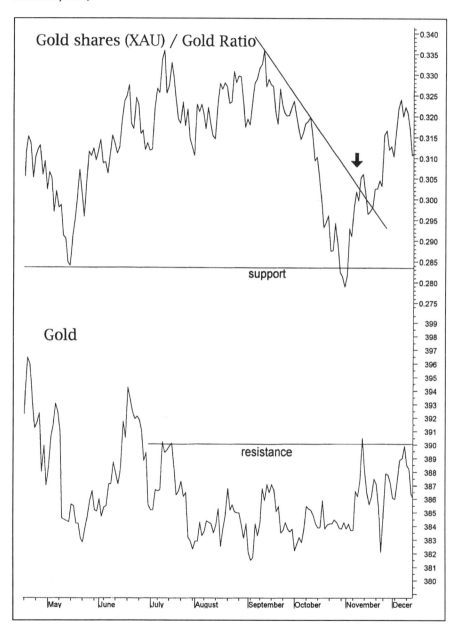

1995 (helped by rising bond prices), as shown in Figure 9.4. Not only did bank shares have good *absolute* 1995 gains, they managed to outperform a strong stock market as shown by the rising relative strength line. Notice the upside breakout by the RS line during May and the pullbacks in the RS line during July and November 1995 bouncing off the uptrend line. May 1995 would have been a good time to rotate funds into bank shares. The successful tests of the trendline indicated it was okay to *hold* bank shares.

Figure 9.5 shows a ratio (RS line) of drug shares divided by the S&P 500. Notice how well trendline analysis, combined with simple trend analysis, worked on this chart. The falling ratio line from 1992 through 1993 showed that drug stocks were not the place to be during that time. However, the breaking of the downtrend line in mid-1994 and the upside breakout a few months later screamed that it was time to rotate back into drug stocks. As the ratio line shows, drug stocks continued to outperform the S&P 500 through the end of 1995.

ROTATION WITHIN SECTORS

Relative strength analysis can even be applied within sectors. For example, transportation stocks can be further subdivided into airlines, rails, and trucking stocks. That means that it is possible to fine-tune your rotation of funds even further. Suppose your work determines that it is a good time to move some funds into transportation stocks. Let's suppose that the economy is strengthening and the Dow Jones Transportation Average is showing good relative strength. Do you just throw funds into the whole sector or should you be more selective?

Figure 9.6 is a relative strength line of airline stocks divided by the Dow Jones Transportation Average. The chart shows two distinctly different trends. During the first half of 1995, airline stocks outperformed the transportation average. The second half (marked by the break of the uptrend line at midyear) showed underperformance. Clearly, the visual investor would have been better off with funds in other transportation stocks (or a more diversified transportation fund) during the second half of that year. Note, however, that the ratio line had bounced off major support at the lows set a year earlier and had broken its downtrend line at the end of 1995. That upturn in the ratio indicated it was time to rotate funds back into airlines again. An investor could accomplish that by switching from a general transportation fund to one that emphasizes airlines.

Figure 9.4   Banking stocks had a good absolute performance during 1995 and even managed to outperform a strong stock market on a relative basis. Notice how well the uptrend line worked to define the bank/S&P ratio's uptrend. *(MetaStock, Equis International, Inc.)*

Bank stocks / S&P 500 Ratio

Figure 9.5 This chart shows what drug stocks did relative to the rest of the market from 1992 to 1995. The relative strength ratio bottomed in mid-1993 and turned up in mid-1994. Since then, drug stocks have outperformed the market. *(MetaStock, Equis International, Inc.)*

Figure 9.6   This relative strength chart shows the airlines outperforming the transports during the first half of 1995 (A) and underperforming during the second half (B). After bouncing off support, the ratio line is moving back up again (C). *(MetaStock, Equis International, Inc.)*

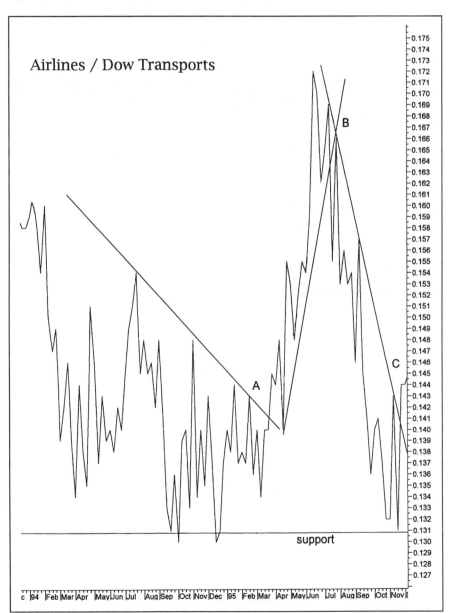

ROTATION FROM ONE SECTOR TO ANOTHER

The previous discussion showed how to utilize relative strength lines to look at groups within sectors, like transportation stocks. Figures 9.7 through 9.9 apply the same principle between separate sectors. Figure 9.7 shows a ratio of the Dow Jones Transportation Index divided by the Dow Utility Index. When the line is rising, rotate toward the transports. When it is dropping, you want to favor the utilities. Figure 9.8 is a relative strength chart comparing semiconductor stocks to the S&P 500. 1995 saw technology stocks soaring and leading the rest of the market higher. Semiconductor stocks were right at the forefront of the technology surge—except that something went wrong during September of that year.

The semiconductor RS line peaked in August and showed a second declining peak during September. Finally, the RS line broke its major uptrend line at the end of the month, signaling a negative shift in its relationship to the S&P 500. The topping process in the RS line and its final breakdown was a clear signal that it was time to rotate funds out of the semiconductor sector. Just to show the damage that took place in the ensuing months, Micron Technology lost two-thirds of its value (falling from 90 to 30), while the semiconductor index fell close to 50 percent. But that's only part of the rotation story. Where did investors put the money coming out of semiconductor stocks?

FOOD STOCKS SHINE IN LATE 1995

Figure 9.9 shows where some of the money went in late 1995. The S&P Food/S&P 500 ratio line in Figure 9.9 shows that food stocks had been out of favor earlier in 1995. Right around the time that chip stocks were peaking (September) the RS line for food stocks started rising. The breaking of downtrend line *a* by the defensive food stocks occurred almost simultaneously with the chip stocks breaking their uptrend line (shown in Figure 9.8). Investors became more defensive at that point, and funneled funds into defensive groups like food, beverage, and drug stocks. The astute visual investor, however, was able to easily spot these shifts in investor preference and switch out of semiconductors just as their run was ending, and into food stocks, whose run was just beginning.

SUMMARY

Momentum investing is based on the idea of concentrating one's funds in those *sectors* of the market that are rising *faster* than the rest of the market

Figure 9.7   During most of 1995, transportation stocks outperformed utility stocks. Although both sectors gained, transports were the better performer. *(MetaStock, Equis International, Inc.)*

Dow Transports / Dow Utilities ratio

Figure 9.8   The breaking of the uptrend line in the semiconductor relative strength line gave plenty of warning that it was time to rotate some funds elsewhere. *(MetaStock, Equis International, Inc.)*

Phlx Semiconductor Index / S&P 500

Figure 9.9   Food stocks are defensive. They outperformed during 1994 when the rest of the market was weak. After a relatively poor 1995, food stocks regained favor near the end of the year as traders became more defensive. *(MetaStock, Equis International, Inc.)*

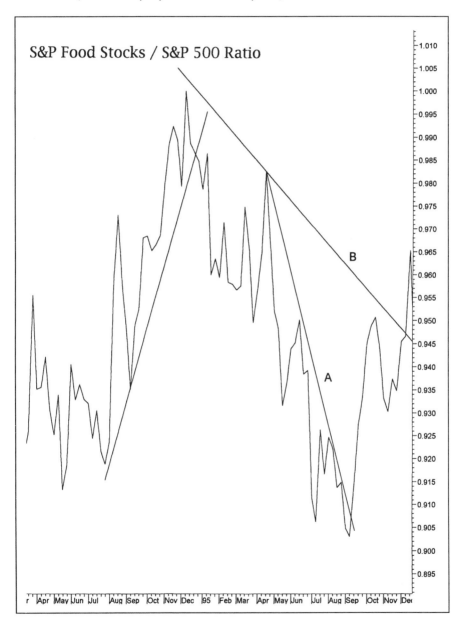

S&P Food Stocks / S&P 500 Ratio

and avoiding those sectors that are *underperforming*. There are actually two elements to momentum investing: earnings momentum and price momentum. Our focus here is on price momentum. *Relative strength,* or ratio, analysis is the best way to compare any two entities for the purpose of measuring relative strength. Ratio analysis can compare two asset classes (e.g., commodities versus bonds), stock sectors versus the broader market (semiconductors versus the S&P 500), stock groups within sectors (airlines versus the rails), or individual stocks versus their respective stock groups or the S&P 500. Ratio analysis has an endless number of uses in comparing any two entities. It can also be used on the international front to compare competing global markets. The *top down* approach to investing means identifying the best sectors first and then the best stocks within those best sectors.

The first three sections of this book present the basics of *charting,* explain some of the more useful trend *indicators,* and offer some *intermarket analysis* to help understand the nature of market and sector rotation. This chapter covers the extremely valuable concept of *relative strength analysis.* Armed with these tools and insights, we're now ready to devote ourselves to the question of *sector analysis* and its application through the use of *mutual funds.*

SECTION 4

Mutual Funds

10

Sectors and
Industry Groups

INTRODUCTION

The material in the preceding nine chapters should provide you with the tools to perform your own visual analysis of the various financial markets. We have deliberately avoided an exhaustive description of the market indicators themselves in order to stress *how* they are used across a broad spectrum of markets and asset classes. With so many investment choices available to the average investor today, both on a domestic and a global scale, some relatively simple system is needed to aid in the search for superior performance.

These next three chapters focus exclusively on market groups. This chapter applies these visual tools to various industry groups within the stock market to show how they work. We also discuss where information on these indexes can be obtained. Once you've decided which industries to invest in, several open-end mutual funds allow you to make your desired switches with a phone call. Chapter 11 deals primarily with *open-end mutual funds*. Although it isn't necessary to perform chart analysis on the mutual funds themselves, you can do so if you wish. Chapter 12 covers the global markets to show how these tools can be used in the international realm.

STANDARD & POOR'S GROUP DATA

The stock *industry* charts used in this book come from two principal sources. The first is the Standard & Poor's Corporation (25 Broadway, New York, NY 10004). Standard & Poor's divides the stock market into 10 sectors, which are further subdivided into 88 industry groups. There is a difference between a sector and an industry. A *sector* is a much broader category such as *Basic Materials,* which includes seven *industry groups* such as aluminum, chemicals, containers, gold mining, metals, paper and forest products, and steel. Other sectors include Capital Goods, Consumer Cyclicals, Consumer Staples, Energy, Financials, Technology, Transportation, and Utilities. Each of these sectors has its own industries. It's important to know what industries are included in each sector as well as which stocks are included in each industry.

The best source of information on the S&P industry groups is that organization's own publications. *The Standard & Poor's Industry Reports* provides a monthly review of 80 S&P industries and over 1,000 stocks. The editor of that publication, Sam Stovall, has authored the *Standard & Poor's Guide to Sector Investing* (McGraw-Hill, 1995), which provides a wealth of information for the sector investor. Among other valuable insights, he shows how sector performance can be tied to the business cycle (Figure 10.1). Transportation and Technology stocks, for example, do well early in an expansion while Basic Materials and Energy are late cycle performers. Consumer Staples are favored early in an economic contraction, while Utilities, Financials, and Consumer Cyclicals do best late in a contraction. Stovall also shows which sector mutual funds match up the best with the various S&P industry groups.

DATA VENDORS

For charting purposes, data on the S&P industry groups is also available to the general public through data vendors. Two popular vendors that provide such data are *Dial Data* (56 Pine Street, New York, NY 10005) and *Telescan* (10550 Richmond Avenue, Suite 250, Houston, TX 77042). The data can easily be accessed with a computer modem. Once you have the data, you can perform all of the chart analysis you want, utilizing any visual tool you want, especially relative strength analysis. The tools of market analysis are applied to industry groups in the same way as to any other market.

Figure 10.1   Sector rotation within the economic cycle. (*Source: Sam Stovall*, The Standard & Poor's Guide to Sector Investing [*McGraw-Hill, 1995*]).

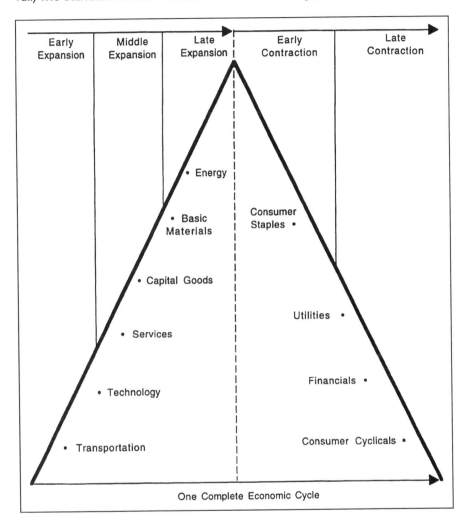

EXCHANGE TRADED INDEX OPTIONS

Another valuable source of sector data is the stock exchanges themselves. Over the past few years, stock exchanges have been introducing a large number of options based on sectors of the market. Here again, the data is easily obtained through a data vendor or the newspaper. One advantage of following the sector options is that they are actively traded and can be monitored throughout the trading day. Their data is also published in the financial press. If you are so inclined, you can actually implement trading positions in the sector options for either trading or hedging purposes.

The Philadelphia Stock Exchange (PHLX)

The three principal options exchanges are the Chicago Board Options Exchange (CBOE), the American Stock Exchange (AMEX), and the Philadelphia Stock Exchange (PHLX). Although the Philadelphia Exchange has the fewest listings, some of its popular index options include the semiconductor index (SOX), the gold/silver index (XAU), the Keefe, Bruyette & Woods bank index (BKX), and a utility index (UTY). The semiconductor index, for example, includes 16 leading chip designers, developers, manufacturers, and distributors. It is especially helpful for trading or monitoring the entire chip sector in one basket.

The PHLX gold/silver index (XAU) includes nine mining stocks and is very popular among investors for tracking the direction of gold-mining stocks. The bank index (BKX) is composed of 24 geographically diverse money center and regional banks. It's always a good idea to know what stocks are in an index option and how the various stocks are weighted. It's useful to know, for example, that Barrick Gold accounts for over a third of the weighting of the XAU index. Obviously, the more heavily weighted stocks have a greater influence on the index. More complete and up-to-date data on the PHLX options can be obtained from the Philadelphia Stock Exchange, 1900 Market Street, Philadelphia, PA 19103.

Chicago Board Options Exchange (CBOE)

It isn't our purpose here to provide a detailed listing of all available index options, but to give a general idea of what's available. Among the sector indexes traded at the CBOE are biotech, chemicals, computer software, environmental, gaming, health care, insurance, retail, telecommunications, transportation, technology (with a separate Internet Index), a real estate investment trust (REIT) index, a Mexico Index, and a Latin American Index. More data can be obtained at the Chicago Board Options Exchange, LaSalle at Van Buren, Chicago, IL 60605.

American Stock Exchange (AMEX)

This exchange also offers an assortment of index options. Some of the better known are airlines, computer technology, natural gas, oil (XOI), pharmaceutical, securities broker/dealers, North American telecommunications, the Morgan Stanley Technology Index, the Internet Index, and a Mexico Index. Several international index options are also offered by both the AMEX and the CBOE. Since these listings are constantly changing, check with the various exchanges for the most recent data. More information on the AMEX options can be obtained at the American Stock Exchange, 86 Trinity Place, New York, NY 10006.

INVESTOR'S BUSINESS DAILY

Financial newspapers provide valuable sector and industry information. One easy way to track activity in various sectors and industries is to read *Investor's Business Daily*, available at your newsstand. This visually oriented paper includes data on the performance of various stock sectors, as well as 197 industries, in table form. In addition, charts of selected industry groups with their relative strength lines are shown.

A booklet containing more detailed information on the composition of the 197 IBD industry groups, *Industry Group & Ticker Symbol Index*, can be obtained from *Investor's Business Daily*, 12655 Beatrice Street, Los Angeles, CA 90066. *Investor's Business Daily* also publishes a large number of market charts and indicators each day, which can be extremely useful to the visual investor. Among them is a chart of the IBD Mutual Fund Index, which includes 23 diversified growth stock funds. The chart includes 50- and 200-day moving averages along with a relative strength line measuring the Mutual Fund Index against the S&P 500.

THE WALL STREET JOURNAL AND BARRON'S

Dow Jones & Co. also calculates sector and industry tables. That information is published daily in *The Wall Street Journal* and weekly in *BARRON'S*. Dow Jones shows eight stock market sectors, subdivided into more than 90 industries. While the exact number of sectors and their makeup may differ slightly from publisher to publisher, the similarities in most cases are much greater than the differences. Dow Jones also publishes sector and industry data on world markets in *The Wall Street Journal*. It shows a table of the six leading and six lagging Dow Jones World Industry Groups along with the three leading stocks in each group. The *WSJ* also presents a more elaborate table showing the performance of all sectors and industry groups in five different regions—the world, the United States, the Americas, Europe, and the Asia/Pacific region. This information allows investors to track various industry groups around the globe. You'll also find close linkages within those industry groups, even on a global basis.

MUTUAL FUND DATA

The examples in this chapter focus on analysis of the industry group charts themselves. We're simply using these S&P industry charts and exchange traded options as vehicles in our sector analysis. Bear in mind, however, that our final goal is to use mutual funds to implement these trading strategies. The investor can perform the required analysis on any sector chart and then simply choose a mutual fund that matches that index. Chapter 11 deals more directly with mutual funds that match up with the various stock groups in the S&P industry indexes. Our primary source for sector mutual fund analysis will be Fidelity Investments, which includes no less than 35 sector funds.

Matching Groups to Mutual Funds

The charts that follow show the trend action of various stock sectors and industry groups, employing relatively simple trend-following techniques. Their purpose is to show how a handful of simple indicators can go a long way in identifying important turns in sectors and groups. Once the analysis is performed, the visual investor simply has to match up a mutual fund with the sector or group being analyzed. Utilizing sector mutual funds in the Fidelity family, each index shown in the following charts is matched up with a fund that could be used to implement a rotation strategy.

Chart	Industry Group	Mutual Fund
Figure 10.2	Auto stocks	Fidelity Automotive Fund
Figure 10.3	Homebuilding stocks	Fidelity Select Construction & Housing
Figure 10.4	Utilities	Fidelity Select Utilities
Figure 10.5	Natural gas stocks	Fidelity Select Natural Gas
Figure 10.6	Telephone stocks	Fidelity Select Telecommunications
Figure 10.7	Biotech stocks	Fidelity Select Biotechnology
Figure 10.8	Biotech stocks	Fidelity Select Biotechnology
Figure 10.9	High-Tech stocks	Fidelity Select Technology
Figure 10.10	Semiconductor stocks	Fidelity Select Electronics
Figure 10.11	Food stocks	Fidelity Select Food & Agriculture

Figure 10.2   By using the 40-week average, investors could have exited autos during the spring of 1994 (A). The move back above the average in mid-1995 (B) and its successful retest (C) in late 1995 suggested rotation back to an auto fund. *(MetaStock, Equis International, Inc.)*

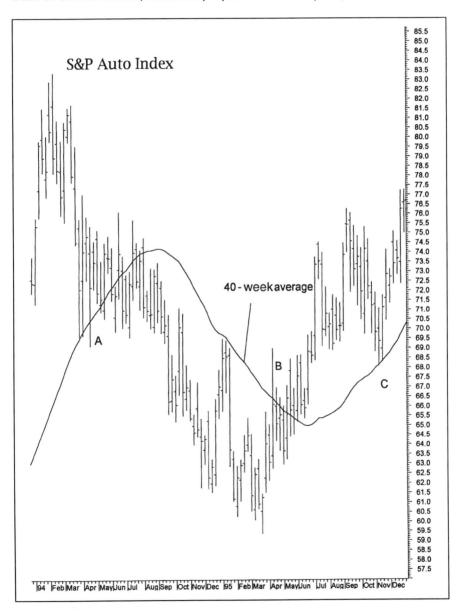

Figure 10.3   Homebuilding stocks fell below the 40-week average in the spring of 1994 (A) and stayed beneath the average until the summer of 1995. The upside breakout at point B suggested rotation back into this industry group. *(MetaStock, Equis International, Inc.)*

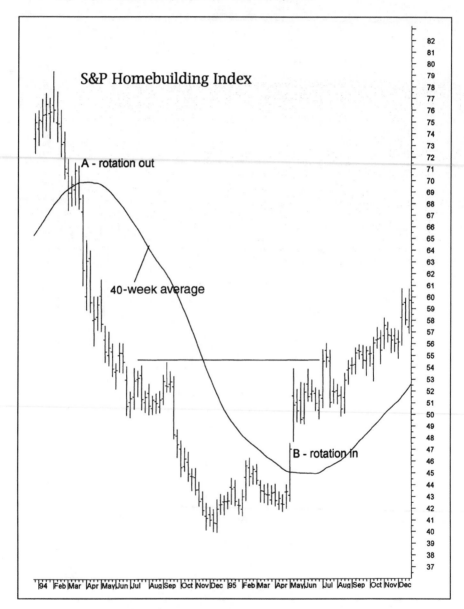

Figure 10.4   The simple 40-week average provided excellent trend signals from late 1993 through 1995. The break below the average during September 1993 (A) warned investors to rotate out of utilities. The move back above the average in early 1995 (B) suggested rotation back into utilities. *(MetaStock, Equis International, Inc.)*

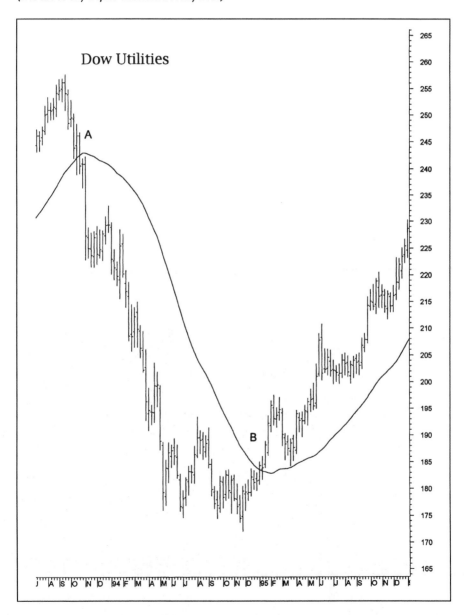

Figure 10.5   During 1995, natural gas stocks (heavy line) were much stronger than the Dow Utilities (thin line). An investor would have been better off in a natural gas fund instead of a utility fund that emphasized electric utilities. *(MetaStock, Equis International, Inc.)*

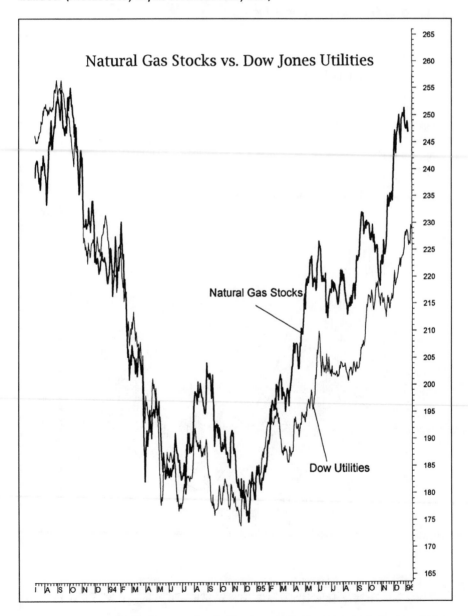

Figure 10.6   This relative strength chart shows that an investor did better in a telecommunications fund than in a general utilities fund during 1995. *(MetaStock, Equis International, Inc.)*

Figure 10.7   A classic example of a bear market turning into a bull. Biotech stocks broke their downtrend line at point A, signaling the onset of a basing pattern. The upside breakout at point B and a successful retest at point C gave clear visual signals to move back into this group. *(MetaStock, Equis International, Inc.)*

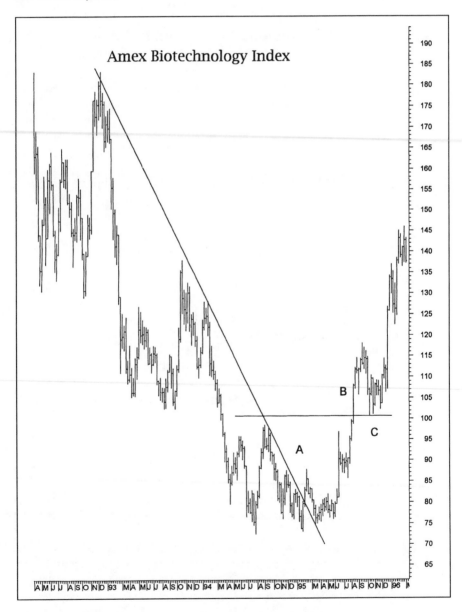

Figure 10.8   Simple charting techniques helped pinpoint entry into biotech stocks during 1995: the move above the 40-week average (A), the bullish breakout (B), the retest of the breakout point (C), and another breakout (D). *(MetaStock, Equis International, Inc.)*

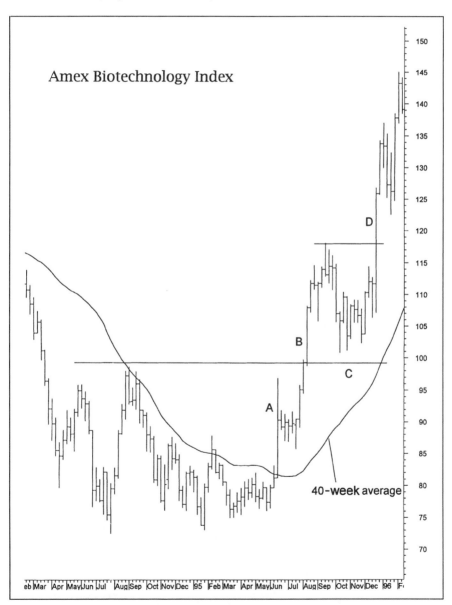

Figure 10.9   The relative strength line shows that biotechs began to outperform high-techs in late summer of 1995. The beginning of 1996 saw a dramatic surge in biotech stocks relative to high-tech stocks. It is no wonder
that investors sold tech funds and bought into biotech funds. *(MetaStock,
Equis International, Inc.)*

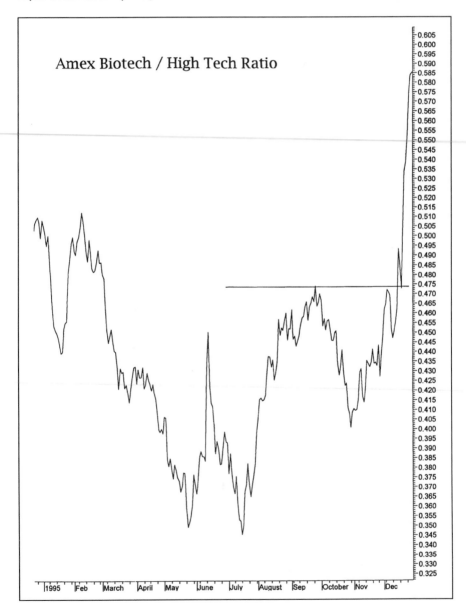

Figure 10.10   A number of chart signals warned of trouble in chip stocks: a double top with the breakdown at point A, trading below a falling 50-day average, and breaking of the 200-day average at point B. *(MetaStock, Equis International, Inc.)*

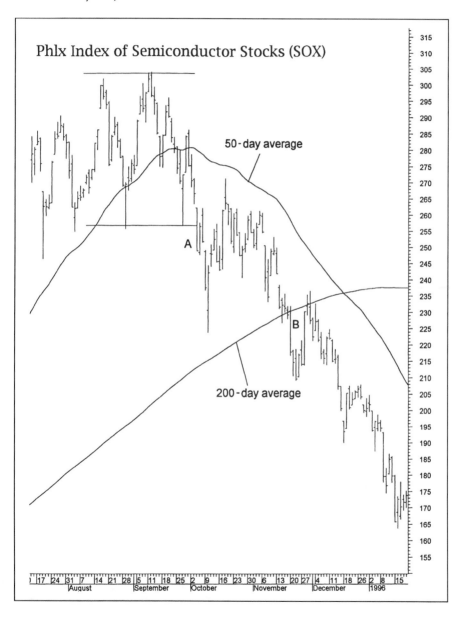

Figure 10.11   The peak in chip stocks during September 1995 coincided
with a surge in food, beverage, and tobacco stocks. A food and agriculture
mutual fund would have been a good place to switch some funds as a
defensive move. *(MetaStock, Equis International, Inc.)*

Figure 10.12   The SOX Index (*top*) and its related sector fund (*bottom*) peaked together in September 1995. *(MetaStock, Equis International, Inc.)*

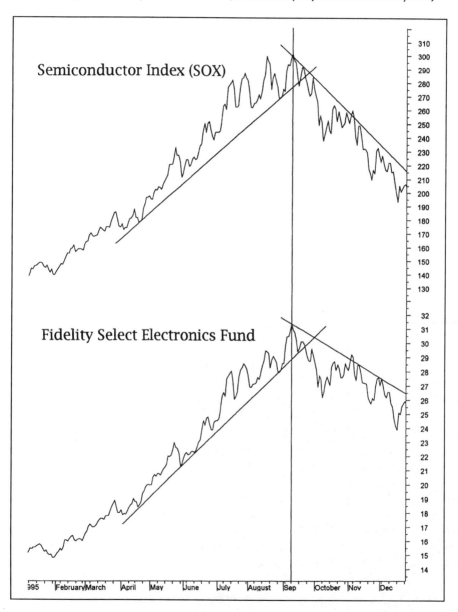

Figure 10.13   There's usually a pretty close correlation between an industry index (*top*) and its related sector fund (*bottom*). (*MetaStock, Equis International, Inc.*)

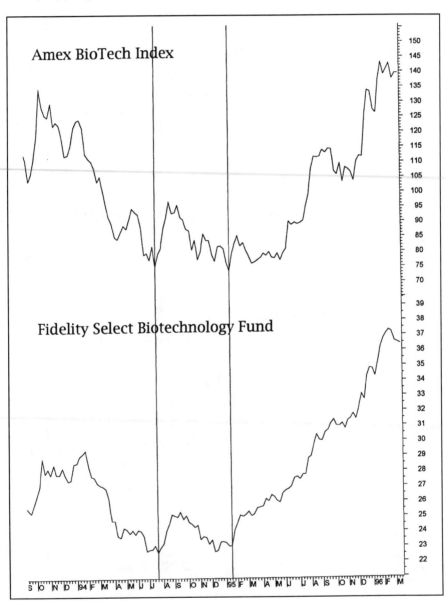

SUMMARY

The preceding list is just a sampling of the funds that are available to the investing public. We are using Fidelity Investments simply because that family of funds offers the greatest number of choices. Many of these sector funds are also available in other fund families such as Franklin, Invesco, T. Rowe Price, Vanguard, and Merrill Lynch. The tools of sector investing needn't be limited to such narrow portions of the market. Many funds are indexed to broader market categories such as the S&P 500 (representing larger stocks) and the Russell 2000 (representing smaller stocks). Relative strength analysis of those two sectors could help an investor decide which type of fund to emphasize at any given time.

These tools apply to bond funds as well. A bullish analysis of the bond market would suggest a more aggressive approach to a bond mutual fund such as Benham Target Maturities Trust, which invests in zero coupon U.S. Treasury bonds. This series of funds does especially well during periods of rising bond prices (falling rates). During a period of rising rates, a bond fund could be rotated with an energy fund or a fund that invests in basic material stocks that benefit during a period of rising prices and rising interest rates. It isn't necessary to analyze the mutual funds themselves, since they usually correlate closely with their respective industry indexes (see Figures 10.12 and 10.13). However, we perform chart analysis on the mutual funds themselves in Chapter 11.

11
Mutual Funds

INTRODUCTION

It's already been emphasized that chart analysis of mutual funds is an additional, though not necessary, step. The trader can analyze the various readily available industry and sector charts and then match up that chart to a suitable mutual fund. Chart analysis can be performed on the mutual funds themselves if that's what you wish to do. There are at least two reasons for doing so. One is for purposes of confirmation. A buy or sell signal on an industry index chart should be confirmed by a similar signal on the mutual fund that corresponds to that index. A second reason is because the industry charts and mutual funds are not *perfectly* correlated.

Sometimes action in the mutual fund chart will lead the industry index, and sometimes it's the other way around. Figure 10.13 in the previous chapter, for example, shows the Fidelity Select Biotechnology Fund turning up a couple of months before the American Stock Exchange index of biotech stocks early in 1995. If you had been monitoring just the AMEX index, you would have gotten a late start in that sector. By charting both, you can spot early signs of trending action in either one.

WHAT WORKS ON MUTUAL FUNDS?

The good news is that most charting techniques work quite well on mutual funds. Even better news is that the *simpler* trend-following techniques work extremely well. Simple *trendlines* along with *support* and *resistance* analysis can be used. *Moving averages* are very useful, as are oscillators like *momentum* and the *relative strength index* (see Figures 11.1 through 11.6). *Moving average convergence divergence (MACD)* and the *MACD histogram* can be used with great effect (see Figures 11.7 and 11.9). Such price patterns as *double bottoms* and *head and shoulders* can often be seen on the mutual fund charts (see Figures 11.3 and 11.10).

All of the examples shown in this chapter utilize the previously mentioned indicators and techniques to show that it's not necessary to delve too deeply into the more esoteric technical indicators to identify winning and losing mutual funds. That is in keeping with the theme of this book, which is to demonstrate that some of the simpler charting techniques work extremely well in the mutual fund arena and that a person need not become a charting expert to derive some benefit.

SOURCES OF INFORMATION

Most data vendors provide mutual fund data that is suitable for charting. Once you have your charting software and computer modem, you can collect data and chart accordingly. All of the techniques shown in this book can be accomplished with such better known software packages as *Meta-Stock* and *SuperCharts.* For more research data on mutual funds, one publication that specializes in that area is *Morningstar, Inc.* (225 West Wacker Drive, Chicago, IL 60606).

That publisher produces a number of services covering the open-end and closed-end mutual fund business, both in printed form and on floppy and CD-ROM disks that are suitable for computer analysis and charting. They also produce data on international equities and American depository receipts (ADRs). ADRs are foreign stocks traded on the American stock exchanges that allow investors to buy and sell individual foreign stocks denominated in U.S. dollars. We deal with closed-end funds and ADRs in the next chapter.

BLENDING FUNDAMENTAL AND TECHNICAL DATA

Although this book deals primarily with the charting (visual) aspects of market and mutual fund analysis, it cannot be emphasized enough that

Figure 11.1   Simple trendline analysis identified a major upturn in housing stocks in early 1995. *(SuperCharts, Omega Research)*

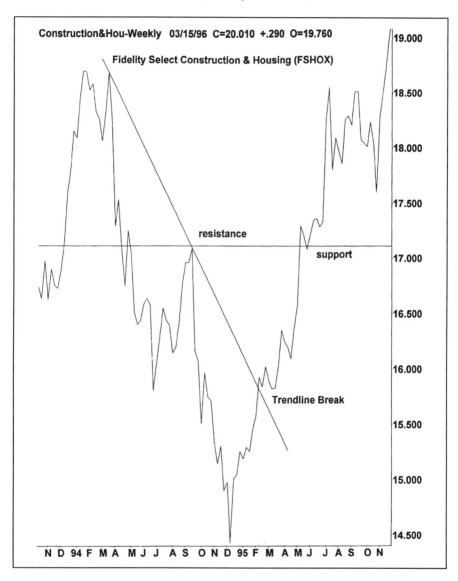

Figure 11.2   Simple moving average analysis applied to a natural gas fund. The 10-week average crossing over the 40-week average at point A was a bullish signal as was the breakout above the 1994 highs at point B. *(Super-Charts, Omega Research)*

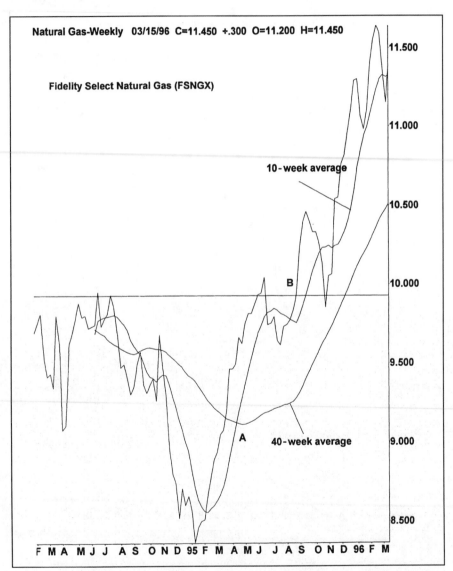

Figure 11.3   Many traders use the 50-day moving average to time fund switches. This biotech fund rose above its moving average line (point B) in January 1995 and remained above the line for the balance of 1995. Major double bottom pattern was completed at point A. *(SuperCharts, Omega Research)*

Biotech-Daily 03/15/96 C=36.430 -.200 O=36.430 H=36.430

Fidelity Select Biotechnology Fund (FBIOX)

50-day average

31.000
30.000
29.000
28.000
27.000
26.000
25.000
24.000
23.000

A
B
1
2

A M J J A S O N D 95 F M A M J J A S O N

Figure 11.4   The fall below the 10-week average during September 1995 was the first warning of negative action in semiconductor stocks. The 10-week momentum chart fell below zero during October 1995 suggesting a negative turn in the trend. *(SuperCharts, Omega Research)*

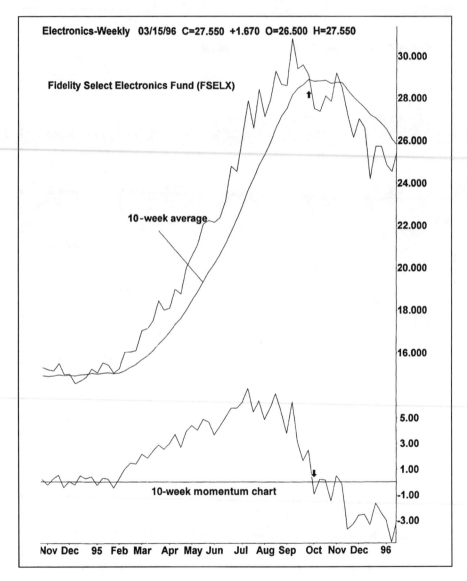

Figure 11.5   The breaking of support during December 1995, accompanied by a falling 50-day average, were clear signals to rotate some funds out of this technology fund. *(SuperCharts, Omega Research)*

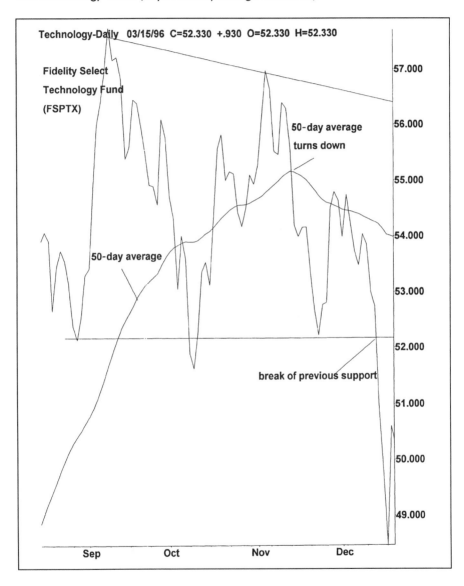

Figure 11.6   The 14-week RSI line showed a negative divergence from August through November 1995 from an overbought condition above 70. *(SuperCharts, Omega Research)*

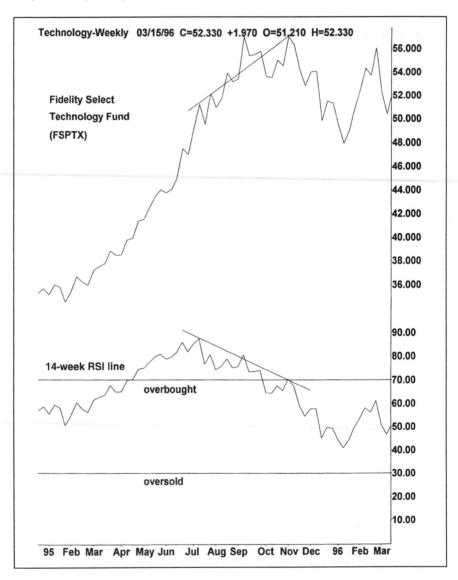

Figure 11.7   The weekly MACD histogram (*bottom*) fell below its zero line for the first time during 1995, flashing a bearish warning for this fund. (*SuperCharts, Omega Research*)

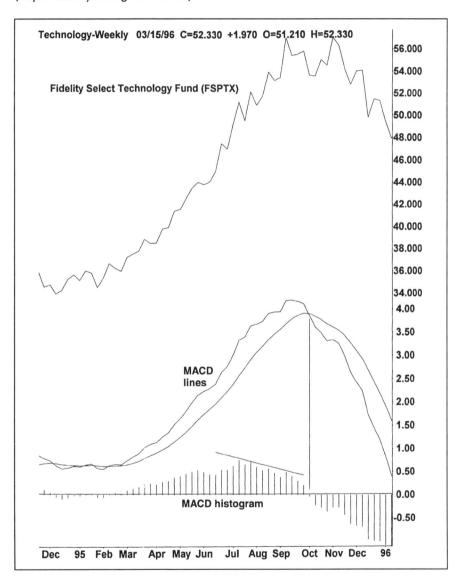

Figure 11.8 A comparison of these two funds shows that the peak in technology stocks in early September 1995 caused a rotation into the more defensive food and agriculture fund (*bottom*). *(SuperCharts, Omega Research)*

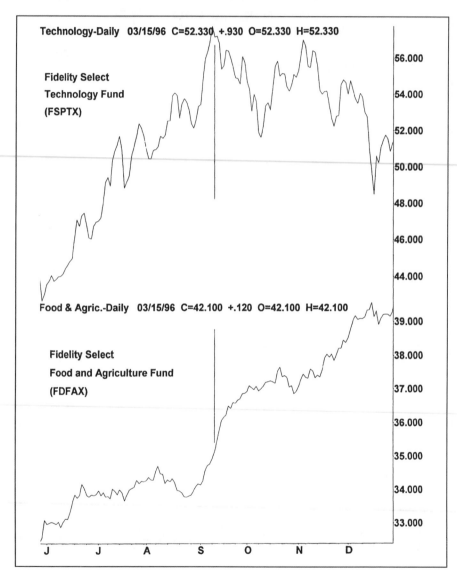

Figure 11.9   The actual peaks and troughs in the weekly MACD histogram (*bottom*) coincide with the turning points in this energy fund. Actual buy (B) and sell (S) signals are given on the crossing of the zero line. The last signal was a buy in early December 1995. (*SuperCharts, Omega Research*)

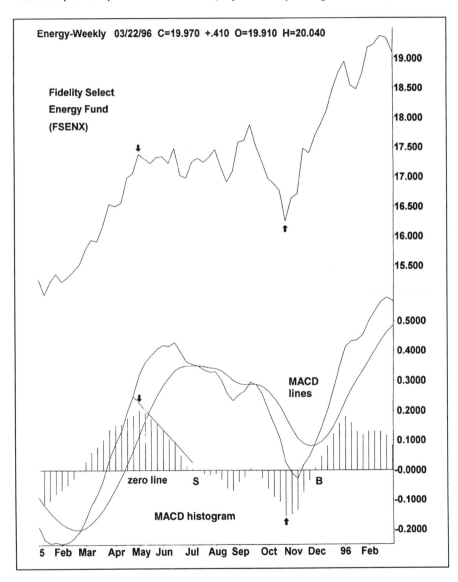

Figure 11.10   This gold fund may be completing a bullish inverse head and shoulders pattern. *(SuperCharts, Omega Research)*

investors should be aware of the fundamental economic background that effects the various financial markets. *Morningstar,* for example, provides a unique rating system that takes into account both profitability and risk. An investor might limit visual analysis to those funds that have the highest (four or five star) *Morningstar* ratings for example. Or the visual investor might check the *Morningstar* pages to obtain more details on a fund that looks attractive from a charting standpoint. That way the investor has both the fundamental and technical factors working together. Another service that covers the mutual fund business, including fund rankings and historical performance data, is *Lipper Analytical Services* (74 Trinity Place, New York, NY 10006).

OPEN- VERSUS CLOSED-END FUNDS

There are two types of mutual funds. Both types allow investors to buy and sell baskets of stocks, but in different ways. The *open-end* mutual fund takes in new cash from investors at any time and is usually purchased through a fund family, such as Fidelity or Vanguard. The *closed-end* fund has a fixed amount of assets and is traded like any other stock on a stock exchange. The closed end fund has an opening price, a high and low range for the day, and a closing price. Volume figures are also available. That being the case, the closed end fund can be analyzed like any other individual stock.

Over the past decade, the open-end fund has surpassed the closed-end fund in investor popularity. While the number of open-end funds exploded to approximately 8,600 by the start of 1996, the closed-end fund population numbered around 500, which actually represented a decline over the prior three years. We're not going to debate the relative merits of the two types of funds here, but want to make you aware that both exist. Most of our comments in this book have been directed at the open-end fund, since that is where most of the interest has been. However, one place where the closed-end variety makes more sense is in the international realm, especially with the growing availability of single country funds. We'll take a look at the usefulness of closed-end funds to help implement a strategy of global diversification in Chapter 12.

ANOTHER LOOK AT RELATIVE STRENGTH ANALYSIS

Chapter 9 explained the merits of relative strength analysis and its particular importance in mutual fund selection. Relative strength analysis adds an important dimension to market analysis by telling us how one fund is performing relative to the general market or how it is performing relative to other fund competitors in the same category. We also pointed out that simple relative strength, or ratio, analysis could be performed with most software charting packages. You should be aware, however, that there are mutual fund charting services that go beyond the popular charting packages and that raise relative strength analysis, in particular, to a new height of usefulness.

Investors FastTrack

One such program is called *Investors FastTrack* (P.O. Box 77577, Baton Rouge, LA 70879). This service provides mutual fund data via an 800 phone number for a flat fee each month. FastTrack's software also provides some unique charting capabilities that go well beyond what is available in the more conventional packages. The number of indicators are not as broad-based as other packages, but include those believed to be most useful for mutual fund charting. They include trendlines and channels, moving averages, MACD histograms, RSI, and stochastics. Possibly the most unique feature is a relative strength indicator called *AccuTrack*.

AccuTrack

AccuTrack is basically a relative strength line that compares two different funds or a fund to a market index. AccuTrack fluctuates around a zero line. When the AccuTrack line is above zero (positive) and rising, the fund in question is performing better than its counterpart and could be bought. When the AccuTrack line is below zero (negative) and falling, it is under-performing and should probably best be avoided. Used in this way, actual buy and sell signals are given to suggest when an investor might want to do some switching between funds. Among the examples given in its manual is a comparison of the NASDAQ Composite Index to the Dow Jones Industrial Average.

When the AccuTrack indicator is positive (NASDAQ outperforming), an investor would favor a small-cap fund. When AccuTrack is negative (Dow outperforming), a large-cap fund would be the preferred vehicle. There are several other creative examples in the FastTrack manual of how the Accu-Track indicator can be used to choose between two competing funds. Accu-Track is an indicator based on the concept of relative strength that can be extremely helpful in the mutual fund selection process. All the charts are color coded to make for easier and more striking visual impressions. The investor who wants to specialize in chart analysis of mutual funds themselves might want to consider a more sophisticated data and charting package, like *FastTrack*. The fact that the data and charting software are provided by the same company also simplifies the collection and analytical process. (See Figures 11.11 through 11.14 for examples of FastTrack charts.)

Telechart 2000 by Worden Brothers

Another very popular data and charting service that specializes in mutual fund analysis is *TeleChart 2000 by Worden Brothers* (Worden Brothers, Inc. Five Oaks Office Park, 4905 Pine Cone Drive, Durham, NC 27707). Their mutual fund data service was ranked first in *Technical Analysis of Stocks & Commodities* magazine's Readers' Choice Awards for 1994 and 1995. (TeleChart 2000 also ranked first for stock data in 1995.) One advantage of using a data vender that specializes in mutual fund data is that they adjust the raw mutual fund net asset value (NAV) for dividend distributions in order to determine a fund's true return. You might want to make sure that this is the case with any data vendor you choose. TeleChart 2000 mutual

Figure 11.11   Fidelity Magellan Fund versus Dow Industrial Index. *(FastTrack)*

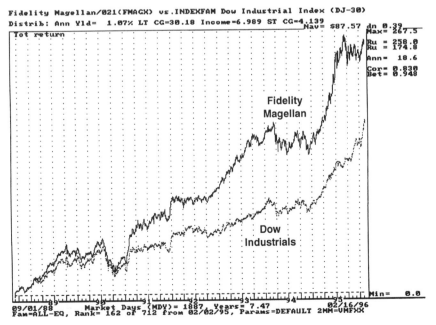

Figure 11.12   Fidelity Magellan Fund versus Dow Industrial Index. *(FastTrack)*

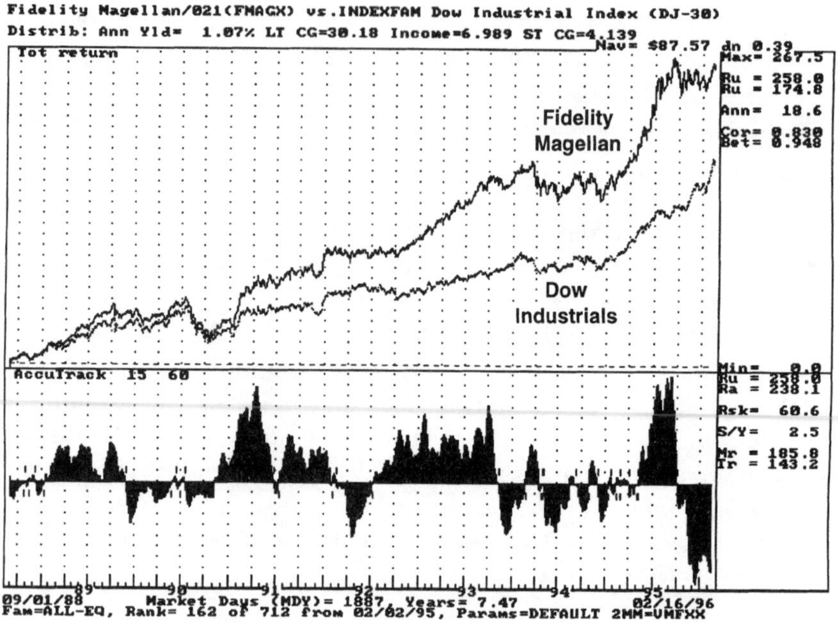

fund and stock data can also be used on such popular charting packages as *MetaStock* and *SuperCharts*. Or you could use TeleChart's own $29 charting software, which, however, can only be used with TeleChart data. (TeleChart's charting package also took first place in *TA* magazine's Readers' Choice Awards for charting packages under $200.)

CHART EXAMPLES

The accompanying charts apply some tools of chart analysis directly on open mutual fund charts representing various stock market industry groups during 1995. For the most part, the mutual funds chosen correspond with industry indexes shown in Chapter 10. Figure 11.1, for example, shows how simple trendline analysis helped identify an upturn in the Fidelity Select Construction & Housing Fund (homebuilding group) during the first quarter of 1995. The crossing of the 10- and 40-week moving averages signaled an uptrend in the Fidelity Select Natural Gas Fund (see Figure 11.2). Fidelity's Biotechnology Fund formed a pretty obvious double bottom during the second half of 1994 (see Figure 11.3). An upside breakout

Figure 11.13   NASDAQ Composite versus Dow Industrial Index. *(FastTrack)*

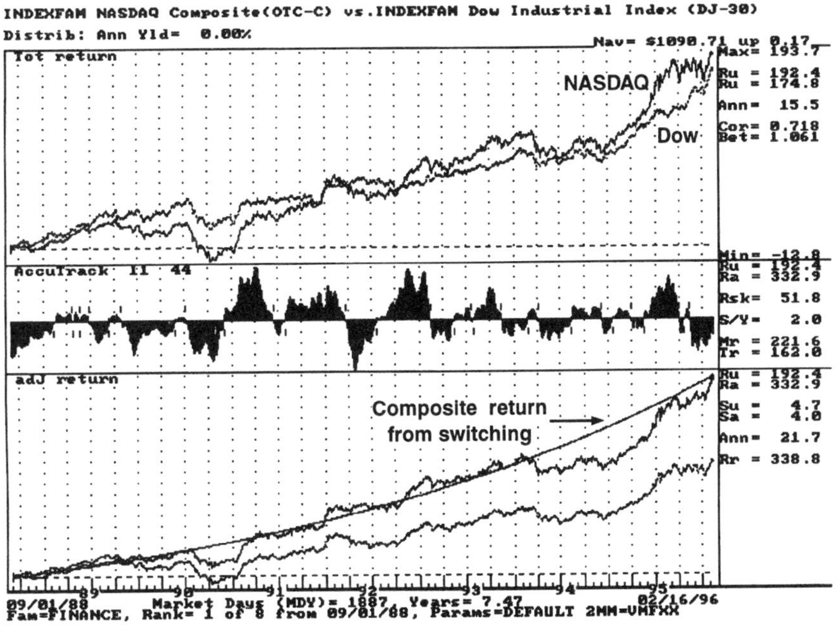

INDEXFAM NASDAQ Composite(OTC-C) vs.INDEXFAM Dow Industrial Index (DJ-30)
Distrib: Ann Yld=   0.00%

during March 1995 was clearly visible. Once the uptrend was established, the 50-day moving average line (10 weeks) did a good job of containing the upward trend by providing support during corrections.

During the summer of 1995, technology stocks were flying. However, some cracks in the bullish story began to show up on the charts of the technology indexes themselves and their respective mutual funds. Figures 11.4 through 11.7 use moving averages, chart support, momentum, RSI, and the MACD histogram to show the clear deterioration in the Fidelity Select Electronics Fund (semiconductors in particular) and the Select Technology Fund (technology in general).

There were plenty of visual warnings to move money out of that sector during the summer and fall of 1995, months before the fundamental story started to turn sour. Figure 11.8 shows that the more defensive Fidelity Select Food and Agriculture Fund started to move higher during September 1995 at the same time that the Technology Fund was peaking. Energy stocks, which had been laggards for much of 1995, began to rally sharply during the fourth quarter of 1995—another defensive play (see Figure 11.9). The final chart of the Fidelity Select American Gold Fund

Figure 11.14   Fidelity Select Energy Service versus Fidelity Select Transportation. *(FastTrack)*

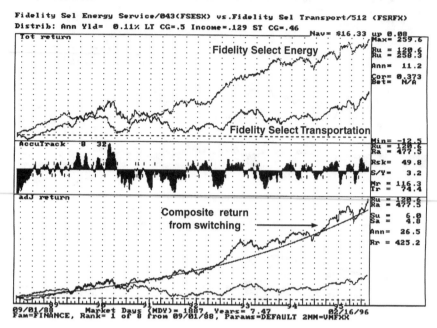

shows a potentially bullish inverse head and shoulders pattern (see Figure 11.10).

These charts show that price patterns and trends can readily be seen on the charts of mutual funds. That being the case, the visual investor has an advantage over those who choose to ignore market action. In the case of semiconductor funds, the breakdown that became evident during the summer and fall of 1995 warned of trouble on the fundamental front that didn't become clear until the beginning of 1996, after semiconductor stocks had suffered heavy losses. It was a classic case of the market discounting weakening fundamentals long before the fundamentals became known. The visual investor with even a basic knowledge of charting is in an excellent position to spot changes in trends among various sectors of the market and to act accordingly.

SOME CHARTING ADJUSTMENTS ON MUTUAL FUNDS

Some adjustments have to be made when analyzing open-end mutual funds. Only one price is available on a daily basis—the net asset value

(NAV) that is released after the close of business. The NAV tells us what the fund is actually worth, based on the closing values of the stocks included in the fund. There is no opening price and no high and low price range for the day. As a result, line charts that connect closing prices are used in place of bar charts. (It isn't possible to construct candlestick charts, since that technique requires an opening price along with high and low prices.)

However, the indicators described in this book can still be used, since they are based primarily on *closing* prices. The relative strength index (RSI) can still be used, for example, to measure overbought and oversold readings (see Figure 11.6). Traditional momentum and rate of change (ROC), as well as the MACD indicators, can still be used (see Figures 11.4 and 11.7). However, volume analysis isn't possible on an open-end fund, since volume figures are not released with the NAV values.

SUMMARY

Chart analysis can be performed on mutual funds with a few adjustments. *Open-end* mutual funds data can be collected and charted like any other market, except that only *closing* net asset values (NAV) are available. Simple indicators like *trendlines* and *moving averages* work especially well, along with basic elements of charting like *support, resistance,* and *pattern identification.* All of the price-based indicators described in this book can also be applied to any mutual fund. There are two types of mutual funds—open- and closed-end. *Open-end* funds, which are the most popular, take in investor funds at any time. Open-end funds also allow easy switching between funds with a phone call. *Closed-end* funds are usually listed on a stock exchange and can be traded like any other individual stock. Both types of funds allow investors to trade baskets of stocks. More specialized mutual fund data services like *Investors FastTrack* and *TeleChart 2000* greatly simplify the collection of mutual fund data and provide both data and charting capability for a modest monthly fee.

12
Global Investing

INTRODUCTION

One of the great advantages of the visual approach to market analysis is the ability to monitor large numbers of markets. Each segment of the U.S. market is represented by some type of index, whether it be bonds, commodities, currencies, the stock market in general, or its respective stock sectors and industry groups. By following a selected group of indexes, the trader or investor is able to spot significant trend changes anywhere on the financial spectrum. The same can be said for global investing. It's relatively easy to keep track of the major bond and stock markets around the world. Currency charts are also readily available. Data on the major global markets can be collected and analyzed in much the same way that an investor analyzes domestic markets.

That being the case, the problem of global investing is greatly simplified. Armed with the handful of visual tools already discussed in this book, the trader is able to make more informed decisions. Those decisions would include whether it is an opportune time to increase one's overseas exposure and, if so, where. Fortunately, the mutual fund universe encompasses many open- and closed-end funds that allow an individual investor to move easily into and out of the stock markets of individual countries and entire geographic regions.

WHY GO OVERSEAS?

Why can't an American investor concentrate on the domestic American markets, which are the largest and most liquid in the world? Of course, you can do that. If you do, however, you deprive yourself of the chance to participate in profitable moves taking place in foreign markets. You also lose some benefits of *diversification,* which argues for spreading one's invested funds across a broad spectrum of financial markets.

During 1995, the U.S. market racked up gains of 30 percent, while foreign markets gained only 5 percent. During 1993, however, foreign markets surged 38 percent, while the U.S. market rose only 5 percent. Emerging markets, which are admittedly the riskiest of overseas investments, have gained an average of 18 percent since 1989, outpacing the S&P 500's 15 percent. Some financial advisors recommend keeping as much as a third of one's assets in foreign markets to lower overall risk while increasing portfolio returns.

The ability to *rotate* a portion of one's assets is a basic principle of investing that should be considered on a global as well as domestic basis. Consider this: Many Americans wouldn't hesitate to buy a Japanese car if they felt it was superior to an American model—why not buy the *stock* of the company that makes that car instead of an American auto stock? The principle is the same. As a consumer, you're willing to purchase foreign-made products if they provide better quality and value. That same attitude should apply to investing.

CURRENCY CONSIDERATIONS

One of the complicating factors when investing overseas is the problem of *foreign exchange* values. Generally speaking, a strong dollar would seem to discourage foreign investing since profits gained in foreign markets are reduced by the losses in their respective foreign currencies. For example, a falling Japanese yen (or rising dollar) reduces the profits an American investor would gain from a rising Japanese stock market. This is because profits made in yen eventually have to be converted to U.S. dollars. Conversely, a stronger yen (or weaker dollar) increases the profits made by an American in the Japanese market. A falling dollar would seem to encourage foreign investing by Americans.

To compensate for currency problems, many mutual funds *hedge* their dollar positions in an attempt to neutralize the effects of fluctuating exchange rates. If this is a concern to you, you might want to limit your overseas exposure to those funds that do actually hedge in the currency markets.

Consider, however, that some foreign markets *benefit* when their currency is falling relative to the U.S. dollar. In the second half of 1995, central bankers made a concerted effort to prop up the U.S. dollar, especially against the German mark and the Japanese yen. The attempt was successful, and the dollar rallied sharply. The German and Japanese markets started to rally and became two of the better performing global markets (see Figures 12.1 and 12.2). While it's true that some of the profits made in those markets were lost in the currency conversion, it's also true that the rising dollar was a major factor in those stock market gains.

Currency Considerations Often Balance Out

All this would seem to suggest that movement in the dollar may not be as important as it would first appear. The profits lost in currency conversion because of a stronger dollar are often offset by foreign stock market gains *caused* by the stronger dollar. In other words, currency considerations are often neutralized by stock market action. There are times, however, when a plunging currency can have a devastating effect on a stock market. In late 1994 and early 1995, a plunging Mexican peso contributed greatly to a sharp fall not only in the Mexican market but in Latin America in general. In late 1995, a stabilized peso helped attract investors back to Latin America.

In the case of Mexico, a falling currency had a negative effect on its stock market. American investors got a double whammy—falling Mexican shares and a falling peso. To make matters worse, the doubling in Mexican shares in terms of the peso during the second half of 1995 produced much smaller profits in dollar terms. All of which suggests that it's generally a good idea to keep an eye on the currency charts, especially if one is investing in Latin America. Some mutual funds allow investors to participate from trends in the *currencies* themselves. (See Figure 12.14.)

Just Follow the Charts

Foreign markets are usually quoted in local currencies and in U.S. dollar terms. From an American investor's standpoint, quotes in dollar terms are the most realistic since they represent true profits and losses (after conversion back to dollars). However, quotes in local currencies are a truer representation of local market action—another tradeoff. One of the basic premises of market analysis is that markets *discount* all relevant factors.

Figure 12.1   German stocks (which are export-oriented) rallied on a falling Mark at points A and B during 1995. The profits lost to an American investor from the falling Mark were balanced by stock market gains. (*SuperCharts, Omega Research*)

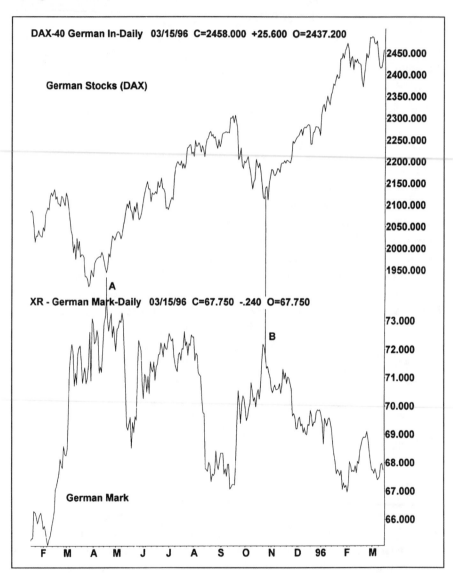

Figure 12.2   Another example of a foreign stock market rallying on a weaker currency. A weak foreign currency is not always bad for foreign investors. (*SuperCharts, Omega Research*)

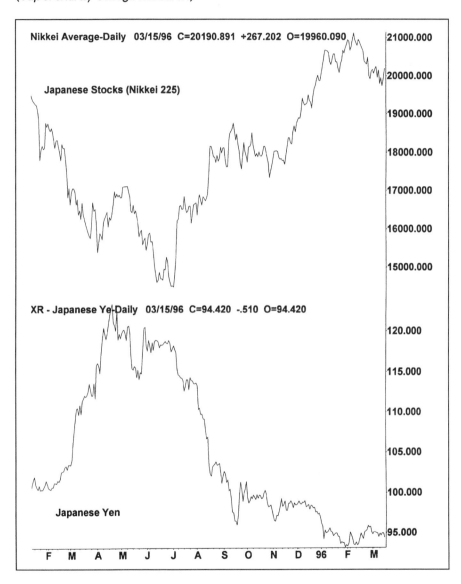

One of those factors is currency fluctuation. My suggestion would be to concentrate on the stock market charts and take your cue from them. Let the currency considerations take care of themselves. One advantage of *American depository receipts (ADRs)* and closed-end *country funds* is that they are traded on American exchanges and, as a result, are quoted and charted in dollar terms.

AMERICAN DEPOSITORY RECEIPTS

American depository receipts (ADRs) represent shares of foreign stocks that are traded on American stock exchanges. More specifically, ADRs are negotiable certificates representing ownership of a certain number of shares in a foreign company. They are issued by depository banks in the United States and are traded on American exchanges or in the over-the-counter market. As such, they are quoted just like any other stock and can be charted accordingly. ADRs represent one way of participating in foreign markets. Unfortunately, they are probably the riskiest. Generally speaking, the narrower one's focus, the greater the risks. This is true of all investing. An investor who chooses an ADR has to consider whether the stock it represents is in the right region of the world, the right country, and the right industry group. There are still times, however, when ADRs may be the preferred vehicle. One such case is Telefonos de Mexico (Telmex).

This Mexican stock, which is traded on the New York Stock Exchange (symbol: TMX) has the largest capitalization in the Bolsa Index of Mexican stocks (approximately 30 percent). As a result of its heavy weighting, this stock has a powerful influence on movements in the Mexican market. Furthermore, many Americans view Telmex as a proxy for the Mexican market. This accounts for the fact that Telmex shares often make the most active list on the Big Board when the Mexican market is active. An American investor who wants some Mexican exposure can obtain it by taking a position in the Telmex ADR. The fact that Telmex is quoted in U.S. dollars also simplifies currency considerations. Telmex (and most liquid ADRs) can also be analyzed very effectively with charts (see Figures 12.3 and 12.4). In most cases, however, an investor is probably better off investing in a *basket* of foreign stocks. There are two ways available—*closed-end* and *open-end* mutual funds. Let's deal with the closed-end variety first.

CLOSED-END FOREIGN FUNDS

Closed-end funds are similar to regular mutual funds except that their shares trade on a stock exchange like any other stock. After their initial

Figure 12.3   Even a casual analysis of Telmex in late 1994 showed a break-down (see arrow). The ADR hit a 52-week low during December 1994 and dropped all the way to 25. Needless to say, the Mexican market also collapsed. (*SuperCharts, Omega Research*)

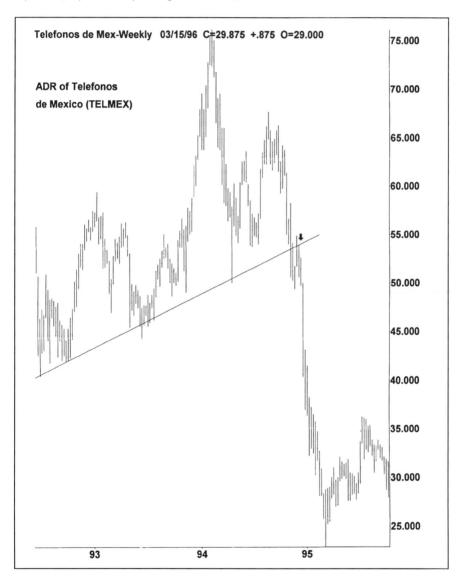

Telefonos de Mex-Weekly   03/15/96   C=29.875 +.875 O=29.000

ADR of Telefonos
de Mexico (TELMEX)

Figure 12.4   This bellwether of the Mexican market appears to be forming a double bottom near 25. A close above 36 is needed to turn the trend higher. (*SuperCharts, Omega Research*)

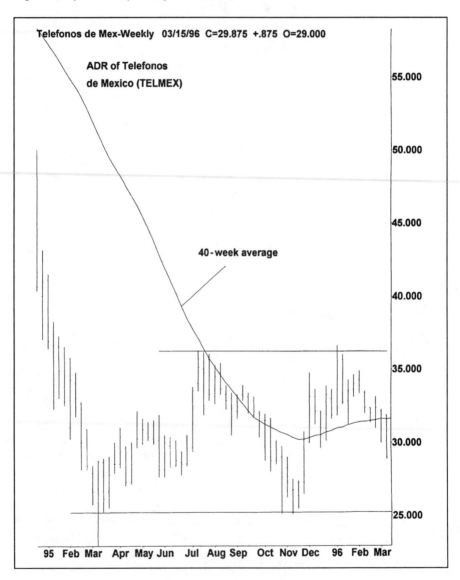

Telefonos de Mex-Weekly   03/15/96 C=29.875 +.875 O=29.000

ADR of Telefonos
de Mexico (TELMEX)

55.000

50.000

45.000

40-week average

40.000

35.000

30.000

25.000

95 Feb Mar Apr May Jun   Jul Aug Sep Oct Nov Dec   96 Feb Mar

offering, closed-end funds don't issue new shares. Since the number of shares is fixed and closed-end funds are not subject to the whims of mutual fund money flows, these funds are able to invest in less liquid global markets that might not be suitable to an open-end mutual fund. Closed-end funds also allow the investor to participate in a basket of stocks representing small, individual foreign markets.

Smaller markets, like Ireland, are only available through a closed-end country fund. (During 1995, for example, the Irish stock market gained 25 percent in dollar terms—making it the best performer among the world's smaller markets.) Other examples of *country* funds include Argentina, Brazil, China, France, Germany, India, Japan, Korea, Malaysia, Mexico, Spain, Taiwan, and Thailand. In addition to closed-end funds that specialize in *single* countries, there are also *regional* funds that invest in geographic regions. Examples include *Asia Pacific, Latin American Discovery,* and *Templeton Emerging Markets,* to name a few. For investors who wish to diversify globally by focusing on individual countries or regions, the closed-end fund is one way to go. Happily for our purposes, closed-end funds can be charted just like any other stock (see Figures 12.5 and 12.6).

OPEN-END FUNDS

The *open-end* mutual fund is the most popular way to invest abroad. There are a large number of *international* funds to choose from. Fidelity Investments alone manages 19 international equity funds with over $10 billion in assets. In response to a growing investor appetite for international funds, Fidelity launched six new country/regional funds in November 1995. International funds are broken down into three categories—*broadly diversified, regional/single country,* and *emerging markets.*

Among the *country* funds Fidelity offers are Canada (see Figures 12.7 and 12.8), France, Germany, China, Japan (see Figure 12.12), and the United Kingdom. Fidelity's *regional* funds include Europe (see Figure 12.9), Latin America (see Figure 12.10), Nordic Countries, Pacific Basin, and Southeast Asia (see Figure 12.11). One of Fidelity's more speculative international funds is the *Emerging Markets Fund,* which invests in the developing markets of Asia and Latin America.

The more broadly diversified Fidelity funds include Diversified International, Global Balanced, International Growth and Income, and Worldwide. Fidelity also offers a Global Bond Fund and three currency funds—British Pound, German Mark and Japanese Yen. As a rule, the most conservative funds are the broadly diversified global funds that

Figure 12.5   The break of the major up trendline in late 1994 warned of a serious breakdown in Mexican stocks and a clear signal to move funds elsewhere. (*SuperCharts, Omega Research*)

Mexico Fund-Weekly   03/15/96 C=13.875 +.625 O=13.125 H=14.125

The Mexico (Closed End) Fund (MXF)

Figure 12.6 A successful retest of its March 1995 low suggests the Mexican fund may be turning higher. The Mexico fund is traded in U.S. dollars. (*Super-Charts, Omega Research*)

Figure 12.7 The Toronto 300 broke its downtrend line in March 1995, signaling a new upleg in the Canadian stock market. Fidelity's Canada Fund tracked the T-300 closely during 1995 and also turned up in the spring. (*SuperCharts, Omega Research*)

Figure 12.8   The 14-day RSI (*bottom*) did a nice job of pinpointing buying opportunities on dips below the oversold 30 level. The last buy was in October 1995 (see arrow). (*SuperCharts, Omega Research*)

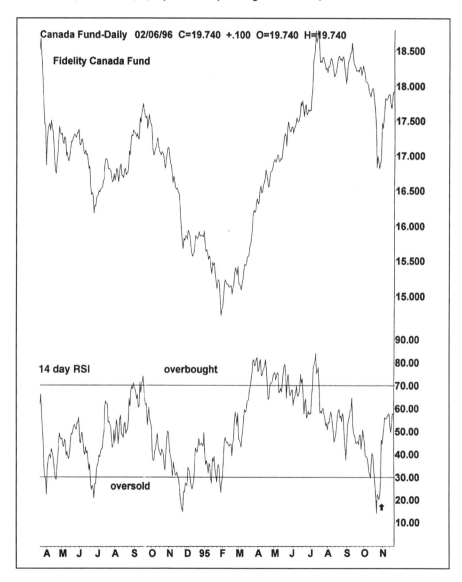

Figure 12.9   Fidelity's Europe Fund is a regional fund. This fund broke out to the upside during the spring of 1995, suggesting an uptrend in Europe. That bullish analysis will hold as long as the fund remains above its 200-day moving average. (*SuperCharts, Omega Research*)

Figure 12.10   The Latin America fund appears to be basing in early 1996, but still has to rise above resistance. The MACD histogram has already turned positive. (*SuperCharts, Omega Research*)

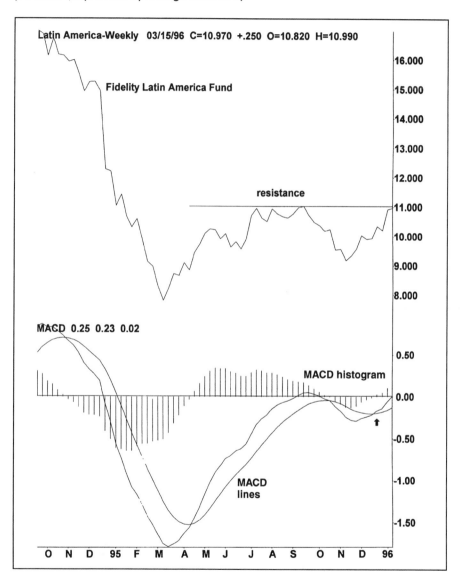

Figure 12.11   Fidelity's Southeast Asia fund (excluding Japan) appears to be in the final stages of an inverse head and shoulders bottom at the start of 1996. (*SuperCharts, Omega Research*)

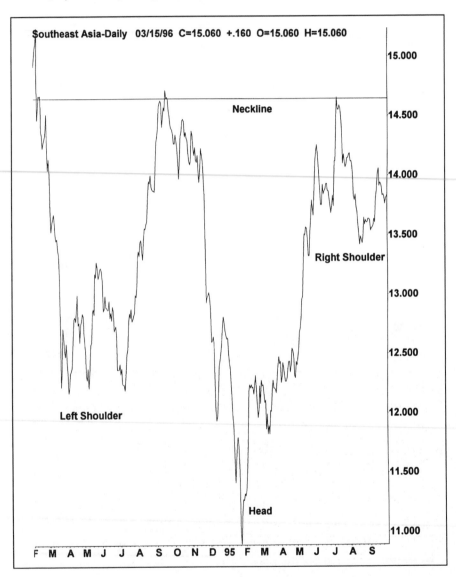

invest all over the world. The more speculative choices are single country and regional funds, as well as the emerging market funds.

Once again, we're using Fidelity as an example of what's available. Other fund families offer international funds as well, although not as many as Fidelity. From an analytical viewpoint, the investor who chooses a broadly diversified international fund doesn't need much ongoing analysis. However, the decision to invest in specific regions like Latin America or Asia requires some analysis, as does the even more difficult decision to invest in specific countries. Fortunately, data on all of these funds can be collected and analyzed. Or, if you prefer, you can analyze the stock markets, the bond markets, and the currencies of the individual countries themselves.

CHART EXAMPLES

The accompanying charts show what some of the international funds looked like at the beginning of 1996. Canada and Europe had been rallying for some time along with the United States. Latin America was showing signs of basing, as was Southeast Asia, which looked even better (see Figures 12.15 and 12.16). One of the best looking individual markets, from a charting perspective, was the Japanese market which had just hit a 52 week high and was beginning to outperform the U.S. market (see Figures 12.12 and 12.13).

One of the principles of sector rotation is to siphon *some* money out of a market that has achieved a long profitable run (like the United States in 1995) and to move *some* funds into the poor performers (like Japan) that are just showing signs of turning up. On a regional scale, that would also suggest some rotation out of Canada and Europe, which had a relatively good 1995, and into Latin America and Southeast Asia, which lagged behind in 1995 but were just showing signs of rebounding at the start of 1996. The second factor favoring these laggards was their low *correlation* to the United States.

WATCH CORRELATION TO ACHIEVE DIVERSIFICATION

The reason an individual invests overseas is to achieve *diversification.* In order to do so, however, the investor should also consider the degree of *correlation* of foreign markets to the U.S. market. It doesn't make a lot of sense, for example, to place a significant portion of one's international portfolio into countries that have a high correlation to the American mar

Figure 12.12   Japan was one of the worst global performers in 1995. The Japanese Fund has just set a 52-week high and appears to have achieved a bullish breakout. (*SuperCharts, Omega Research*)

Japan-Daily   03/15/96   C=12.190   +.070   O=12.190   H=12.190   L=12.190

Fidelity's Japan Fund

200-day average

bullish breakout

14.500
14.000
13.500
13.000
12.500
12.000
11.500

J   J   A   S   O   N   D   95   F   M   A   M   J   J   A   S   O   N   D   96

Figure 12.13   The relative strength (ratio) line shows the Japanese market beginning to outperform the American stock market in mid-1995 to early 1996. This formation suggests some rotation in funds from the United States to Japan. (*MetaStock, Equis International, Inc.*)

Figure 12.14   This chart suggests that the major uptrend in the Japanese
Yen ended in 1995. That would argue against investing in a Yen fund. (*Meta-
Stock, Equis International, Inc.*)

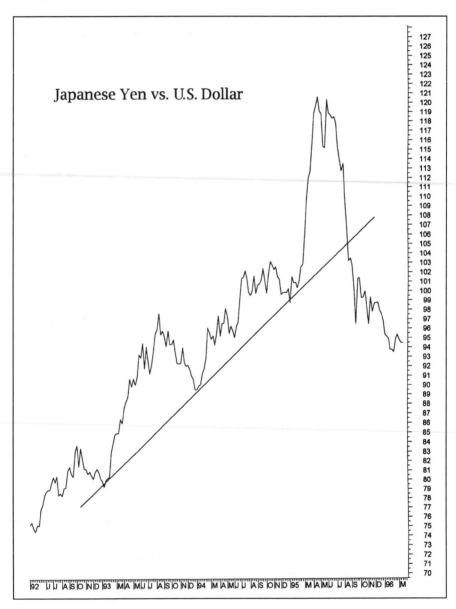

Japanese Yen vs. U.S. Dollar

Figure 12.15   This fund trades on the New York Stock Exchange (symbol = GRR) and is charted and traded like any other stock. Notice the double bottom and bullish breakout in early 1996. This fund is one way to benefit from the rally in Asia. (*MetaStock, Equis International, Inc.*)

Asia Tigers Closed End Fund (GRR)

Figure 12.16   This closed-end emerging markets fund is traded on the NYSE (symbol = EDF). Its price traded above its 40-week average in June 1995 and broke out to the upside in January 1996. Emerging market funds generally invest in Asia and Latin America. (*MetaStock, Equis International, Inc.*)

ket. Of all the global markets, Canada and the United Kingdom have the highest correlation to the American market. During the period from 1990 to 1995, Britain had the highest correlation to the United States (.65) and Canada the next highest (.57). Other countries or regions with high correlations to the United States were the Netherlands, Belgium, and Norway (Source: *Morningstar American Depositary Receipts*). Since these markets usually move in sync with the U.S. market, less diversification is achieved by investing in their markets.

Better diversification is achieved by favoring foreign countries or regions that show historically low correlation to the U.S. market. During the same five-year period ending in 1995, the lowest correlations were seen between the United States and Italy (.16), South Korea (.20), Indonesia (.22), Chile (.24), Brazil (.26), Argentina (.27), Japan (.27), and Mexico (.29). The only global market to achieve a *negative* correlation to the United States over that five-year span was the South African Gold market (–.18). These correlation figures suggest that better diversification is achieved by emphasizing Latin American and Asian markets (along with South African Gold). These markets are the most likely to rise when most other global markets (including the United States) are falling, which is the reason one looks to diversify globally in the first place. The downside is that these markets will usually underperform when other markets are rising, as happened in 1995.

SUMMARY

The question of where to invest one's money has an important *international* dimension. Some of the most profitable stock markets can be found overseas. *Currency* considerations add an element of risk to foreign investing. As a result, many funds *hedge* their currency exposure to eliminate that element of risk. The charting principles discussed throughout this book can be applied to foreign markets in the same way as domestic markets. Price data on foreign markets is easily obtained by computer modem and is suitable for charting. It's not necessary to become a charting expert to benefit. Just follow the lines on the charts. Three ways to invest globally are through *American Depositary Receipts (ADRs), closed-end country* and *regional funds,* and *open-end international funds.* If an investor wishes to be more active in selecting country and regional funds, the use of the visual approach should prove very useful. Keep global *correlations* in mind when looking for maximum diversification. Generally speaking, countries or regions with low correlations to the United States provide better diversification.

CONCLUSION

___

WHY IT'S CALLED *VISUAL INVESTING*

We have followed two overriding themes throughout this book. One is to introduce the reader to *visual* investing by explaining, in simple language, some of the charting techniques that professionals have used for decades. The second theme is to show how to use these visual tools for sector and global investing, primarily through mutual funds. We've chosen to call this approach *visual investing* for two reasons. The first is because that's just what it is. We look at pictures of markets. The pictures tell us just what a market is doing. It is going up or down. That's all that really counts. That's the bottom line. Why it's going up or down isn't that important.

The Media Will Always Tell You Why Later

You can pick up your newspaper or turn on your television and learn *why* markets did what they did that day. The reasons seem clear and reasonable. There's only one problem. If the reasons were so clear, why weren't you told about them *beforehand,* when you still had time to act on them? Media explanations also have a way of shifting with market trends. At 10:00 in the morning, you may be told that an economic report is bullish while the markets rise. After the markets close lower the same day, you may be told at 5:00 P.M. that the same report that was bullish at 10:00 A.M. was really bearish *on closer examination* (and shame on you for not knowing that at 10:00 when you invested your money). There's a world of difference between *predicting* and *reporting.* That's where visual analysis comes in. You'll be able to spot market trends and act on them long before the media explains to you *why* they happened.

Visual Analysis Is More User Friendly

The second reason for using the term *visual analysis* is to lessen the intimidating effect that this form of analysis has had on many investors in the past, under the general heading of *technical* analysis. Many investors are turned off by exotic-sounding terminology and incorrectly assume that the techniques are too difficult to grasp. By calling it what it actually is—*visual analysis*—we hope to encourage a wider understanding and appreciation of these valuable tools among the investing public. Everyone looks at charts. Economists look at charts of economic indicators. Security analysts look at charts of prices and earnings. Even presidential candidates use charts. Why shouldn't you?

Keep It Simple

Another consistent theme is *simplicity.* Don't get bogged down trying to master a lot of formulas or esoteric theories. Keep it simple. Concentrate instead on price *trends;* learn to spot significant *support* and *resistance* levels; look for important *breakouts* or *breakdowns;* understand the role *volume* plays in confirming price action; draw *trendlines* and keep an eye on them after you've drawn them; use *moving averages* to help keep track of trends; follow one or two of the popular *oscillator* systems; learn to tell the difference between markets that are *trending* and those that are not; learn to recognize a couple of the more obvious *price patterns.* Watch *relative strength.*

Before you make any investment, ask yourself this basic question: "Is the market I'm about to put my money into going up or down?" You'd be surprised how many people have trouble answering that question. The investing community is full of people who keep buying stocks that are falling and selling those that are rising. We all have a tendency to make the study of market trend more complicated than it has to be. That point was brought home to me by one of my children. I often sit in front of my computer scanning the various markets. My small son would sit on my lap and look at the pictures on the screen. I would often ask, "Which way is that line going?" He would say either "up" or "down." He wasn't predicting anything, just reading the direction of the price line on the chart. But he was always right. I've often wondered why adults have such difficulty telling up from down.

THE SECOND THEME—SECTOR INVESTING

Our second overriding theme is the *universality* of the visual approach and its application to *sector* and *global* investing. These visual techniques can be applied to any market, including commodities, currencies, bonds, and individual stocks. Our main emphasis in this book is the use of visual analysis for sector investing. One of the factors that makes this approach so appealing is that you don't have to know much about the line on the chart. Is it going up or down? Are technology stocks rising or falling? You may have to wait a month to get the semiconductor book-to-bill ratio, but you can see what the stocks are doing any time you want. You don't have to wait. Which way are gold stocks trending? Is the Japanese market rising or falling? Which global stock markets are rising, and which ones are falling? Simply look at the charts. Which way are interest rates trending? Look at the line on the chart. Is the price of oil rising or falling? Which way is the price line moving? The visual approaches covered in this book can be applied to all markets anywhere in the world, even if you don't know that much about them.

APPLICATION TO MUTUAL FUNDS

With the explosion of mutual fund investing over the past decade, and the increasing tendency for mutual funds to track smaller sectors of the market, the ability to track and analyze mutual funds has become critically important. Fortunately, these visual techniques can be applied to different market sectors and industry groups represented by those mutual funds as well as the mutual funds themselves. Investors have a lot of decisions to make. Is this a good time to buy a bond fund? How does the stock market look? What sectors of the market are doing well, and which aren't? Which stocks are the leaders in the various industry groups? What do the global markets look like? Is this a good time to invest abroad and, if so, where? It's a lot of ground to cover. Fortunately, with computers and easy access to market data, together with a handful of visual tools, the task has been made a good deal easier.

CLOSING THOUGHTS

For the past five years, I've had the unique opportunity to present these visual techniques on television in my role as technical analyst for CNBC. The time limitations of TV reports and the need to explain complex ideas forced me to become very selective in what I could show and how I could show it. In other words, I've been forced to simplify. In addition, I've had to find ways to explain technical ideas in a nontechnical way to a largely nontechnical audience. The results of that analysis have been there for all to see. It was mainly a lot of phone calls and mail from CNBC viewers that prompted the writing of this book.

It became clear that many investors were impressed and intrigued by the visual techniques they saw on the screen, but didn't know quite how to start doing it themselves. They didn't know what software programs to use, what indicators to focus on, or where to get more information on books and educational services. This book was written largely with those viewers in mind. I've tried to provide a good starting point that utilizes the benefits of the latest computer technology and, at the same time, captures the mood and the challenges of mutual fund investing. If I've done my job, you should have more than enough information to get started and enough reference sources to learn more when you're ready to do so. Good luck.

Getting Started

THE COMPUTER

Where do you go from here and how do you get started? You're going to need three things to do visual analysis in the proper way. The first is a *computer,* preferably an *IBM* or *IBM compatible.* With computers getting cheaper as they get more powerful, (under $2,000), don't skimp on computer power and memory. It's recommended that the computer have a *486 processor* with *8 megabytes* of memory. *Windows* capability is needed. A *CD-ROM* is also highly recommended to handle the large amounts of historical data that many vendors make available. You'll also need a *modem* to collect price data.

Before buying a computer, *select your software first.* All software packages tell you what their computer requirements are. If you don't have a computer, check with some of the leading software vendors to see what their hardware requirements are. There usually isn't that much difference among the software providers. But it's still a good idea to check the software needs first.

Whether or not you already have a computer, you'll need two additional things—*software* and *data.* Charting software enables the computer to perform the visual analysis. However, you still need price data to perform the analysis on. The data comes from a *vendor* and is usually collected over a phone modem. With your 486 IBM-compatible computer, charting software, and price data, you're ready to start applying all of the techniques explained in this book.

SOME WELL-KNOWN PLACES TO START

It's always difficult to know where to begin searching for the proper software and data vendors. The following Resources section lists the names and addresses of several of each. Two names that stand above the rest in the software field are MetaStock and SuperCharts. You can't go wrong with either one. Some popular data vendors are Dial Data, Telescan, and TeleChart 2000. Fortunately, there are also many resources to help you learn more about chart analysis and to keep you abreast of ongoing developments. Books and magazines are available.

TECHNICAL ANALYSIS MAGAZINE

One magazine that stands alone in this field is *Technical Analysis of Stocks & Commodities* (4757 California Avenue S.W., Seattle, WA 98116-4499). This monthly publication is a wealth of technical information. In addition to articles, it includes reviews of books and software products. The ads showing the different computer products alone are probably worth the cost of a subscription.

Each January, *TA* magazine publishes a bonus issue that includes its *Readers' Choice Awards.* This poll of the magazine's readers rates various computer services in 20 categories, along with addresses and phone numbers. It is a valuable reference source in looking for products with high customer satisfaction. The 1995 Readers' Choice Awards (published in January 1996) is one of the sources used in choosing the services highlighted in the Resources section.

Another magazine that includes valuable technical material is *Futures* (219 Parkade, P.O. Box 6, Cedar Falls, IA 50613).

THE MARKET TECHNICIANS ASSOCIATION

This is the premier technical association in the United States. Based in New York (One World Trade Center, Suite 4447, New York, NY 10048), the *Market Technicians Association* (MTA) is comprised of professional technical analysts and affiliates. Monthly meetings are held in New York, with an annual seminar held each May at a different site within the United States.

A monthly newsletter is supplemented by a journal of articles published three times a year. The MTA has instituted the Certified Market Technicians (CMT) program, which is a three-step process enabling applicants to receive the professional CMT designation. Many investors go through the program simply for its educational benefit. Membership includes access to the MTA library and a computer bulletin board. MTA members also become colleagues of the International Federation of Technical Analysts (IFTA), which is a global body including organizations in more than 20 countries.

COURSES AND SEMINARS

The *New York Institute of Finance* (2 Broadway, 5th Floor, New York, NY 10004-2283; [800] 227-NYIF) has at least a half-dozen courses covering various aspects of technical analysis, taught by practicing Wall Street professionals. The NYIF also publishes and sells financial books. Various organizations hold educational seminars on a year-round basis.

An organization that provides seminars on technical trading is *Financial Trading Seminars* (74-09 37th Avenue, Room 422, Jackson Heights, NY 11372; [800] 458-0939). The group also sells technical books and produces educational videotapes.

Financial magazines such as *Technical Analysis of Stocks & Commodities* and *Futures* usually provide listings of upcoming seminar dates and locations.

The *American Association of Individual Investors (AAII)* (625 North Michigan Avenue, Chicago, IL 60611-3110; [312] 280-0170 or [800] 428-2244) holds day-long seminars on various aspects of investing for both members and nonmembers.

COMPUTRAC UNDER NEW NAMES

Computrac is a name long recognized as a pioneer in charting software and also for highly regarded educational seminars held in the United States and abroad. Computrac itself no longer exists. However, *Telerate Seminars* (a division of Dow Jones Telerate and successor to Computrac) continues to produce seminars (Telerate Seminars, 701 Poydras Street, New Orleans, LA 70139-9998; [504] 592-4550). An intensive four-day seminar on technical analysis is presented each fall in New Orleans or at some other site in the United States. The Computrac software has been continued by some former employees since Dow Jones Telerate divested itself of the product.

The software product still exists and is now called SMARTrader Professional (DOS version) and SMARTrader for Windows. It can be purchased from Stratagem Software, Inc., 520 Transcontinental Drive, Suite B, Metairie, LA 70001; (800) 779-7353.

ADDITIONAL TECHNICAL MATERIAL

Technical analysis is a large field. Although we have covered many of the most useful techniques, there is a lot more to the subject. The bibliography at the end of this section includes a sampling of books that are recommended reading. We also tell you where you can get those books. The better-known software packages provide a user's manual that includes a brief explanation of the various technical approaches and indicators as well as reference sources for the various techniques. The user's manual becomes especially helpful if you choose to expand to some of the other indicators and charting tools available with the software. Some of the more popular software packages also have *user groups* scattered around the world. Ask your charting software company if they know of any.

MUTUAL FUND DATA

For those seeking more information on the mutual fund industry, an excellent source is *Morningstar* (Morningstar Inc., 225 West Wacker Drive, Chicago, IL 60606). The firm provides a number of different services covering open- and closed-end funds, as well as international funds. Morningstar also provides historical data on floppy disk and CD-ROM that lets you compare and analyze over 2,500 mutual funds.

Another firm that produces valuable material on the mutual fund industry is *Lipper Analytical Services* (74 Trinity Place, New York, NY 10006).

Resources

A complete listing of software and data vendors would be a long list indeed. Our purpose here is simply to get you started. Therefore, we're giving you a *short* list of products and companies. We've chosen those with the highest ratings by *Technical Analysis* magazine's Readers' Choice Awards. Many fine products may not be included in our short list due to their newness or specialization. As you gain more experience, you might want to shop around and try some of those other products as well.

CHARTING SOFTWARE

According to *Technical Analysis* magazine, the $200 to $400 category will cover the needs of 95 percent of investors; those just starting out will most likely begin with a product in that category.

$200–$499

MetaStock, Equis International, 3950 S. 700 East, Suite 100, Salt Lake City, UT 84107; (800) 882-3040.

SuperCharts, Omega Research, 9200 Sunset Drive, Miami, FL 33173; (800) 556-2022.

$0–$199

TeleChart 2000, Worden Brothers Inc., Five Oaks Office Park, 4905 Pine Cone Drive, #12, Durham, NC 27707; (800) 776-4940. (Only runs with TeleChart 2000 data.)

Analyzer 3.0, Telescan, 10550 Richmond, Suite 250, Houston, Texas 77042.

FastTrack, Investors FastTrack, P.O. Box 77577, Baton Rouge, LA 70879.

MarketExpert, AIQ Systems, P.O. Drawer 7530, Incline Village, Nevada 89452.

StreetSmart, Charles Schwab & Co., 101 Montgomery Street, San Francisco, CA 94104.

Windows on Wall Street, MarketArts, 1810 N. Glenville Drive, Suite 124, Richardson, TX 75081.

The Technician, Equis International (see previous MetaStock listing).

Wall Street Analyst, Omega Research (see previous SuperCharts listing).

DATA VENDORS

Real-Time Data

Signal, Data Broadcasting Corporation, 1900 S. Norfolk, Suite 150, San Mateo, CA 94403.

BMI (Bonneville), 3 Triad Center, Suite 100, Salt Lake City, UT 84180.

DTN Wall Street, Data Transmission Network, 9110 W. Dodge Road, Suite 200, Omaha, NE 68114.

Telescan, 10550 Richmond, Suite 250, Houston, Texas 77042.

Knight-Ridder, 30 S. Wacker Drive, Suite 1810, Chicago, IL 60606.

Stock Data

Worden Brothers, Inc., Five Oaks Office Park, 4905 Pine Cone Drive #12, Durham, NC 27707. (Price data can be used on most charting software, although their TeleChart 2000 software will only run with their own data.)

Dial Data, GMI, 56 Pine Street,, New York, NY 10005; (800) 935-7788.

Telescan, 10550 Richmond, Suite 250, Houston, TX 77042; (800) 324-8246. (Telescan data will run with most charting software and also provides its own charting capability.)

Mutual Fund Data

Worden Brothers (See previous listing.)

Dial Data (See previous listing.)

Dow Jones & Co., P.O. Box 300, Princeton, NJ 08543.
Data Transmission Network (See previous DTN Wall Street Listing.)
FastTrack (See previous listing.)
Morningstar, 225 W. Wacker Drive, Chicago, IL 60606.
Prodigy, P.O. Box 791, White Plains, NY 10601.
Signal (See previous listing.)
Telescan (See previous listing.)

Futures Data
Dial Data (See previous listing.)
Signal (See previous listing.)
Commodity Systems Inc., 200 W. Palmetto Park Road, Boca Raton, FL 33432.

RECOMMENDED BOOKS

The following list is a selection of books that deal more extensively with matter touched on in this book. Most of the descriptive comments are taken from the *Traders Press* catalog (see following bookseller listing).

Cyberinvesting, David Brown (chairman and CEO of Telescan, Inc.) and Kassandra Bentley (New York: John Wiley & Sons, 1995). Shows how to unleash the potential of PCs for stock investing, using fundamental and technical analysis.

How to Make Money in Stocks, William O'Neil (New York, McGraw-Hill). A blend of technical and fundamental analysis by the publisher of *Investors Business Daily* and *Daily Graphs.*

Intermarket Technical Analysis, John Murphy (New York: John Wiley & Sons, 1991). Explains how various markets relate to each other.

Pring on Momentum, Martin Pring (Gloucester: Intl. Institute for Economic Research, 1993). Explains such technical studies as the McClellan oscillator, stochastics, and MACD and ADX lines.

Schwager on Futures: Technical Analysis, Jack Schwager (New York: John Wiley & Sons, 1996). An excellent overview of technical analysis with major emphasis on practical applications.

Secrets for Profiting in Bull and Bear Markets, Stan Weinstein (Burr Ridge: Irwin Professional Publishing, 1988). The editor of *Professional Tape Reader* reveals his methods for chart analysis.

Standard & Poor's Guide to Sector Investing, Sam Stovall (New York: McGraw-Hill, 1995). The basics of sector investing, utilizing 88 S&P industry groups and related mutual funds.

Technical Analysis from A to Z, Steven Achelis (Chicago: Probus, 1995). Reference source for over 100 indicators and an excellent companion to popular software packages by the president of Equis International and developer of MetaStock software.

Technical Analysis of the Futures Markets, John Murphy (Englewood Cliffs: Prentice-Hall, 1986). "The most comprehensive and standard reference for technical analysis" (Traders Press catalog); has an accompanying Study Guide.

Trading for a Living, Alexander Elder (New York: John Wiley & Sons, 1993). Blends psychology, market analysis, and computer-oriented trading methods; has an accompanying Study Guide.

Understanding Fibonacci Numbers, Edward Dobson (Greenville: Trader's Press, 1984). Primer on what Fibonacci numbers are and how traders use them, by the President of Traders Press.

WHERE TO BUY FINANCIAL BOOKS

It's not always easy to find the type of financial books listed above. Your best bet is a mail order firm that specializes in financial and technical books. *Traders Press* (see following) provides a 70-page catalog describing all of the technical books indexed by author, subject, and title. Each listing includes a brief description to aid in your search for the right book. Videotapes are also available.

TRADERS PRESS, P.O. Box 6206, Greenville, SC 29606; (800) 927-8222.

TRADERS LIBRARY, P.O. Box 2466, Ellicott City, MD 21041; (800) 272-2855.

ONLINE HELP

Online services like *CompuServe* and *Prodigy* provide informative data on investing in general and some technical analysis. *MetaStock,* for example, provides free technical support for its charting software on CompuServe and Prodigy. CompuServe also provides a data retrieval service that is compatible with popular charting packages ([800] 848-8990). CompuServe even offers a discount to MetaStock users through the MetaStock Quote Club. A growing amount of information is also available on the *Internet's World Wide Web.*

Web Sites

The amount of financial information available on the Internet has grown enormously and will continue to do so. One way to sift through the available resources is the personal finance section of the *Whole Internet Catalog*. Some sites devoted to mutual funds are the *Mutual Funds Home Page* and *Networth* (which features analysis by *Morningstar*).

Stock quotes are available through services like *PCQuote*. Data and charting capability can be found through services like *Stockmaster* (created by MIT) or *TIPnet* (produced by Telescan). For those who want to keep up with their favorite financial publications, Web sites can even be found for *MONEY* magazine and *The Wall Street Journal*.

Appendix A

Market Breadth

Gregory L. Morris

INTRODUCTION

When you go to the doctor, one of the first tests the nurse will do is take your blood pressure. This gives an immediate indication or reading of your internal workings and alerts the doctor to anything that is not normal. The stock market has a similar reading that is called *market breadth*.

Market breadth involves some basic data that is available about the market every day. The primary components of breadth are: advancing issues, declining issues, up volume, down volume, new highs, and new lows. While there are more components, these six make up the bulk of the breadth calculations.

One significant advantage of breadth is that each stock carries an equal amount of weight in the calculation of the breadth indicators. Most market averages, such as the Dow Industrials, S&P 500 Index, and NASDAQ Index are *capitalization-weighted indices*. This means that the stocks which have the greatest market capitalization carry the greatest weight in the index.

DEFINITIONS

Advances (advancing issues): Each trading day a stock will rise, fall, or stay the same. If it rises, it is an advancing issue. At the end of the day, each stock market will tally the advancing issues and list them as *advances*.

Declines (declining issues): Similar to advances, if the stock falls in price for the day, it is called a declining issue and the total of all declining issues on that exchange will be listed as *declines*.

Unchanged (issues that have no change in price): When an issue closes a day at the same price as the previous day, it is deemed an unchanged issue. The total number of unchanged issues on each exchange is listed as UNCHANGED.

Up volume: The total trading volume for all of the *advances* for the day.

Down volume: The total trading volume for all of the *declines* for the day.

New highs: Whenever a stock trades at a price that is higher than it has been in the last 52 weeks (1 year), it is called a *new high*. Each day the total of all stocks reaching new highs is listed as *new highs*.

New lows: Whenever a stock trades at a price that is lower than it has been in the last 52 weeks, it is called a *new low*. Each day a number of stocks making new lows are listed as *new lows*.

DAILY DATA EXAMPLE

The following information is typical of what you will find for the New York Stock Exchange in the business section of most newspapers. Keep in mind that there are similar listings for the American Stock Exchange and the NASDAQ or Over the Counter Exchange.

Stocks on New York stock exchange	Total issues	2400
Stocks closing at a higher price	Advances	1350
Volume of stocks advancing	Up volume	185M
Stocks closing at a lower price	Declines	680
Volume of stocks declining	Down volume	95M
Stocks closing at a new 52 week high	New highs	125
Stocks closing at a new 52 week low	New lows	45

ADVANCE-DECLINE LINE

There are a multitude of indicators using market breadth data. All are attempting to uncover strengths or weaknesses in the market that are not readily visible from the typical market indices. One of the most popular, and possibly the best, is the *advance-decline line*.

The advance-decline line uses only two of the breadth components, as you might have guessed: *advances* and *declines*. To calculate the advance-decline line, each day you subtract the declines from the advances. If there were more declines than advances, the result would be a negative difference. Next you add all of these differences together on an ongoing basis. This is sometimes referred to as cumulative adding. Here is an example, along with spreadsheet formulas:

	A	B	C	D	E
				Difference	Cumulation
1	Date	Advances	Declines	= (B – C)	= SUM(D2:D?)
2	Day 1	1350	680	670	670
3	Day 2	1200	850	350	1020
4	Day 3	800	1000	–200	820
5	Day 4	650	1220	–570	250
6	Day 5	1100	1100	0	250
?	etc.				

Column E contains the numbers that make up the advance-decline line. Plotting these numbers along with an exchange index will reveal some interesting, and not always obvious, information.

Figure A.1 shows the extreme weakness that occurred in the NASDAQ market during the last half of 1995. Only in the beginning of 1996 did the NASDAQ advance-decline line start an up move, breaking above its long downtrend line. Even so, the AD line is still well below its high point.

NEW HIGHS/NEW LOWS

Another popular breadth indicator is the plot of new highs and new lows. There are a number of ways to manipulate the data, but a simple plot of both reveals all the information. You can see that whenever new highs reach an extreme, the market has a topping tendency. Similarly, whenever new lows reach an extreme, the market is near a bottom.

Figure A.2 shows how the new lows helped identify the market low in late 1994. In a bear market or downtrending market, the new lows will dominate the action as shown here. Similarly, in an uptrending market, the new highs will show most of the action.

MCCLELLAN OSCILLATOR

Sherman McClellan developed this breadth indicator using only advance and decline data. It is widely followed by the financial media. The basic con-

Figure A.1   The NASDAQ Advance-Decline Line displayed exceptional weakness in late 1995 relative to the Index (*top*). (*MetaStock, Equis International, Inc.*)

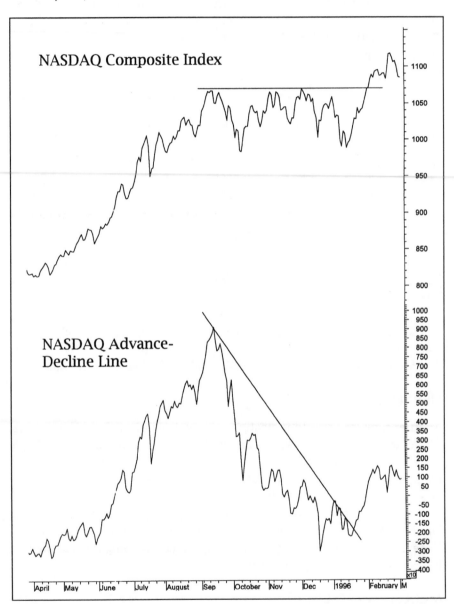

Figure A.2   The New York Composite Index. (*MetaStock, Equis International, Inc.*)

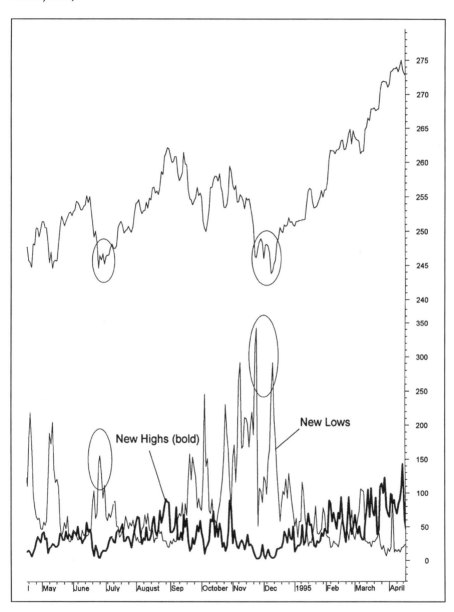

Figure A.3   (*Top*) New York Composite Index; (*bottom*) McClellan Oscillator. (*MetaStock, Equis International, Inc.*)

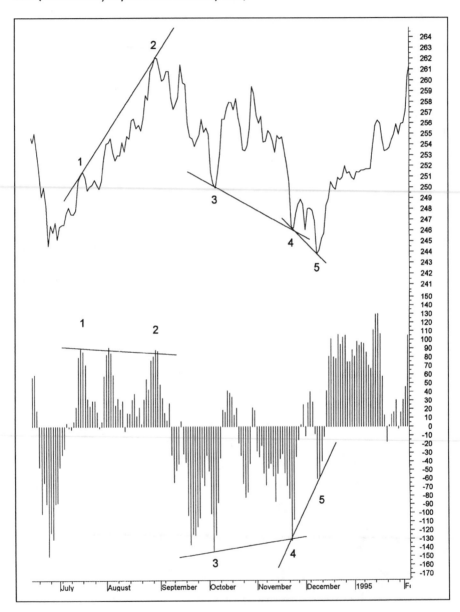

Figure A.4   (*a*) New York Composite Index; (*b*) New York Advance-Decline Line; (*c*) New York new highs (bold) and new lows; (*d*) McClellan Oscillator and Summation Index. (*MetaStock, Equis International, Inc.*)

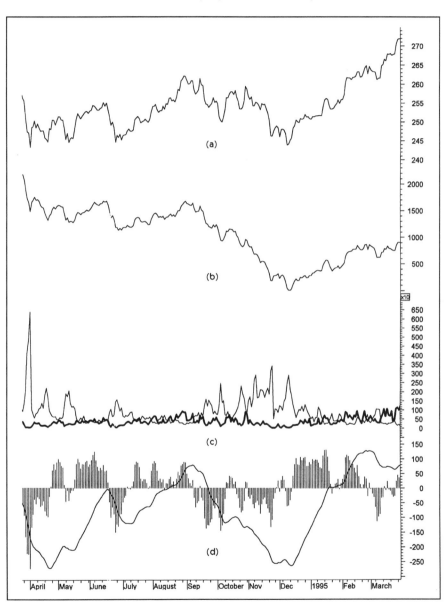

cept behind the McClellan oscillator is the difference between two smoothings of the advance-decline difference. The formula is simply the 19-period exponential average of the difference between advancing issues and declining issues, minus the 39-period exponential average of that difference.

19 exp avg (advances – declines) – 39 exp avg (advances – declines)

The McClellan oscillator is an excellent tool to use for identification of divergences. The up move that began in July 1994 at Point 1 looked quite strong (see Figure A.3). However, the McClellan oscillator got weaker and displayed a negative divergence at Point 2. Two examples of divergence occurred in the down move from late August 1994 until December 1994. The first, between Points 3 and 4, showed slight divergence and hinted at the downtrend abating. Points 4 and 5 offered an abrupt change in divergence and suggested an immediate bottom at Point 5.

Analysts often use a move above zero as a buy signal and a drop below zero as a sell signal. Readings above +100 and below –100 are interpreted as *overbought* and *oversold,* respectively.

MCCLELLAN SUMMATION INDEX

The McClellan summation index is a further derivation of the McClellan oscillator, in that the McClellan oscillator is summed or accumulated on a daily basis to obtain the summation index. This provides a longer-term view of the McClellan concept and can be seen by the single line overlayed on the McClellan oscillator in Figure A.4. Figure A.4 also shows the advantage of viewing multiple breadth indicators on the same chart for comparison purposes.

INFORMATION SOURCES

G. Morris Corporation (9500 Forest Lane, Suite 550, Dallas, TX 75243; [214] 690-1284 or [800] 298-4995) provides over 16 breadth indicators for the New York and NASDAQ markets that integrate seamlessly with these Windows-based analysis software programs: MetaStock for Windows, SuperCharts, TradeStation, and Windows on Wall Street.

Appendix B

Japanese Candlesticks

Gregory L. Morris

OVERVIEW

Only in the last few years has a centuries-old charting and analysis technique from Japan been used in the West. This fascinating method of viewing data and identifying short-term trend changes offers a totally new and powerful way of analyzing market data. It should be stated here that there are two related, but distinct, subjects when discussing Japanese candlesticks. The first is the technique of displaying the data in candlestick form, and the second is the pattern identification process of using these candlesticks in defined combinations.

CANDLESTICK CHARTING

Once you get used to using candlestick charts, you may not want to return to common bar charts. So much more visually appealing, candlestick charts hold a wealth of information not readily available in bar charts. The data used are the same, just the way that it is displayed is different. Following is a single day of trading showing the difference between the common bar (left) and the candlestick.

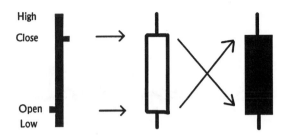

The box in the candlestick is called the *body* and represents the difference between the opening price and the closing price. The two small lines above and below the body are the *shadows* and represent the high and low for the day. If the body is white (or not filled) it means that the closing price was higher than the opening price. The black body means the closing price was lower than the opening price. The Japanese place great significance on the opening and closing prices—the high and low only occasionally come into use in their analysis.

When you view a chart showing many days of candlesticks, information that was not obvious with bar charts seems to leap off the screen or page. Figure B.1 shows this.

Different shapes of body/shadow combinations have different meanings. Long bodies are referred to as *long days,* whereas short bodies with long shadows are called *spinning tops.* When the opening and closing prices are equal, it is called a *Doji* day.

CANDLE PATTERN ANALYSIS

When particular combinations of the individual candlesticks occur, a pattern unfolds helping to identify trend reversals or continuation of trend. These candle patterns can consist of anywhere from one to five candlesticks (days) and visually portray the change in psychology of the traders over the period of the pattern. They are visual pictures of short-term trading psychology. There are approximately 70 Japanese candle patterns that identify both trend reversals and trend continuations.

Reversal Patterns

All candle patterns are directly related to the short-term trend of the market. Therefore, when the market being analyzed is in an uptrend, only bearish reversal patterns are considered. These patterns help traders mark the

Figure B.1   A comparison of bar and candlestick charts. (*MetaStock, Equis International, Inc.*)

end of the uptrend and many times, the beginning of a new downtrend. Similarly, in a downtrend, the bullish reversal patterns help identify the end of the down move. Reversal candle patterns, used in conjunction with other technical indicators, provide the trader with an early warning system for trend reversals.

One of the best patterns for trend reversal is the bullish *morning star.* This is a three-day pattern that only shows up in a downtrend and consists of three candlesticks. The first day of the morning star convinces traders that the downtrend is continuing because the close of the day is much lower than the open (a long, black day). However, on the open of the second day, prices gap lower, trade in a narrow range and close near the open, but not above the previous day's close (a spinning top). While the downtrend still seems to be in place, confidence is somewhat shaken because of the small move between opening and closing prices on this second day. The third day finally produces the evidence needed to scare even the bravest of shorts. Prices open higher on a gap and trade higher to close at least above the midpoint of the body of the first day of the pattern. A reversal of trend from down to up is almost assured.

Most reversal patterns have opposite cousins; one for bullish signals and one for bearish signals. The opposite pattern to the morning star is called the *evening star* and works similarly but is used to identify the reversal of an uptrend in the market.

Continuation Patterns

A pattern that helps identify the fact that the current trend is going to continue is more valuable than may first appear. Each trading day, a decision needs to be made whether to enter, exit, or remain in a trade. The continuation pattern offers guidance for these decisions. If you are already long in a position and a bullish continuation pattern appears, you could add to your position, or at least be comforted that the trend has further to go.

Filtered Candle Patterns

A technique known as *filtering* helps eliminate bad signals and vastly improves candle pattern reliability. One must first understand how an indicator moves in order to grasp this concept. In this example, *stochastics %D* is used. Stochastics %D oscillates between 0 and 100. One of the interpretations for this indicator is that when %D rises above 80 and then falls below 80, a sell signal is generated (see Figure B.2). Similarly, when it drops below 20 and then rises above 20, a buy signal occurs.

What do we know about using %D? We know that when it enters the area above 80 or below 20, a signal will eventually occur. I call the area above 80 and below 20 the *presignal area*—the area that %D must get to before it can generate a signal of its own.

Filtered candle patterns utilize this presignal area—only candle patterns that occur when %D is in its presignal area are considered. This means that if a reversal candle pattern occurs when %D is at 55, the pattern is ignored. It should be stated here that only reversal candle patterns are filtered—we are looking only for trend reversal signals. Looking at Figure B.3, the double-headed arrows represent the filtered patterns while the single-headed arrows are normal candle patterns. As you can see, the filtered patterns picked the tops and bottoms with uncanny accuracy.

SUMMARY

Japanese candlestick charting and candle pattern analysis are valuable tools to assist the investor or trader with analysis and market timing decisions. There are two points that I strongly believe to be true. The first is: Once you become accustomed to viewing market data in candlestick form, you may not want to see another bar chart. The second is: Japanese candle patterns, used in conjunction with other technical indicators (filtering), will almost always offer a signal prior to price-based indicators used alone.

INFORMATION SOURCES

Books

Morris, Gregory L. *Candlestick Charting Explained.* Chicago: Irwin, 1995. (Originally published as CandlePower in 1992.)

Nison, Steve. *Japanese Candlestick Charting.* New York: New York Institute of Finance, 1991.

Nison, Steve. *Beyond Candlesticks.* New York: John Wiley & Sons, 1994.

Figure B.2   Using stochastics as a filter with candlesticks. (*MetaStock, Equis International, Inc.*)

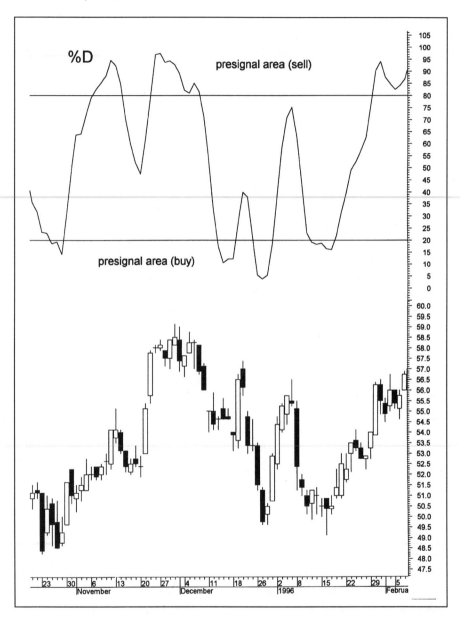

Figure B.3   CandlePower 5.0. (*Worth Systems, Inc.*)

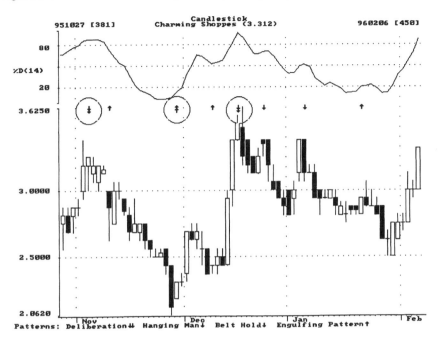

Software

North Systems, Inc. *CandlePower 5.0.* Salem, Oreg.; (503) 364-3829. Note:
    This is the software used to identify the candle patterns in this section.

G. Morris Corporation, *Indicators & Trading Systems.* Dallas, Tex.; (800)
    298-4995.

Glossary

Advance-decline line: One of the most widely used indicators to measure the *breadth* of a stock market advance or decline. Each day (or week) the number of advancing issues is compared to the number of declining issues. If advances outnumber declines, the net total is added to the previous cumulative total. If declines outnumber advances, the net difference is subtracted from the previous cumulative total. The advance-decline line is usually compared to a popular stock average, such as the Dow Jones Industrial Average. They should trend in the same direction. When the advance-decline line begins to diverge from the stock average, an early indication is given of a possible trend reversal.

ADX line: *Average directional movement* line; measures the degree of trend or direction in a market. A rising ADX line suggests a strong trend; a falling ADX line reflects little or no trend in a market. (See *Directional movement.*)

Arms index: Developed by Richard Arms, this contrary indicator is a *ratio* of the average *volume* of *declining* stocks divided by the average volume of *advancing* stocks. A reading below 1.0 indicates more volume in rising stocks. A reading above 1.0 reflects more volume in declining issues. A 10-day average of the Arms index over 1.20 is oversold, while a 10-day average below .80 is overbought.

Ascending triangle: A sideways price pattern between two converging trendlines, in which the lower line is rising while the upper line is flat. This is generally a bullish pattern. (See *Triangles.*)

Bar chart: On a daily bar chart, each bar represents one day's activity. The vertical bar is drawn from the day's highest price to the day's lowest price (the *range*). A tic to the left of the bar marks the opening price, while a tic to the right of the bar markets the closing price. Bar charts can be constructed for any time period, including monthly, weekly, hourly, and minute periods.

Bollinger bands: Developed by John Bollinger, this indicator plots trading bands two standard deviations above and below a 20-period moving average. Prices will often meet resistance at the upper band and support at the lower band.

Breakaway gap: A price gap that forms on the completion of an important price pattern. A breakaway gap usually signals the beginning of an important price move. (See *Gaps.*)

Candlesticks: A form of Japanese charting that has become popular in the West. A narrow line (*shadow*) shows the day's price range. A wider *body* marks the area between the high and close. If the close is above the open, the body is white; if the close is below the open, the body is black. (See Appendix B, *Japanese Candlesticks.*)

Channel line: Straight lines drawn parallel to the basic trendline. In an uptrend, the channel line slants up to the right and is drawn above rally peaks; in a downtrend, the channel line is drawn below price troughs and slants down to the right. Prices will often meet resistance at *rising* channel lines and support at *falling* channel lines.

Confirmation: Having as many market factors as possible agreeing with one another. For example, if prices and volume are rising together, volume is *confirming* the price action. The opposite of confirmation is *divergence.*

Continuation patterns: Price formations that imply a pause or consolidation in the prevailing trend. The most common types are *triangles, flags,* and *pennants.*

Descending triangle: A sideways price pattern between two converging trendlines, in which the upper line is declining while the lower line is flat. This is generally a bearish pattern. (See *Triangles.*)

Directional movement: This indicator, called *DMI,* plots a positive +DI line measuring buying pressure and a negative –DI line measuring selling pressure. The pattern is bullish as long as the +DI line is above the –DI. The formula utilizes the past 14 time periods. The *ADX line* is derived from this system and is based on the *spread* between the +DI and –DI lines.

Divergence: A situation where two indicators are not confirming each other. For example, in *oscillator* analysis, prices trend higher while an oscillator starts to drop. *Divergence* usually warns of a trend reversal. (See *Confirmation.*)

Double top: This price pattern displays two prominent peaks. The reversal is complete when the middle trough is broken. The *double bottom* is a mirror image of the top.

Down trendline: A straight line drawn down and to the right above successive rally peaks. A violation of the down trendline usually signals a reversal of the downtrend. (See *Trendlines.*)

Dow theory: One of the oldest and most highly regarded technical theories. A Dow theory buy signal is given when the Dow Industrial and Dow Transportation Averages close above a prior rally peak. A sell signal is given when both averages close below a prior reaction low.

Elliott wave analysis: An approach to market analysis that is based on repetitive wave patterns and the *Fibonacci* number sequence. An ideal Elliott wave pattern shows a five-wave advance followed by a three-wave decline. The Fibonacci number sequence (1, 2, 3, 5, 8, 13, 21, 34, 55, 89, 144 . . .) is constructed by adding the first two numbers to arrive at the third. The ratio of any number to the next larger number is 62 percent, which is a popular Fibonacci retracement number. The inverse of 62 percent, which is 38 percent, is also used as a Fibonacci retracement number. The ratio of any number to the next smaller number is 1.62 percent, which is used to arrive at Fibonacci price targets. Elliott wave analysis incorporates the three elements of pattern (wave identification), ratio (Fibonacci ratios and projections), and time. Fibonacci time targets are arrived at by counting Fibonacci days, weeks, months, or years from prominent peaks and troughs.

Envelopes: Lines placed at fixed percentages above and below a moving average line. Envelopes help determine when a market has traveled too far from its moving average and is *overextended.*

Exhaustion gap: A price gap that occurs at the end of an important trend, and signals that the trend is ending. (See *Gaps.*)

Exponential smoothing: A moving average that uses all data points but gives greater weight to more recent price data. (See *Moving average.*)

Fibonacci numbers: See *Elliott wave analysis.*

Flag: A continuation price pattern, generally lasting less than three weeks, which resembles a parallelogram that slopes against the prevailing trend. The flag represents a minor pause in a dynamic price trend. (See *Pennant.*)

Fundamental analysis: The opposite of visual analysis. Fundamental analysis relies on economic supply and demand information, as opposed to market activity.

Gaps: Gaps are spaces left on the bar chart where no trading has taken place. An *up gap* is formed when the lowest price on a trading day is higher than the highest high of the previous day. A *down gap* is formed when the highest price on a day is lower than the lowest price of the prior day. An up gap is usually a sign of market strength, while a down gap is a sign of market weakness. Three types of gaps are *breakaway*, *runaway* (also called *measuring*), and *exhaustion* gaps.

Head and shoulders: The best known of the reversal patterns. At a market top, three prominent peaks are formed with the middle peak (or head) slightly higher than the two other peaks (shoulders). When the trendline (neckline) connecting the two intervening troughs is broken, the pattern is complete. A bottom pattern is a mirror image of a top and is called an *inverse head and shoulders.*

Intermarket analysis: An additional aspect of market analysis that takes into consideration the price action of related market sectors. The four sectors are *currencies, commodities, bonds,* and *stocks.* International markets are also included. This approach is based on the premise that all markets are interrelated and impact on one another.

Island reversal: A combination of an *exhaustion gap* in one direction and a *breakaway gap* in the other direction within a few days. Toward the end of an uptrend, for example, prices gap upward and then downward within a few days. The result is usually two or three trading days standing alone with gaps on either side. The island reversal usually signals a trend reversal. (See *Gaps.*)

Key reversal day: In an uptrend, this one-day pattern occurs when prices open in new highs, and then close below the previous day's closing price. In a downtrend, prices open lower and then close higher. The wider the price range on the key reversal day and the heavier the volume, the greater the odds that a reversal is taking place. (See *Weekly Reversal.*)

Line charts: Price charts that connect the *closing* prices of a given market over a span of time. The result is a curving line on the chart. This type of chart is most useful with overlay or comparison charts that are commonly employed in intermarket analysis. It is also used for visual trend analysis of *open-end mutual funds*.

MACD histogram: A variation of the *MACD* system that plots the *difference* between the *signal* and *MACD* lines. Changes in the spread between the two lines can be spotted faster, leading to earlier trading signals.

MACD lines: Developed by Gerald Appel, the *moving average convergence divergence* system shows two lines. The first (MACD) line is the difference between two exponential moving averages (usually 12 and 26 periods) of closing prices. The second (signal) line is usually a 9-period EMA of the first (MACD) line. Signals are given when the two lines cross.

McClellan oscillator: Developed by Sherman McClellan, this oscillator is the difference between the 19-day (10 percent trend) and 39-day (5 percent trend) exponentially smoothed averages of the daily net advance decline figures. Crossings above the zero line are positive and below zero are negative. Readings above +100 are overbought while readings below −100 are oversold. (See Summation Index.)

Momentum: A technique used to construct an overbought-oversold oscillator. *Momentum* measures price *differences* over a selected span of time. To construct a 10-day momentum line, the closing price 10 days earlier is subtracted from the latest price. The resulting positive or negative value is plotted above or below a zero line. (See *Oscillators*.)

Moving average: A trend-following indicator that works best in a trending environment. Moving averages smooth out price action but operate with a time lag. A simple 10-day moving average of a stock, for example, adds up the last 10 days' closing prices and divides the total by 10. That procedure is repeated each day. Any number of moving averages can be employed, with different time spans, to generate buy and sell signals. When only one average is employed, a buy signal is given when the price closes above the average. When two averages are employed, a buy signal is given when the shorter average crosses above the longer average. There are three types: *simple, weighted, and exponentially smoothed* averages.

On-balance volume: Developed by Joseph Granville, *OBV* is a running cumulative total of upside and downside volume. Volume is added on up days and subtracted on down days. The OBV line is plotted with the price line to see if the two lines are confirming each other. (See *Volume*.)

Open interest: The number of options or futures contracts that are still unliquidated at the end of a trading day. A rise or fall in open interest shows that money is flowing into or out of a futures contract or option, respectively. In futures markets, rising open interest is considered good for the current trend. Open interest also measures liquidity.

Oscillators: Indicators that determine when a market is in an *overbought* or *oversold* condition. Oscillators are plotted at the bottom of a price chart. When the oscillator reaches an upper extreme, the market is overbought. When the oscillator line reaches a lower extreme, the market is oversold. (See *Momentum, Rate of change, Relative strength index,* and *Stochastics.*)

Overbought: A term usually used in reference to an *oscillator.* When an oscillator reaches an upper extreme, it is believed that a market has risen too far and is vulnerable to a selloff.

Oversold: A term usually used in reference to an *oscillator.* When an oscillator reaches a lower extreme, it is believed that a market has dropped too far and is due for a bounce.

Pennant: This continuation price pattern is similar to the *flag,* except that it is more horizontal and resembles a small *symmetrical triangle.* Like the flag, the pennant usually lasts from one to three weeks and is typically followed by a resumption of the prior trend.

Percent investment advisors bullish: This measure of stock market bullish sentiment is published weekly by Investor's Intelligence of New Rochelle, New York. When only 35 percent of professionals are bullish, the market is considered oversold. A reading of 55 percent is considered to be overbought.

Price patterns: Patterns that appear on price charts and that have predictive value. Patterns are divided into *reversal* and *continuation* patterns.

Put/call ratio: The *ratio* of *volume* in *put options* divided by the volume of *call options* is used as a contrary indicator. When put buying gets too high relative to call buying (a high put/call ratio), the market is *oversold.* A low put/call ratio represents an *overbought* market condition.

Rate of change: A technique used to construct an overbought-oversold oscillator. Rate of change employs a price *ratio* over a selected span of time. To construct a 10-day rate of change oscillator, the last closing price is divided by the closing price 10 days earlier. The resulting value is plotted above or below a value of 100.

Ratio analysis: The use of a *ratio* to compare the *relative strength* between two entities. An individual stock or industry group divided by the S&P 500 index can determine whether that stock or industry group is outperforming or underperforming the stock market as a whole. Ratio analysis can be used to compare any two entities. A rising ratio indicates that the numerator in the ratio is outperforming the denominator. Trend analysis can be applied to the ratio line itself to determine important turning points.

Relative strength index (RSI): A popular oscillator developed by Welles Wilder, Jr. and described in his self-published 1978 book, *New Concepts in Technical Trading Systems.* RSI is plotted on a vertical scale from 0 to 100. Values above 70 are considered to be overbought and values below 30, oversold. When prices are over 70 or below 30 and diverge from price action, a warning is given of a possible trend reversal. *RSI* usually employs 9 or 14 time periods.

Resistance: The opposite of *support.* Resistance is marked by a previous price peak and provides enough of a barrier above the market to halt a price advance. (See *Support.*)

Retracements: Prices normally retrace the prior trend by a percentage amount before resuming the original trend. The best known example is the 50-percent retracement. Minimum and maximum retracements are normally one-third and two-thirds, respectively. *Elliott wave analysis* uses *Fibonacci* retracements of 38 percent and 62 percent.

Reversal patterns: Price patterns on a price chart that usually indicate that a trend reversal is taking place. The best known of the reversal patterns are the *head and shoulders* and *double* and *triple* tops and bottoms.

Runaway gap: A price gap that usually occurs around the midpoint of an important market trend. For that reason, it is also called a *measuring* gap. (See *Gaps.*)

Sentiment indicators: Psychological indicators that attempt to measure the degree of bullishness or bearishness in a market. These are *contrary indicators* and are used in much the same fashion as overbought or oversold oscillators. Their greatest value is when they reach upper or lower extremes.

Simple average: A moving average that gives *equal* weight to each day's price data. (See *Exponential smoothing* and *Weighted average.*)

Stochastics: An overbought-oversold oscillator popularized by George Lane. Time periods of 9 and 14 are usually employed in its construction. Stochastics uses two lines—%K and its 3-day moving average, %D. These two lines fluctuate in a vertical range between 0 and 100. Readings above 80 are overbought, while readings below 20 are oversold. When the faster %K line crosses above the slower %D line and the lines are below 20, a buy signal is given. When the %K crosses below the %D line and the lines are over 80, a sell signal is given. There are two stochastics versions: *fast* stochastics and *slow* stochastics. Most traders use the slower version because of its smoother look and more reliable signals. The formula for *fast* stochastics is:

$$\text{fast } \%K = \left[\frac{\text{latest price} - \text{lowest low for } n \text{ periods}}{n \text{ period highest high} - \text{lowest low}} \right] 100$$

$$\text{fast } \%D = \text{3-day average of fast } \%K$$

In the formula, *n* usually refers to the number of days, but can also mean months, weeks, or hours. The formula for *slow* stochastics is:

$$\text{slow } \%K = \text{fast } \%D$$

$$\text{slow } \%D = \text{3-day average of slow } \%K.$$

Summation index: A cumulative *sum* of all daily *McClellan oscillator* readings that provides longer-range analysis of market breadth. Used in the same way as an *advance-decline line*. (See Appendix A.)

Support: A price, or price zone, *beneath* the current market price, where buying power is sufficient to halt a price decline. A previous reaction low usually forms a support level.

Symmetrical triangle: A sideways price pattern between two converging trendlines in which the upper trendline is declining and lower trendline is rising. This pattern represents an even balance between buyers and sellers, although the prior trend is usually resumed. The breakout through either trendline signals the direction of the price trend. (See *Ascending* and *Descending triangles*.)

Technical analysis: The study of market action, usually with price charts, which includes volume and open interest patterns. Also called *chart analysis, market analysis* and, more recently, *visual analysis.*

Trend: Refers to the direction of prices. Rising peaks and troughs constitute an *uptrend;* falling peaks and troughs constitute a *downtrend.* A *trading range* is characterized by horizontal peaks and troughs. Trends are generally classified into *major* (longer than six months), *intermediate* (one to six months), or *minor* (less than a month).

Trendlines: Straight lines drawn on a chart below reaction lows in an uptrend, or above rally peaks in a downtrend, that determine the steepness of the current trend. The breaking of a trendline usually signals a trend reversal.

Triangles: Sideways price patterns in which prices fluctuate within converging trendlines. The three types of triangles are the *symmetrical,* the *ascending,* and the *descending.*

Triple top: A price pattern with three prominent peaks, similar to the *head and shoulders* top, except that all three peaks occur at about the same level. The *triple bottom* is a mirror image of the top.

Up trendline: A straight line drawn upward and to the right below reaction lows. The longer the up trendline has been in effect and the more times it has been tested, the more significant it becomes. Violation of the trendline usually signals that the uptrend may be changing direction. (See *Down trendline.*)

Visual analysis: A form of analysis that utilizes charts and market indicators to determine market direction.

Volume: The level of trading activity in a *stock, option,* or *futures* contract. Expanding volume in the direction of the current price trend confirms the price trend. (See *On-balance volume.*)

Weekly reversal: An upside weekly reversal is present when prices open lower on Monday and then on Friday close above the previous week's close. A downside weekly reversal opens the week higher but closes down by Friday. (See *Key reversal day.*)

Weighted average: A moving average that uses a selected time span, but gives greater weight to more recent price data. (See *Moving average.*)

Index